The Pinochet Case:
Origins, Progress and Implications

The Pinochet Case:
Origins, Progress and Implications

Edited by

Madeleine Davis

Institute of Latin American Studies

LONDON

© Institute of Latin American Studies, 2003

Published by
Institute of Latin American Studies
31 Tavistock Square
London wc1h 9ha
http://www.sas.ac.uk/ilas/publicat.htm

British Library Cataloguing-in-Publication Data
A catalogue record for this book is available
from the British Library

ISBN 1 900039 52 4

Contents

Notes on Contributors

Alan Angell Lecturer and fellow of St Antony's College, Oxford and Director of the Latin American Centre, University of Oxford. He has written extensively on Chilean politics. His most recent book (with Pamela Lowden and Rosemary Thorp) is *Decentralizing Development: The Political Economy of Institutional Change in Colombia and Chile* (Oxford, 2001).

Alexandra Barahona de Brito Professor at Moderna University, Senior Associate Researcher at the Institute of Strategic and International Studies, and Visiting Fellow of the Institute for Social Sciences, (all in Lisbon), formerly Visiting Fellow at the Centre of International Studies at Princeton University in 1999. Her publications include *Human Rights and Democratisation* (Oxford, 1997) and *The Politics of Memory* (co-edited, Oxford, 2001), along with a number of articles on human rights, democratisation, and European–Latin American relations.

Francisco Bravo López Legal advisor on human rights, Chilean Interior Ministry, lecturer in history and law. He has represented relatives of victims detained and disappeared or politically executed in legal proceedings ongoing in Chile. Relevant publications include 'Los Nudos Jurídicos sobre procesos de violación a los derechos humanos en Chile,' *Revista Gaceta Jurídica*, no. 226 (1999).

Madeleine Davis Lecturer in Politics at Queen Mary, University of London, and Associate Fellow of the Institute of Latin American Studies. She has research interests in the intellectual history and political practice of the left, as well as in aspects of Latin American politics. Recent relevant publications include *The Pinochet Case* (London, 2000).

Juan E. Garcés Lawyer, awarded the Right Livelihood Award (Alternative Nobel Prize) in 1999 for his leading role in preparing the Pinochet case. He is the author of a number of works in the fields of law and politics, including: 'Crimen de Estado y Humanidad,' *Le Monde Diplomatique*, Madrid, September

1997; *Soberanos e Intervenidos. Estrategias globales, americanos y españoles*, (Madrid, 1996); *Orlando Letelier. Testimonio y vindicación* (Madrid, 1995); *Allende et l'expérience chilienne* (Paris, 1976).

Carlos Huneeus Executive Director, CERC, Chile, and Lecturer, Pontificia Universidad Católica de Chile. His main research interests are in comparative politics, regime change and democratisation, and his publications include: *El régimen de Pinochet*, (Santiago, 2000) and *La UCD y la transición a la democracia en España* (Madrid, 1985).

Brian Loveman Professor of Political Science, San Diego State University. He has written extensively on Chilean and Latin American politics, and in particular the role of the armed forces. His publications include: *Chile, Legacy of Hispanic Capitalism* (3rd edition, Oxford, 2001); *For La Patria: Politics and the Armed Forces in Latin America* (Wilmington, DL, 1999); (with Thomas M. Davies) *The Politics of Antipolitics, The Armed Forces of Latin America* (3rd edition, Lincoln, NE, 1997); *The Constitution of Tyranny: Regimes of Exception in Spanish America* (Pittsburgh, PA, 1993), and (all with Elizabeth Lira) *Arquitectura política y seguridad interior del Estado 1811-1990* (Santiago, 2002), *Las suaves cenizas del olvido: vía chilena de reconciliacion política*, (2nd edition Santiago, 2000) *Las ardientes cenizas del olvido: vía chilena de reconciliación política 1932-1994* (Santiago, 2000).

Carlos Malamud Professor of Latin American History, Universidad Nacional de Educación a Distancia (Spain) and Senior Analyst, Real Instituto Elcano de Estudios Internacionales y Estratégicos, Madrid. Relevant publications include *El caso Pinochet. Un debate sobre los límites de la impunidad* (Madrid, 2000).

Antonio Remiro Brotóns: Professor of International Law and International Relations, Universidad Autonoma de Madrid. He is the author of *El caso Pinochet: los límites de la impunidad* (Madrid, 1999).

Naomi Roht-Arriaza Professor of Law, University of California, Hastings College of Law. Her research has focused on issues of accountability for violations of human and environmental rights. She is the author *of Impunity and Human Rights in International Law and Practice* (New York and Oxford, 1995) and of numerous articles on impunity, amnesties and related topics.

Diana Woodhouse: Professor of Law, Oxford Brookes University. Her main research interests are accountability, the interplay between law and politics and judicial/executive relations. Her publications include: (as editor) *The Pinochet Case: A Legal and Constitutional Analysis* (Oxford, 2000); *Ministers and Parliament: Accountability in Theory and Practice* (Oxford, 1994), *In Pursuit of Good Administration; Ministers, Civil Servants and Judges* (Oxford, 1997) and *The Office of Lord Chancellor* (Oxford, 2001).

Foreword

This volume is in large part based upon a conference on *The Pinochet Case* held in London in November 2001, and organised by the Institute of Latin American Studies (ILAS) in association with the Institute of Advanced Legal Studies. Nine of the chapters presented here are revised versions of research papers presented at the conference. Two, those by Antonio Remiro Brotóns and Alexandra Barahona de Brito, were solicited subsequently. The editor and contributors would like to acknowledge the contributions of a number of individuals and organisations. The Ford Foundation, Santiago gave financial support. Martin Abregú, the Program Officer for Rights and Citizenship, and Augusto Varas, the Representative at the Santiago office, were exceptionally helpful from the inception of the project. James Dunkerley, Director of ILAS, gave his support throughout with characteristically unfailing generosity. The editor received invaluable assistance from the staff of ILAS, in particular John Maher, Tony Bell and Olga Jiménez. Thanks are due to Barry Rider, Director of the Institute of Advanced Legal Studies, and his staff, for their assistance in arranging and hosting the conference upon which this volume is based. A number of people participated in the conference as paper-givers, panel chairs or commentators: Clive Nicholls QC; Lord Justice Stephen Sedley; Reed Brody; Philippe Sands; David Sugarman; Avrom Sherr; Rachel Sieder; Pilar Domingo; Helen Duffy. The editor and contributors are indebted to them for the expert criticism and lively debate that has doubtless informed and improved many of the contributions to this book.

CHAPTER I

Introduction:
Law and Politics in the Pinochet Case

Madeleine Davis

On 1 July 2002 the Rome Statute came into effect, giving birth to the new International Criminal Court (ICC). On the same day the Chilean Supreme Court halted legal proceedings against Augusto Pinochet, judging him mentally unfit to stand trial. Pinochet's arrest in London in October 1998 came a few months after the 120 signatories to the Statute had committed themselves to the institution of a permanent international tribunal empowered to investigate and punish grave breaches of international law. Although the drama of the Pinochet case was played out in national courts, it provided a crucial practical test of the seriousness and depth of the commitment by sovereign states to apply the principle of universal jurisdiction for certain internationally recognised crimes. This principle, though enshrined in the Geneva Conventions, had been applied in limited and inconsistent fashion thereafter, a situation that the establishment of the ICC was intended to remedy. Pinochet, we now know, will not himself be punished by the ICC or by any other court for the murder, torture and forced disappearance of thousands of Chilean and non-Chilean nationals of which he stands accused. However, the case against him was only one part of a much broader investigation. Its outcome – he escaped first extradition to Spain from the UK and subsequently trial in his own country not by being exonerated, but only by reason of mental incapacity – does not signal any definitive resolution of the critical issues raised by the attempt to prosecute him.

Some five years after Pinochet's arrest, and taking into account developments in national and international jurisprudence occurring as a result of or alongside his case, how can we assess the overall significance of what happened? This book brings together lawyers, political scientists and historians from Latin America, Europe and the USA in order to address this question. It adopts historical, comparative, legal and political perspectives in order to analyse and explain the origins, course and implications of the Pinochet affair. Thus, while the arrest and detention of Pinochet in London in 1998 provides a unifying focus and point of departure for the research presented here, the issues addressed cover a broad span, ranging from historical analysis of the legal and political foundations of military impunity in colonial Spanish America, through the conduct and handling of the Pinochet affair by judiciaries and politicians in Spain, Chile and the UK, to reflections and prognoses for the future practice of international law and politics.

The Pinochet case: an overview of events[1]

Pinochet's arrest while recovering from surgery during a private visit to London was the result of a legal process set in motion in Spain some two years earlier.[2] Unable to seek justice in their home countries as a result of domestic amnesties conceded at the time of transition to democratic rule, Argentine and Chilean exiles, victims and relatives of victims of the authoritarian military dictatorships of the Southern Cone took their cases to courts in Spain, aided by human rights organisations, lawyers and politicians. In 1996 two separate investigations were begun in Spain. The first concerned genocide and terrorism allegedly practised by Argentine military personnel, filed by the Unión Progresista de Fiscales (UPFE, Union of Progressive Prosecutors of Spain), and the other related to similar crimes imputed to a number of Chilean military officers including Pinochet, also filed by the UPFE. Later that year two investigating magistrates of the Spanish Audiencia Nacional agreed to take on these cases, Judge Baltasar Garzón accepting the Argentine case and Judge Manuel García Castellón the Chilean. In the ensuing two years leading up to Pinochet's arrest, the judges heard and sought out a mass of evidence concerning human rights abuses committed by the military regimes. Testimony and documentation came from many sources, including the two countries' own truth commission reports which had documented the deaths or forced disappearances of some 3,197 named individuals in Chile, and some 9,000 in Argentina.

The inclusion in the investigations of crimes against non-Spanish nationals committed outside Spanish territory made it essential to claim universal jurisdiction and to categorise the crimes in a way that would allow this claim to be upheld. Garzón claimed that Spanish law established universal jurisdiction, that the crimes alleged fell within Spanish legal definitions of genocide, terrorism

---

1   For a fuller account see Madeleine Davis, *The Pinochet Case* (London, 2000).

2   Richard Wilson, 'Prosecuting Pinochet: International Crimes in Spanish Domestic Law,' *Human Rights Quarterly*, vol. 21 (1999) gives a useful overview of the origins of the legal proceedings in Spain. See also Rojas, Paz et al., *Tarda pero llega. Pinochet ante la justicia española* (Santiago, 1998).

and torture, and that the domestic amnesties of Argentina and Chile were not a bar to prosecution in Spain, since Spanish law does not recognise such amnesties, which had in any case already been ruled as in contravention of international human rights norms.[3] The Spanish public prosecutor's challenge to these claims, made after Pinochet's arrest, was dismissed by the full court of the Audiencia Nacional, which upheld Spanish jurisdiction in two unappealable decisions issued on 4 and 5 November 1998. Particularly crucial was the Audiencia Nacional's upholding of a broad, 'customary' definition of the crime of genocide, according to which 'national group' meant simply a distinct human group 'characterised by something, integrated into a larger collectivity'.[4] According to this definition, the military regimes' targeting of citizens who did not conform to their notions of national identity and values could be characterised as genocide.

In contrast to the Spanish courts, the UK judiciary was not called upon to address the issue of which courts had jurisdiction over Pinochet's alleged crimes, or to pronounce on the Spanish court's interpretation of genocide, terrorism and torture. Having implemented Garzón's international arrest warrants, the only decision the UK courts had to make was whether Pinochet could be extradited to Spain. In making this decision, the issue of whether Pinochet could claim sovereign immunity from prosecution and arrest became central, and the proceedings turned out to be extremely protracted, lasting seventeen months and involving several High Court rulings and three rulings from the UK's highest court, the Appellate Committee of the House of Lords. The first High Court ruling on 28 October 1998 affirmed that Pinochet could claim immunity from prosecution because the Spanish charges related to acts performed in the exercise of his function as head of state. This ruling was overturned on appeal to the law lords. By a 3:2 majority, the Lords' panel ruled on 25 November 1998 that since international law did not recognise immunity – even sovereign immunity – for crimes such as genocide and torture, Pinochet could be committed to await the Home Secretary's decision on whether to extradite. In a dramatic twist, this ruling was itself set aside when another panel of law lords accepted a petition from Pinochet's defence made on the basis that links between Lord Hoffmann, one of the five judges who had heard the appeal, and Amnesty International (which had intervened in the earlier hearing) were such as to give an appearance of bias. In an unprecedented decision, the second panel judged that Hoffmann's position as an unpaid director of Amnesty International Charity Limited should have automatically disqualified him from

3 Wilson, 'Prosecuting Pinochet,' p. 956.
4 *Auto de la Sala de lo Penal de la Audiencia Nacional sobre la competencia de la justicia española para perseguir delitos de genocidio en Chile*, Madrid, 5 November 1998

sitting, and thus the appeal would have to be heard again. A larger panel of seven law lords was convened and, in a complex decision delivered on 24 March 1999, it ruled by a 6:1 majority that Pinochet could be extradited, but only for crimes of torture and conspiracy to torture committed after 8 December 1998 (the date by which the Convention Against Torture had been ratified in the domestic law of Spain, Chile and the UK). Though reducing the number of extraditable charges to just three, and though based on a much more technical interpretation of the interface between domestic and international law, this ruling still refused Pinochet's claim to immunity, setting an important precedent.

Responsibility for the final decision in extradition cases rests with the Home Secretary, then Jack Straw.[5] Having twice given his authority to proceed with extradition, Straw eventually decided to short-circuit the final legal stages of the case, judging, on the basis of medical examinations that he had requested, that Pinochet was mentally unfit to face trial. The Chilean government had for some time been pressing the humanitarian case for release, after abandoning earlier legal and diplomatic strategies. Although protests by human rights groups, by the Spanish legal team and by the authorities of France, Belgium and Switzerland (who had all lodged their own extradition requests) drew out the final stages of the UK chapter of the case, they were not enough to prevent Pinochet leaving the UK for Chile, on 1 March 2000. His legal ordeal was far from over, however. During the period of his detention in London, and in part as a result of it, the pace of judicial reform and the prosecution of human rights abuses had quickened in Chile. Charges had been filed against him and other officers before his arrest, but with little hope of success. On his return, however, Judge Juan Guzmán Tapía, investigating a rapidly growing number of charges, applied to have Pinochet stripped of the immunity from criminal prosecution afforded him by his life senatorship. In August 2000 the Chilean Supreme Court upheld an earlier decision by the Santiago Appeals Court to remove Pinochet's immunity, and in early 2001 Guzmán began to question Pinochet about his role in the 'Caravan of Death' murders. Persistent efforts by his defence to have the case suspended on the grounds that medical evidence showed that Pinochet was unfit to stand trial eventually came to fruition. However, the outcome – that he was declared to be suffering from 'dementia' – did not signal innocence, and was viewed by his family and supporters as a deep humiliation. The Supreme Court ruling also forced Pinochet to resign his life-membership of the Senate – having been declared mentally unfit to face questions in court he could hardly

---

5 Proposals to streamline the extradition process were given added weight by the Pinochet affair. In June 2002 a draft bill was published, including plans to introduce European-wide arrest warrants, to reduce the role of the Home Secretary, and to give a single right of appeal to the High Court.

claim to be able to take part in Senate debates – and thus precipitated his retirement from Chilean public life. In October 2002 a Chilean court blocked an extradition request for Pinochet from an Argentine judge for his role in the 1974 murder of Carlos Prats in Buenos Aires, again on the grounds of mental incapacity. There is now no realistic prospect that he will face trial.

If in an obvious sense the events of 1 July 2002 marked both a beginning and an end, the issues surrounding both continue to be hotly contested. Pinochet accompanied his withdrawal from political life with an unrepentant reiteration of the 'soldierly sacrifice' he saw himself as having made for Chile. Trials of ex-military personnel in the national courts of Chile and other Latin American countries continue. No sooner had the Rome Statute come into force than its signatories came under intense pressure from the United States government to grant exemption from prosecution by the ICC to US personnel. In July 2002 a US threat to veto future United Nations peacekeeping operations unless the UN Security Council agreed to exempt UN peacekeepers whose governments had not ratified the Rome statute from any prosecution by the ICC resulted in the unanimous passage of Resolution 1422, granting one year's immunity. This was later renewed.[6] US domestic legislation through the American Service-members' Protection Act (ASPA), passed in 2002, allows the US to refuse to participate in UN peacekeeping missions to countries party to the Court, to withhold military aid unless recipient countries agree not to hand over US citizens to the Court, and to use 'all means necessary' to free any US and allied servicemembers taken into custody by the Court.[7] In September 2002 the European Union – strongly urged by the UK – decided to allow its members to sign individual immunity agreements with the US in return for Washington's guarantee that US war crimes suspects will be tried at home. That decision further heightened concern about the effectiveness and impartiality of the court whose first chief prosecutor, Luis Moreno Ocampo, was elected in April 2003.

Both the outcome of the attempt to try Pinochet in Spain and later Chile, and the current controversy over the role of the ICC demonstrate the complex interplay between law and politics in the contemporary world – the overarching

---

6 United Nations Security Council Res. 1422, UN Doc S/Res/1422 (2002). Renewal from 1 July 2003 was granted despite the misgivings voiced by Kofi Annan that the passage of the resolution amounted to a misuse of provisions of the Rome Statute. Kofi Annan, statement to the Security Council, 12 June 2003, available at http://www.un.org/apps/sg/sgstats.asp?nid=389 . For an analysis of US opposition to the ICC see Marc Weller, 'Undoing the global constitution: UN Security Council action on the International Criminal Court,' *International Affairs*, vol. 78, no. 4, 2002, pp. 693-712.

7 Jamie Mayerfeld, 'Who Shall be Judge?: The United States, the International Criminal Court and the Global Enforcement of Human Rights,' *Human Rights Quarterly* 25, (2003), pp. 93-129

theme which runs through this collection. The book is organised into four parts. In the first, the legal, political and historical context of the Pinochet case is analysed. The second part follows the progress of the case through the courts, first in the UK and subsequently in Chile. In the third part, the focus shifts to the way in which the sensitive political issues surrounding the attempt to prosecute Pinochet were handled and perceived by governments and public opinion in Spain, Chile and the UK. The final section analyses the Pinochet affair and other transnational prosecution attempts in the international context, in terms of their implications for the legal and political culture of recently democratised Latin American countries, for the future of democratic governance, and for the development of international law.

The Chilean dimension

Arguments concerning the nature and quality of Chilean democracy were deployed during the period of Pinochet's detention in the UK both by those who wanted to see him extradited, and by those who did not. The former claimed that it would be impossible to try him in Chile, because Chilean democracy was in critical respects limited and incomplete as a result of the restrictions placed upon it by the outgoing dictator, who remained as head of the armed forces for eight years after the restitution of civilian rule. Among the latter, on the other hand, were those who professed concern that Pinochet's trial abroad threatened to jeopardise the stability of Chile's fledgling democracy and polarise Chilean society. In their different ways and for different purposes, both claims oversimplified the situation in Chile, but they also raised anew long running debates about the extent to which justice for past human rights crimes may or should be pursued in countries that have undergone transitions to democracy. In Chile what effectively happened at the time of transition was that a (limited) truthtelling about human rights abuses was conceded in return for impunity for the perpetrators. Whether such trade-offs stabilise democracy or weaken the rule of law and impede the consolidation of democratic rule remains a subject of controversy. Several of the contributions to this volume engage with these issues as they relate to the Chilean situation, in contrasting but complementary ways.

Legacies of history

Brian Loveman's approach is historical. Two questions central to the Pinochet case were the extent to which former (or serving) heads of state may enjoy immunity/impunity from prosecution and, relatedly, the ability and willingness of national courts to exercise universal jurisdiction over crimes against humanity. Loveman sets these contemporary issues in historical and regional context by considering the extent to which longstanding constitutional, legal and military traditions in the Spanish Americas and Brazil provide for impunity and weaken civil liberties. Detecting a widespread culture of impunity for crimes committed by military and civilian officials, he argues that this must be understood as the legacy of constitutional and legal traditions in place long before the military regimes of the 1960s–1990s. These regimes used and extended these foundations of impunity, but while the more recent restitution of civilian rule has gone some way toward dismantling the structures providing for impunity, 'protected democracy' must be seen as a long run regional trend rather than simply an outgrowth of the military governments.

Loveman's argument clearly has regional significance, but he focuses primarily on Chile, tracing the developments that embedded 'protected democracy' in institutions, culture and politics. Beginning in the colonial era, he shows how the militarisation of politics and administration in Spain and its colonies created a legal and political framework for impunity which persisted through independence struggles, nation-building and constitution-writing into the twentieth century. The extraordinary scope of military jurisdiction and the routine overlap of civilian and military authority, have bestowed upon the armed forces special responsibilities going well beyond external defence, from the obligation to maintain 'internal order' to the monitoring and supervision of elections. Far from being reversed by independence, this militarisation of politics was entrenched and codified by constitution writers who, Loveman argues, established the principle that defence of 'la patria' may at times outweigh the claims of citizens to the most basic rights and freedoms. Indeed, many of the military edicts and decree laws enacted by Pinochet and other military heads of state were in fact simply reformulations, extensions or strict applications of existing legislation. Despite the formal restitution of civilian rule, there remain, deeply embedded in many countries including Chile, laws and traditions inimical to democracy and to the guarantee of fundamental rights and freedoms.

Loveman's contribution raises a number of difficult questions. While the very significant progress of the case against Pinochet in Chile represents an important breach of the wall of impunity, Loveman's analysis suggests that the efforts of human rights activists and lawyers cannot by themselves be enough. Dismantling the structures that have facilitated impunity will require a deeper, more uncomfortable examination of the past, and a greater political willingness to challenge accepted practices than has thus far been shown by civilian politicians. If this challenge is not met, Loveman suggests, democracy in the region will remain incomplete, perhaps even precarious.

Political processes in the erosion of pinochetismo

Alan Angell's assessment of 'The Pinochet Factor in Chilean Politics' addresses from a contemporary standpoint the quality of democracy in newly democratising nations. If Loveman's analysis emphasises the legal and constitutional *restrictions* placed on Chilean democracy by the legacy of the past, and inclines toward a pessimistic view, Angell's stresses the democratising potential of political processes. Acknowledging that elements of the 'Pinochet project' have shaped Chilean democracy – broad agreement among significant political forces to maintain the neoliberal economic framework put in place under the dictatorship, a cultural legacy that prioritises individualism over community and implies acceptance of inequality – Angell makes the case that in other respects *pinochetismo* has been eroded. The man himself, he argues, and key aspects of his institutional and political legacy have been marginalised in Chilean political life, a process of marginalisation already quite far advanced before Pinochet's arrest in 1998.

Angell's analysis goes some way toward undermining claims that the Pinochet case would be a 'bombshell' thrown into Chilean democracy. In fact, the arrest elicited a relatively restrained response from Chilean politicians and military leaders, and failed to generate the expected level of internal political controversy. Incremental changes have occurred at a number of levels – in the institutional structure bequeathed by Pinochet, in civil–military relations, in judicial circles, and in public opinion – despite the tight grip exerted by Pinochet upon the transition and on the civilian governments succeeding him. 'Formal constitutional rules are not necessarily a guide to the real power of particular institutions', Angell argues, and thus changes in constitutional and legal *behaviour*, as well as some success in securing institutional reforms, have resulted in a gradual permeation of the spirit of democracy through governmental structures.

This emphasis on the autonomy of national processes is shared by Carlos Huneeus, who in chapter 9 examines the effects of Pinochet's arrest on the conduct of Chilean politics, both in terms of its immediate impact upon party politics during the 1999 presidential election campaign, and in the context of some longer term trends. Pinochet emerges from his account as a 'strong' dictator, the longest-serving governor in Chilean history, who presided over a regime that was 'modernising' in economic policy, and unapologetically repressive of dissent. This combination of features, together with Pinochet's relatively peaceful handover of power to a civilian government, helps explain the persistence of popular support for him, as well as the unique position he occupied in Chilean political life up until the time of his arrest. Only against this background, and the particular characteristics of Chile's transition to democracy, argues Huneeus, can the actions and attitudes of Chilean political figures be explained.

Huneeus shows that although Pinochet's detention placed politicians of all sides in an uncomfortable situation, the main actors responded with pragmatism and restraint, more mindful of immediate political considerations than of past ones. Thus the call by the Concertación government under Eduardo Frei for Pinochet to be sent home was based upon practical considerations about the possible effects of the case. Army chief Ricardo Izurieta, having already set out upon a path of professionalisation, worked with the government to argue for Pinochet's release and resisted pressure from some right-wing generals who called for more drastic measures. Arms purchases from a French–Spanish consortium remained unchanged. Even the right-wing Unión Demócrata Independiente (UDI – Independent Democratic Union), the political party with the strongest links to Pinochet, concentrated on political advantage. It capitalised on nationalist sentiment by condemning the Spanish and British proceedings as an abuse of sovereignty but was careful to avoid direct associations with Pinochet himself. Far from the image of dangerous polarisation presented by some of Pinochet's supporters abroad, the picture that emerges here of Chilean politics is one of careful strategic manoeuvring. Like Angell, Huneeus stresses the importance of national factors in creating a situation where Pinochet could eventually be tried in Chile: 'external ones can only have internal consequences when there are favourable conditions that allow the effects to spread through the political system'.

The rehabilitation of the judiciary

If Huneeus and Angell make it clear that Pinochet's final humiliation and isolation were the culmination of a number of linked developments, neither deny that his arrest was a critical catalyst for change. This issue is addressed in greater detail by Francisco Bravo López, who examines the obstacles in Chile that prevented or hindered the prosecution of human rights violations committed under military rule. His examination of the manner in which the dictatorship subordinated law to politics, while at the same time claiming to be acting 'legally', exposes the cruel ironies faced by thousands of Chileans who sought to have the torture, murder and forced disappearance of their loved ones recognised as criminal acts sponsored by the state. Between 1973 and 1990 the combination of institutional restrictions with a subservient judicial culture meant that even where the law did contain adequate formal provisions for the prosecution of abuses – for example, covering the treatment of persons subject to arrest – these provisions were not enforced by the courts. Despite persistent efforts on the part of individuals and human rights organisations to file and investigate complaints, the courts did nothing effective to prevent or punish unlawful detention, torture, solitary confinement and murder in secret – that catalogue of horrors for which the phrase 'detained-disappeared' has become shorthand.

Bravo López concurs with Huneeus and Angell in seeing the transition to democracy as controlled by the dictatorship for its own ends, so through much of the 1990s there was little improvement in legal doctrines. From 1996 a combination of structural reforms and generational change within the judiciary brought about a gradual shift in legal culture. That process of change was accelerated by the fallout from the Pinochet case, the continuation of which in Chile took many observers by surprise. While undeniably a great change, the decision to remove Pinochet's own immunity from prosecution had antecedents in Chile as well as abroad. It was both a result of and contribution to a new legal and political climate, in which the prospects for investigation and prosecution of human rights abuses have improved. Tracing the progress of the case through the Chilean courts, Bravo López does not see the eventual outcome for Pinochet himself as a step backwards. Pinochet escaped trial only on a technicality; he was not declared innocent and nor were the charges against him dropped. Many other investigations are proceeding and are beginning to yield results. Yet Bravo López also points out that although significant advances have been made, these have been largely a result of the application of domestic law, with Chilean courts still displaying only a very limited assimilation of the doctrines of international human rights law.

Law vs politics in the national arena

Three of the chapters focus on the handling of the Pinochet case by politicians and judiciaries in Spain and Britain. Two, those by Diana Woodhouse and myself, address complementary aspects of the case in the UK, dealing respectively with the legal progress of the case and its political significance. Carlos Malamud examines the politics of the case in Spain. Although the governments of both countries insisted that legal proceedings (the initiation of which neither had anticipated or supported) would be allowed to take their course, the interplay between legal and political considerations, and between judicial and executive functions, was more subtle and complex than such assurances suggested, and the eventual outcome of the extradition proceedings resulted from a decision taken in the political rather than the judicial arena. In both Spain and the UK, as all three chapters demonstrate, the crucial issues of international legal and political significance were filtered through domestic priorities and sensitivities.

Woodhouse's focus in chapter 5 is upon the reasoning and decisions of the UK courts. The major issues that the courts were called to address were firstly, whether Pinochet, as a former head of state, was entitled to claim sovereign immunity from prosecution, and, secondly, if such immunity could not be claimed, whether the crimes for which Spain sought his extradition were extraditable under the 1989 Extradition Act. As she explains the progress of the case, Woodhouse identifies features of the way the case was handled that have national and international significance. During its course, no fewer than fifteen judges were involved, twelve of them in the House of Lords. These judges were required to move beyond statutory UK law to engage with the substance and spirit of developing international law, giving them a foretaste of the consequences of the UK's adoption of the Human Rights Act in October 2000. Woodhouse argues that the diversity of judicial reasoning in the Pinochet case leaves open a number of questions about the suitability of the House of Lords as the final court of appeal in important political and constitutional cases.

In the domestic arena, Woodhouse shows how the Pinochet case, and in particular the Hoffmann episode, exposed the procedures and practices of the UK's highest court to criticism – of the way panels are constituted, of the extent and effect of the Lords' reliance on counsel, and of the efficacy of procedures for ensuring impartiality and transparency. In the international context, the decisions arrived at by the Lords in Pinochet 1 and 3 contributed to international jurisprudence regarding crimes against humanity, and to discussions about the need for a coherent system for dealing with such crimes. Although the Lords' decision in Pinochet 3 drastically reduced the number of extraditable charges, it is still highly significant that a majority of judges on both panels rejected the claim of sovereign immunity from prosecution, thus demonstrating their willingness to apply customary international law – a development which Woodhouse argues is a major departure from the norm. Yet the insistence by the panel in Pinochet 3 on a strict application of the double criminality rule simultaneously demonstrated the reluctance of the majority of the Lords to take a clear and unequivocal stand on the broader issues concerning universal jurisdiction. They were not prepared to support Lord Nicholls' view, robustly expressed in Pinochet 1, that, 'international law has made plain that certain types of conduct, including torture and hostage taking, are not acceptable conduct on the part of anyone. This applies as much to heads of state, or even more so, as it does to anyone else; the contrary conclusion would make a mockery of international law.' The status of international legal norms in the domestic law of the UK was thus left unclear.

The political context against which the various hearings took place is examined in my own contribution to this volume. I consider two main issues:

the role of the Home Secretary Jack Straw and the Labour government, and the impact of political and contingent factors on the legal proceedings. With regard to the first, I argue that the matter was handled in a manner typical of New Labour in its first term of office – cautious, technocratic and sensitive to the requirements of pragmatism and the constraints of public and media opinion. The outcome of the UK proceedings – Pinochet's eventual release on medical grounds by decision of the Home Secretary – is best seen against a political and diplomatic context that changed over time. In the early phase of the Pinochet affair in the UK, under intense scrutiny from the media and public opinion and with political and emotive issues to the fore, Straw had little option but to play matters 'by the book'. In the latter stages, a decline of public interest in the case, a change of diplomatic tack by Chile, and the important fact that the denial of immunity had been confirmed by the courts, all made it easier for Straw to use the latitude allowed him under UK extradition law. While Straw's own 'quasi-judicial' role demonstrates quite clearly the entanglement of judicial and executive functions in institutional arrangements, it is harder to measure the impact of political considerations on the behaviour of the courts. Nevertheless, I argue that such considerations, aggravated by the acute embarrassment of the Hoffmann affair, may have played a part, especially in inclining the lords involved in Pinochet 3 toward the use of a narrow and technical reasoning that resulted in the convoluted compromise ruling of March 1999. In the national arena of the UK – as indeed in Spain and Chile – political sensitivities and practicalities constrained the options available to legal and political actors to make an actual trial of Pinochet unlikely.

Carlos Malamud differs from several contributors to this volume in viewing the Spanish role in the Pinochet case as properly a matter for executive rather than judicial decision-making. His analysis of the politics of the case in Spain in chapter 8 focuses on the actions and motivations of politicians and the media in the crucial weeks that surrounded Pinochet's arrest, setting these against a backdrop of strong majority public support for Pinochet's extradition to Spain. Domestic political considerations, he argues, were a primary factor shaping reactions and attitudes. The centre-right government of José María Aznar was placed in a most uncomfortable situation, in particular in November 1998 when called upon to decide whether to transmit Garzón's extradition request formally to the British authorities. While diplomatic and economic relations with Chile were a prime concern, for the government to block the extradition process would have undermined Aznar's efforts to distance himself and his party from associations with the Francoist past, and given credibility to opposition claims that the government was trying to interfere in the judicial process. Effectively, Malamud argues, Aznar's hands were tied. Meanwhile, opposition politicians of

the left sought to gain political advantage from the case by associating themselves with the cause of human rights, and the majority of press opinion was also
strongly in favour of extradition.

Malamud is sharply critical of the self-interest he detects at work in the
attitudes of some political, media and judicial actors (not least Garzón himself).
He gives greater credence to the rather isolated opinions of those who, like
former Prime Minister Felipe González, were uncomfortable with Spain's claim
to jurisdiction over the crimes of the Chilean dictatorship, and who would have
preferred to see Pinochet returned to Chile for trial, or dealt with by an international court. While Malamud concurs with other contributors to this volume
that attempts to apply universal jurisdiction raise difficult questions about the
relative functions of national executives and judiciaries, he goes further than
most in suggesting that the interpretation of genocide upheld by the Spanish
courts (a major plank of the rationale for Spanish jurisdiction) was flawed, and
that Spain's part in the Pinochet case could and should have been seen primarily
as a matter of foreign policy. Some kind of psychological transference factor –
to do to Pinochet what was not done to Franco – may have conditioned the
Spanish public reaction to the case. Of this too Malamud is critical, arguing that
it manifests both hypocrisy and an insensitivity toward the circumstances of the
Chilean transition to democracy, as well as to the right of Chileans to deal with
their own past in their own way. However, a question that may be asked in the
light of more recent developments – the start of a campaign within Spain to
publicise the locations of the mass graves of Republican victims of Francoist
repression and to identify their remains[8] – is whether the Pinochet case has had
a cathartic or galvanising effect upon those who would like to see some kind of
settling of accounts in relation to Spain's own past. Should this prove to be the
case, it would add a new twist to debates about transitional justice; coming to
terms with the past may be an issue relevant not only to newly democratised
nations.

---

8 In August 2002 campaigners who want Spain to set up a truth commission to investigate the
   fate of Franco's victims took their case to the United Nations working group on forced
   disappearances, after the PP refused to start the search for the bodies of an estimated 30,000
   executed and buried in mass graves. In November 2002 the UN working group
   recommended that Spain investigate at least two of the cases they had been presented with
   (they confined themselves to deaths and disappearances that occurred after 1945, when the
   organisation was founded). The Asociación para la Recuperación de la Memoria Histórica is
   coordinating the campaign in Spain. See 'La ONU pide que se investigue donde estan
   enterrados republicanos fusilados tras la guerra,' *El País*, 16 November 2002.

Geo-politics and international law

One obvious and immediate effect of the Pinochet case was to give new or renewed impetus to attempts to prosecute crimes against internationally recognised human rights norms, on the basis of claims to universal jurisdiction. The second House of Lords ruling, denying Pinochet sovereign immunity, was welcomed by some human rights groups as setting one of the most important international legal precedents since Nuremberg. Some five years on from the arrest, however, the application of the 'Pinochet precedent' has been far from consistent. The uneasiness of the international political climate in the wake of the attacks on the United States of 11 September 2001 makes prediction of the likely future development of international law extremely difficult. Will that development – the most tangible signal of which to date is the formal institution of the ICC – help safeguard human rights, prevent large-scale future abuses and provide a mechanism by which individuals responsible for such abuses, whatever position they hold, may be punished? Or will universal jurisdiction, selectively applied under the control of political organs, become one more weapon in the arsenal of the already powerful? The clear preference by the world's pre-eminent military and economic power for a model of international law enforcement that is subject to political control, was manifested powerfully in Bush's declared 'war on terror' as well as in the US campaign to undermine the ICC. The decision in June 2003 by the Belgian Parliament to limit its controversial law allowing universal jurisdiction[9] also does not seem to be a promising sign. At the same time, some significant results have been achieved at the regional or national level in what Naomi Roht-Arriaza identifies as a 'burgeoning field of transnational prosecutions', with domestic amnesties for past human rights crimes undermined and a growing number of high-ranking ex-military personnel facing prosecution. The opportunities, dangers, difficulties and paradoxes of developments in international and national law occurring alongside or after the Pinochet case are explored by a number of contributors to this book.

Challenging impunity in Latin America

Naomi Roht-Arriaza addresses the implications and effects of transnational prosecutions for Latin America, focusing particularly on efforts to seek justice

9 This decision was a result of mounting pressure and corresponding political embarrassment caused to the Belgian government by a number of controversial cases naming high profile individuals including George Bush, Ariel Sharon and Gen. Tommy Franks (commander of US forces in the recent Iraq war). The amendment will limit the reach of the law to cases involving Belgian citizens.

for victims of military repression. The Spanish investigations of the Argentine and Chilean military regimes were based upon the claim that jurisdiction was not available in these countries, where wide-ranging amnesty laws protected the military from scrutiny. A series of decisions by other national courts and the Inter-American Commission finding such amnesty laws to be in violation of international law have helped to devalue them, and encourage a renewed wave of challenges. New interpretations of amnesty laws – for example a recognition of a 'right to the truth', new investigative techniques such as DNA profiling, and the spread of local 'truth trials' – have all facilitated investigations and prosecutions. In 2001 an Argentine judge found the *punto final* (full stop) and due obedience laws (which protected the military from prosecution) to be unconstitutional and to violate international law. We may thus see 'the Pinochet effect' as a catalyst stimulating the action of domestic courts.

Roht-Arriaza welcomes such developments as positive in breaking down impunity, securing justice for past crimes, and making future abuses less likely. However, the resurgence of domestic investigations alongside the proliferation of transnational ones creates a number of difficulties, such as the potential for cases to undermine each other – already a number of incidents relating to Operation Condor are under investigation in several countries, with multiple extradition requests pending for the same defendants. The question of subsidiarity – that is, which country or court has the primary right to prosecute – is also critical. Events relating to Guatemala, discussed by both Roht-Arriaza and Antonio Remiro Brotóns, exemplify the increasingly apparent complexities of extra-territorial jurisdiction. In December 2000 the Spanish Audiencia Nacional denied Spanish jurisdiction over allegations of genocide, torture and state terrorism levelled at several high-ranking ex-military officers and three former heads of state. The basis for this denial was the subsidiarity principle – it could not be proved, the court decided, that Guatemalan domestic courts were unable to exercise jurisdiction, either as a result of amnesty laws or because the judiciary were subject to political pressures that prevented them from carrying out their functions. This decision, as well as signalling the Spanish courts reluctance to act as a kind of 'mini-ICC', leaves open a number of questions which will have to be addressed in the future, not least by the ICC itself. By what measure is it to be decided that domestic courts are 'unable or unwilling' to act (as the ICC statute demands) in order for extra-territorial jurisdiction to be invoked? Roht-Arriaza raises the possibility that repressive governments in the future may rely on informal means such as corruption or intimidation to prevent investigations, and that the impunity thus fostered may prove more difficult to challenge from outside the country than formal amnesty laws.

Democracy, sovereignty and universality

Transnational prosecution attempts also have political implications for the region and more widely, a theme explored by Alexandra Barahona de Brito in chapter 11. Examining the implications for democratic governance, she argues that the Pinochet case reflects a world uncomfortably poised between the traditional logic of state sovereignty and a new logic of universal jurisdiction. This in turn raises a number of questions about the nature and locus of sovereignty and for our understanding and practice of citizenship. Since the early 1970s, a 'human rights revolution' has introduced and gradually embedded the theory and practice of human rights into the international arena, creating a set of shared norms increasingly backed up by international law and institutions. The 'democratic revolution' – the spread of democracy through the 1980s and onward – has also allowed human rights and civil society organisations greater influence and reach, since democratic systems are more likely to allow such organisations to attain authority and legitimacy. A third key development is the proliferation of transnational networks promoting and pursuing human rights causes – without the cross-border activism of victims' associations, campaigning lawyers and human rights NGOs the Pinochet case would probably not have been possible – while a fourth is the existence of a global public easily reached and quickly mobilised on human rights issues. Such developments have facilitated transnational prosecution attempts, which allow us an insight into some of the opportunities and difficulties that they present.

In common with several other contributors, de Brito sees transnational prosecutions as mounting a challenge to the legitimacy of 'pacted' transitions to democracy. The pursuit of human rights cases in extra-national arenas can, as Roht-Arriaza and Bravo López show, have the effect of opening or reopening the 'justice versus stability' debate of the transitional period, reinvigorating domestic prosecution attempts and sparking reform of the structures and rules guaranteeing impunity. It may also, de Brito suggests, place a question mark over the meaning and quality of democracy and citizenship in newly democratised nations. Should there be a democratic right to seek justice? What right do people have to contest decisions made or accepted by citizens at the time of transition in the courts of other nations? Should such national courts be involved in judging the legitimacy of decisions made democratically in other countries? As de Brito points out, the widespread adoption of international conventions governing human rights norms would seem to justify such involvement, but it also implies a new conception of citizenship and rights. If a new model of transnational citizenship and sovereignty may be seen in the making, the international system does not yet possess the structures and rules that might make this nebulous conception a reality. While the logic of national sovereignty no longer rules supreme, the instruments to pursue universality are as yet weak and contradictory.

Universal criminal jurisdiction in the twenty-first century

The Pinochet case illustrates the increased influence judiciaries may acquire where human rights norms transcend national boundaries. Does this phenomenon amount to or presage 'a judicialisation of politics' and, if so, what are the implications? Contrasting perspectives on this issue are offered by our contributors. De Brito concedes that the potential impact of the pursuit of transnational prosecutions upon international relations gives some foundation to the executive's fear that their control over foreign policy is being usurped. She also points out that if a 'judicialisation of politics' is occurring, we must question the legitimacy of the new role acquired by judiciaries – not simply because they are unelected but also because different national legal systems and jurisprudential traditions may produce inconsistent rulings. Extradition requests from the various European countries for Pinochet were based on different reasonings and interpretations of domestic and international law. Which courts in which countries should be accorded primacy? This is more than a technical difficulty, as de Brito recognises. In an international society that is profoundly unequal in terms of both geo-political power and access to justice, transnational prosecutions may simply reflect such inequality, whether through the reassertion of 'old territorialities' or new patterns of power.

Antonio Remiro Brotóns and Juan Garcés, themselves lawyers, question the motives of those who, like Kissinger and others in the current US administration, have professed concerns that the application of universal jurisdiction will lead to the 'judicialisation of politics' or 'the politicisation of justice'. Some of those who see the application of state justice to international crimes as a process of politicisation simultaneously make support for the ICC conditional on its activity being subject to the control of political organs. The Clinton government was concerned to ensure a judicial model that would be dependent on the permanent members of the UN Security Council for its initiatives, and the Bush administration has gone further in insisting that justice must be applicable only to others. Aware that the currency of rules or norms claimed to be 'universal' is critically limited as long as the powerful may choose to exempt themselves, Remiro Brotóns and Garcés offer differing perspectives on the contemporary situation that may help elucidate the question of whether recent developments favouring the application of international criminal jurisdiction will have beneficial effects.

Remiro Brotóns examines three critical issues for the present and future

practice of international law; first, how far individuals responsible for internationally recognised crimes can be investigated using the principle of universality; second, what is the extent of immunity from prosecution of agents of
other states; and third, what should be the relationship between national judges
and international courts in preventing and punishing human rights crimes. In
relation to the first, Remiro Brotóns' survey of recent relevant cases and precedents reveals an unclear situation. While Spain's claim to exercise universal
jurisdiction in the Pinochet case had precedents in the decisions of other
national courts, Chile's insistence on its sole jurisdiction was never tested in an
international court. As has been repeatedly claimed by lawyers involved in the
Pinochet investigation, the Geneva Conventions commit those states that are
party to them to investigate serious infringements of the regulations, on the
basis of universal jurisdiction. Thus national judges in almost every country
have the jurisdiction to investigate such crimes wherever committed and
whatever the nationality or domicile of their perpetrators. The manner in which
this principle has been interpreted for operational purposes in international
treaties has tended to set some limitations, however. Thus the question of
whether the exercise of universal jurisdiction by individual states conforms to
the norms of international law is an open one, as is the related question of
whether states have carte blanche to incorporate the principle of universal
jurisdiction in their national criminal law – and if so, over which crimes.
Examining the current state of jurisprudence after the Pinochet case, Remiro
Brotóns concludes that whether or not the courts of a particular state can
exercise extra-territorial jurisdiction over international crimes depends on the
provisions of its internal law and on the constitutional handling of the relations
between customary international law and the criminal jurisdiction of the courts.
Even where the principle of universal jurisdiction is upheld by national courts,
selectivity may be seen in the treatment of cases. As already noted, the Spanish
Audiencia Nacional's decision not to proceed with the investigation of human
rights violations in Guatemala may reflect an unwillingness to take on the role
of 'refuge for all lost causes', at least as much as any genuine deferment to the
principle of subsidiarity.

The Pinochet case was of particular importance in that arguments surrounding the claiming of immunity in respect of international crimes were tested with
regard to the highest level of immunity possible – that of head of state. In the
course of the UK proceedings it was specifically recognised that the crimes of
which Pinochet was accused could not be seen as within the functions of a head
of state. International law has further established, with the trial of Slobodan
Milosevic, that a serving head of state may be tried by an international tribunal.
National courts, however, as Remiro Brotóns points out, are still reluctant to

refuse the immunity enjoyed by foreign agents accused of international crimes (the UK law lords, for example, unanimously agreed that Pinochet would be immune from UK jurisdiction if he were still a serving head of state). A recent pronouncement by the International Court of Justice upholding the immunity of a Congolese minister served with an international arrest warrant by a Belgian judge shows a marked reluctance on the part of the main judicial organ of the UN to accept any risk to the stability of international relations that may be posed by decentralised investigation of crimes, no matter how serious.

Hopes have frequently been expressed that the institution of a permanent International Criminal Court will clarify, if not resolve the kind of inconsistencies outlined above. While agreeing that more effective, and consistent avenues must be established for the investigation of grave international crimes, Remiro Brotóns sounds a note of caution. The ICC has inbuilt limitations: it will not have retrospective jurisdiction; it will only be able to exercise jurisdiction in cases where either the state where the crimes were committed or the state of which the accused is a national is party to the Statute that set up the court; and there are also a number of political preconditions accepted in the Statute that may limit its scope. There is a danger that the existence of the ICC may be used as an argument to prevent individual states from investigating international crimes – in the course of the Pinochet affair, for instance, Chile expressed its hope that the court would be operative as soon as possible, along with the concern that the Spanish magistrates were attempting to 'usurp its competencies'. Nor should the denial of criminal immunity to those accused of international crimes become the sole prerogative of the ICC, as some have proposed. While the preamble to the ICC Statute reaffirms its intention to put an end to impunity and the duty of each state to exercise criminal jurisdiction, Remiro Brotóns points out that the project of the Statute has already been weakened, first to attract the support of the Clinton administration, and subsequently by Bush's pursuit of exceptions and limitations to the Court's power to investigate alleged crimes by United States personnel.

US hostility to the ICC project is placed in historical and contemporary perspective by Juan Garcés, in a wide ranging and polemical contribution with which, because of its provocative and timely theme, we open the body of this volume. Garcés himself played a leading role in initiating the Spanish investigations into the activities of the southern cone dictatorships. These investigations uncovered a mass of evidence concerning the extent of US involvement and complicity in human rights crimes. Partly as a result of pressures from investigating lawyers, the Clinton government in 1999 ordered the declassification of thousands of CIA and State Department documents. These have confirmed much of what was already suspected about covert US involvement in the coup which ousted Allende in 1973, in the establishment of interrogation and torture centres under the Pinochet dictatorship, and in the planning and execution of other crimes, including some committed outside Chile. Following the arrest of Pinochet attempts have been made to question Henry Kissinger, who served as national security adviser and subsequently secretary of state from 1969–1977 under Presidents Nixon and Ford. Refusing to answer questions, Kissinger has recently set out his own vision of the imperatives for US foreign policy in the future,[10] a vision which Juan Garcés robustly criticises.

Garcés identifies the starting point of the contemporary international order as 1945, when revulsion at Nazi atrocities prompted states to make the landmark decision to place international relations under the rule of law, a decision enshrined in the principles set out in the UN Charter. The basic legal principles were then established by the Nuremberg Statute, the 1948 Treaty for the Prevention and Punishment of Genocide, and the Universal Declaration of Human Rights, adopted in 1948. Against this vision of universalism, Garcés sets in stark contrast the views of Kissinger, which have their roots in a much older tradition. For Garcés, Kissinger makes power the guiding principle of relations between states, in a way that recalls the absolutism of the European *anciens régimes* rather than the republican ideas accompanying the birth of the United States. His interpretation of the role of the United States in the world has the twin notions of 'balance of power' and 'spheres of influence' at its centre, as essential foreign policy instruments. These are used both to justify intervention in other states, and the prevention of the division of the world into antagonistic blocs. A foreign policy based upon such a world-view, Garcés suggests, assumes the right to act outside international law and to guarantee impunity for its US practitioners. Dire warnings that the application of universal jurisdiction threatens to substitute 'the tyranny of judges for that of states'[11] are revealed here as caricatures based upon a wilful and ignorant misinterpretation of the relevant rules and concepts. Kissinger's portrayal of the concept of universal jurisdiction as of recent vintage, for example, is simply false, ignoring the fact that certain crimes such as piracy have been subject to universal jurisdiction for centuries, while the principles on which extradition law is based go back to the seventeenth century and to the founding of modern states.

Garcés offers a robust defence of developments that many of our contributors have viewed with greater ambivalence. Far from endangering national sovereignty, he suggests, the development of international law by placing limits

10 Henry Kissinger, *Does America Need a Foreign Policy? Toward a Diplomacy for the 21st Century* (New York, 2001).

11 Kissinger, *Does America Need a Foreign Policy?*, p. 273.

on interventionism and unilateralism actually contributes to the strengthening of domestic sovereignty and democracy as well as to the peaceful regulation of relations between states. By contrast, interventionism of the kind Kissinger sanctioned in Chile and elsewhere makes a mockery of state sovereignty and international legality. The opposition of these two perspectives is of critical and timely importance.

PART I
Context

CHAPTER 2

Kissinger and Pinochet
facing universal jurisdiction

Juan E. Garcés

The international prosecution of Pinochet, which took place from July 1996 onwards following proceedings by the Spanish Audiencia Nacional to begin the initial investigation, occurred at a time when important international strategic concepts were attracting reconsideration.

First, in 1999, came President Clinton's executive order to declassify thousands of US Government documents containing information on criminal policies put into practice by the Pinochet regime.[1] Second, the Hinchey Amendment, passed in 1999 by both parties in the US Congress[2] obliged the CIA to inform Congress about its clandestine activities in Chile concerning three matters: the violent death of President Allende in 1973; the takeover of power by Pinochet; and the crimes committed by state officials under Pinochet's authority. In its response of September 2000[3] the CIA directorate publicly recognised, for the first time, the fact that,

some clandestine contacts of the CIA were involved in human rights abuses. The CIA, at the direction of and with the full concurrence of senior US policymakers, maintained official contacts with various security services. At the same time, the CIA maintained clandestine contacts with selected members of the Chilean military, intelligence and security forces, both to collect intelligence and carry out the covert actions described above. There is no doubt that some CIA contacts were actively engaged in committing and covering up serious human rights abuses. As a result of lessons learned in Chile, Central America and elsewhere, the CIA now carefully reviews all contacts for potential involvement in human rights abuses and makes a deliberate decision balancing

---

1 Chile Project 199900030.

2 Section 311 of the Intelligence Authorisation Act for Fiscal Year 2000 (Hinchey Amendment)

3 *The Hinchey Report on CIA Activities in Chile*, 18 September 2000, published by the House of Representatives, available at http://foia.state.gov/Reports/Hinchey Report. asp#toc

the nature and severity of the human rights abuse against the potential intelligence value of continuing the relationship. These standards, established in the mid-1990s, would likely have altered the amount of contact we had with perpetrators of human rights violators in Chile had they been in effect at that time.

Both decisions mark the beginning of a process of self-critical reconsideration in the highest political spheres in Washington of the strategies adopted during the Cold War. Analysis of the information contained in the documents made public will undoubtedly have an influence on future events. In this chapter I offer some reflections and observations, and raise a number of questions that remain to be answered.

1973–1990: the international context for the rise and consolidation of a criminal state in Chile

1945 was the starting point of the modern political world. The difficult and bloody defeat of Nazi fascism enhanced awareness of the need to place international relations under the rule of law. The UN Charter proclaimed three fundamental principles: (1) the freedom of every state to choose democratically its own form of government and economic system; (2) the respect and promotion of fundamental human values (articles 1, 55 and 56); and consequently (3) the supremacy and freedom of each country to determine its internal and external policy in a way compatible with the principles of the United Nations.
The basic principles for the setting out of international law emerged from the rubble and requirements of 1945, in particular those principles that conceived of 'humanity' itself as having rights:

- The principles of the Statute and Sentence of the Nuremberg Trial adopted by the UN General Assembly on 11 December 1946.
- The Treaty for the prevention and sanctioning of the crime of genocide adopted on 9 December 1948.
- The Universal Declaration of Human Rights adopted on 10 December 1948.

However, the roots of the international vision of the administration in office in the United States between 1968 and 1978 go back not to the universalism of 1945 but much further, not to the founding ideals of 1776 but to the *anciens régimes* and the principles laid down in the Peace of Westphalia of 1648: '*cuius regio eius religio*'. Such principles are incompatible with the liberal legacy of the revolutions of 1776 and 1789 that gave birth to the *citoyen* as a legal entity and postulated that government was subordinate to a nation of free citizens. Further, they are incompatible with the ongoing development of the *ius gentium* since the sixteenth and seventeenth centuries, and in effect, they subject international relations to the law of the jungle.

The overseer of US foreign policy between 1968 and 1976, Henry Kissinger, made 'power' and 'force' the guiding criteria for relations between countries, placing these beyond or even in contravention of international law, as he deemed fit. His ideas are an adaptation of the principles of the conservative Holy Alliance inspired by Metternich and of the balance of power theorised by Castlereagh. In a recent publication,[4] Kissinger invokes the principles of the Peace of Westphalia, which he presents as postulates of non-intervention and under their spell attempts to cover up the truth about clandestine and subversive operations against society and governments that occurred worldwide throughout the Cold War. In Chile the result was the establishment in 1973 of a state that practised terrorism, abduction, torture and assassination as instruments of social control.

During the Republican administrations of Richard Nixon and Gerald Ford, Kissinger made use of US government resources to intervene in and subvert states with internal or external arrangements that he disliked, to support financially and diplomatically the establishment of *de facto* regimes that used crimes against humanity to impose their authority, and to support terrorist practices that modernised some of the methods used by the fascist states defeated in 1945 by the Allies. A paradigmatic example is Chile where, in relation to the intervention undertaken during the Nixon administration, the concept of 'destabilisation' was developed to describe the sequence of undercover actions applied during the 1960s and 1970s that finally led in 1973 to an armed insurrection against the democratic institutions.[5]

In accordance with the 1925 Constitution the Chilean people democratically elect their government in presidential elections every six years. On 4 September 1970 a majority of the electorate voted for Salvador Allende. A few hours later Nixon and Kissinger ordered their services to cause a military revolt to prevent him from taking office.[6] The then head of the Chilean Army, General René Schneider, maintained that his duty was to respect the country's democratic institutions. Kissinger co-ordinated a terrorist operation that culminated with the general's death on 22 October 1970.[7]

---

4   Kissinger, *Does America need a Foreign Policy? Toward a Diplomacy for the 21st century* (New York, 2001)

5   See Report by William Colby, Director of the CIA, 24 April 1974 to the Intelligence Oversight Subcommittee of the House Armed Forces Committee; *The Washington Post*, 8 September 1974, article by S. Hersch and L. Stern.

6   See Senate Select Committee on Government Operations with Respect to Intelligence Activities: *Alleged Assassination Plots Involving Foreign Leaders*, US Printing Office, 1975, p. 228; Senate Select Committee on Government Operations with Respect to Intelligence Activities: *Covert Action Report*, US Printing Office, 1975, p. 92.

7   *Ibid*, 'Memorandum of Conversation,' 15 October 1970, held at the White House between Kissinger and others.

Throughout 1971, 1972 and 1973 Kissinger promoted and financed economic, social and political destabilisation operations in Chile, including terrorist operations.[8] On Saturday 8 September 1973 he received the US ambassador in Santiago de Chile, Nathaniel Davis, in his office with the following words: '*So there's going to be a coup in Chile!*'[9] He said this three days before 11 September 1973. With Kissinger's knowledge and support, the military insurrection plunged Chile into more than fifteen years of terror.

Pinochet received Kissinger on 8 June 1976, the day before Kissinger was to appear before the Assembly of the Organization of American States (OAS) in Santiago de Chile. Kissinger's involvement with Pinochet is verified in the *Memorandum of Conversation* of the then Secretary of State:

> In the United States, as you know, we are sympathetic with what you are trying to do here. (…) We wish your government well. (…) I'm going to speak about human rights this afternoon in the [OAS] General Assembly (…) I will refer in two paragraphs to the report on Chile of the OAS Human Rights Commission. I will say that the human rights issue has impaired relations between the US and Chile. This is partly the result of Congressional actions. I will add that I hope you will shortly remove these obstacles (…) I can do no less, without producing a reaction in the US which would lead to legislative restrictions. The speech is not aimed at Chile. I wanted to tell you about this. (…) None of this is said with the hope of undermining your government. I want you to succeed (…) Ninety-five percent of what I say is applicable to all the governments of the Hemisphere. It includes things your own people have said. (…) We want an outcome which is not deeply embarrassing to you. (…) We are not out to weaken your position (…) We want to help, not undermine you.[10]

The government that was overthrown in 1973 was a legally elected democratic government in a constitutional state with full and effective political, social, civic, cultural and religious freedoms. Multi-party parliamentary elections had taken place on the previous 4 March and on 11 September President Allende, according to comments he made two days beforehand to the head of the army, was to read a message to the nation calling for a referendum.[11] In contrast to this democratic practice, Kissinger's protégés imposed something unprecedented in the history of Chile – they suppressed the representative form of government, they closed down congress, they prohibited political parties, elections, freedom

---

8 See *Hinchey Report*, cited in note 3; and the 'Church Commission Report' (*Covert Action in Chile 1963–1973*. 94th Congress 1st Session. COMMITTEE PRINT. Staff Report of the Select Committee to Study Governmental Operations With Respect to Intelligence Activities. UNITED STATES SENATE. December 18, 1975).

9 Nathaniel Davis, *The Last Two Years of Salvador Allende* (Ithaca, NY, 1985), p. 358.

10 Department of State. *Memorandum of Conversation*, 8 June 1976, declassified in 1999.

11 This matter is explained in Juan Garcés, *Allende et l'expérience chilienne* (Paris, 1976).

of the press and civil rights, and installed a system founded on terror, murder and torture.

Court investigations in Europe, the USA, Argentina and Chile have gathered proof of the way in which terrorist activities, abductions, torture, murder and 'disappearances' committed by state officials in Chile, Argentina and Uruguay were co-ordinated in the months and years following the military insurrection on 11 September 1973 in Chile. Documents declassified by the US Government in 1999 and 2000 have confirmed Kissinger's knowledge of the planning and carrying out of these crimes while they were being committed.[12]

Kissinger's retrospective view in 2001

Looking back in 2001, Kissinger adopted an effectively meaningless position. On the one hand, he presented his policy of undercover actions, which totally contravened UN principles, as being one of 'non-intervention' while, on the other, he described the effective application of the principles of the Charter in the trial of those accused of crimes against humanity as 'intervention': 'non-interference in the domestic affairs of other states has been abandoned in favour of a concept of universal humanitarian intervention or universal jurisdiction.'[13]

Here, Kissinger assimilated two different concepts and distorted them both. 'Universal jurisdiction' as a concept and practice is characterised by basic premises such as the fact that it is subject to pre-existing laws adopted by states in treaties that are freely ratified, such as the 1984 treaty that penalises torture, and laws passed in respective national parliaments. These laws are, in turn, subject to control by the courts of justice in constitutional states where the principles of 'nullum crimen sine lege', the right to due process and full guarantees of defence and appeal are enforced. The concept of 'humanitarian intervention' is different in that its application, according to present-day law, is founded on the UN Charter and is subject to the political and not jurisdictional bodies of this organisation.

International law is seen by Kissinger as an obstacle to what he considers necessary, that is a free hand to use instruments of internal or foreign policy

12   See, for example, the document signed by Kissinger, with a report enclosed on 19 July 1976, No. 1976 STATE 178852, on the co-ordination of criminal operations in the countries that participated in *Operación Cóndor*, to which the Embassy in Buenos Aires replied, confirming the involvement of 'Condor' in the co-ordinating of crimes; telegram from the US Embassy in Santiago de Chile to the Department of State, ref. 0071606Z June 1976; CIA, The National Intelligence Daily, 23 June 1976: 'S. America: Anti-Refugee Action,' and July 2 1976, on the co-ordination between Chile, Bolivia, Uruguay, Paraguay, Brazil and Argentina in what this newsletter calls 'Operación Cóndor'; INR afternoon summary, 23 November 1976.

13   Kissinger, *Does America Need a Foreign Policy?*, p. 21.

outside or even in contravention of the law, without having to take international law into account. This non-recognition of the limits of international law by a state is in accordance with the policy sponsored and practised by Kissinger and those who share his perspective.

The politics of 'balance of power'

For Kissinger 'the United States and its allies must stress – against all their inclinations – that their concerns with the balance of power did not end with the Cold War'.[14]

'Balance of power' has been an instrument of policy since at least the seventeenth century. It has been a basic principle of British foreign policy, formulated by Castlereagh,[15] Canning,[16] and practised in the twentieth century by Neville Chamberlain and Winston Churchill. Its legacy to the world is clearly seen in one increasingly devastating hegemonic war after another. From the point of view of the global interests of humanity, the balance of power as an instrument of international policy has had different results to those vaunted by contemporary subscribers to the 1648 Peace of Westphalia.

Kissinger made use of the concept of balance of power to rationalise the setting up of states of terror within the area of influence of the USA, to cause and maintain domestic and international civil wars in Asia (Vietnam, Cambodia, Indonesia, East Timor), Africa (Angola, Mozambique) and Latin America (Chile, Argentina, Uruguay, Bolivia, Brazil, Guatemala). He applied the same concept in 2001 to explain how he envisaged a new hegemonic conflict in Europe, directed at preventing a reunified Germany from acting as a nexus between western and eastern Europe during times of peace. What Kissinger does not explain is that this same nexus, given the means to construct it pacifically and in a way that respected the principles of the UN, would in itself transcend the basic concepts of 'balance of power' and 'spheres of influence', which could lead to an unprecedented era in international relations. He does, however, foresee this risk and asks for a free hand to abort it outside and/or in contravention of international law:

> Germany's willingness to accept a subordinate status in NATO as well as in Europe has diminished. As Russian recovery gains momentum, the traditional temptation of special German relations with Russia has reappeared. (...)

14 *Ibid.*, p. 77.
15 See his State Paper of 5 May 1820, in H.V. Temperley and L.M. Penson (eds.), *Foundations of British Foreign Policy* (Cambridge, 1938), p. 48; C.K. Webster, *The Foreign Office of Castlereagh, 1815–1822* (London, 1947), p. 51.
16 See H.V. Temperley, *The Foreign Policy of Canning, 1822–1827. Holy Alliance and the New World* (London, 1925).

Germany may well seek for itself the role within Europe that France insists Europe should play within the Atlantic Alliance. (...) As Germany's relative role and power grow, and as Russia recovers, there will emerge temptations for a special Russo-German rapprochement based on the Bismarck tradition.[17]

Kissinger's political approach is not unique to him. The policy of the Truman administration towards Europe after the Potsdam Conference (July–August 1945) and of successive US administrations broke with the strategic concepts of the Roosevelt administration. With Truman, the United States adopted and applied the principles of the balance of power and areas of influence for the first time, leading to the dividing of Germany, the rearming of Western Europe and the isolation in Europe of the Western bloc from the Eastern bloc by means of programmes and institutions that sustained the Cold War for 45 years. In 2001 Kissinger disguised the reality of this bloc diplomacy by affirming that if the United States were to abstain from opposing an alignment between Germany and Russia 'the Atlantic relationship would change its character and become more like the traditional European diplomacy of balancing rewards and penalties',[18] which, according to him, would be equivalent to a modernised version of 'appeasement' as practised by Neville Chamberlain in the 1930s up to Hitler's invasion of Czechoslovakia in 1938. Kissinger keeps silent about the fact that it was Chamberlain himself who declared war on Germany in September 1939, one week after Berlin established an alliance with Moscow.

In 2001 Kissinger proposed that the United States intervene to prevent an agreement between what Castlereagh in 1820 called the 'western mass' in Europe (led today by Germany) and the 'eastern mass' (Russia and its surroundings, in 1820 and today). Given that such a 'preventive intervention' would be against international law, Kissinger is in effect declaring that such law must be seen as an enemy by leaders who wish to have a free hand to practice inhuman policies. In other words, in *Does America need a foreign policy? Toward a diplomacy for the 21st Century* Kissinger is postulating the need for a new hegemonic war to succeed the Cold War that ended in 1990. This is the fatal logic inherent to using the idea of the balance of power as a means of guiding international policy.

The criticism that Kissinger makes of the Clinton administration points to the fact that Clinton failed to embrace the criteria practised by the administrations in which Kissinger worked. The Clinton administration espoused a different concept, that of 'collective security' within which international law does have an important role to play and, consequently, those who are in power do not have a free hand to use criminal acts as an instrument of policy. For

17 Kissinger, *Does America Need a Foreign Policy?*, p. 40.
18 *Ibid.*, p. 41.

Kissinger, the concept of collective security 'threatens to dissolve NATO into a multilateral mishmash'.[19] At the beginning of the twenty-first century, the policy of 'balance of power' requires the prevention of any form of basic agreement aimed at overcoming the division of Europe, Asia, and the rest of the world into antagonistic blocs. Kissinger declares 'international law' to be the enemy of such a policy (along with the UN Charter, treaties to prevent crimes against humanity and universal jurisdiction for penalising them).

The legal logic that informs the UN Charter and treaties to prevent international crime is the same, namely to place the world under the *rule of law*. Given the level of current technological development, this is both increasingly necessary and feasible. To overcome the lethal effects of the strategies inherited from the putting into practice of the 'balance of power' concept, the international community needs to strengthen the rule of international law and prevent and penalise international crime. This is a field where Kissinger and those who think like him are insecure.

The spectre of Karl Haushofer[20]

In order to sustain his argument for governing outside international law Kissinger caricatures the transcendence of the division of Europe into 'eastern' and 'western' masses, and presents a Germany that

> without the United States … would lack an anchor to restrain national impulses (even as a member of the European Union); both Germany and Russia would be tempted to view each other as their best foreign policy option. At the same time, the U.S., separated from Europe would become, geopolitically, an island off the shores of Eurasia resembling nineteenth-century Britain vis-à-vis Europe. It would become obliged to conduct the kind of balance of power strategy toward Europe that it has traditionally rejected.[21]

This determination to hide the reality of the past does not bode at all well, showing a tendency to view the present in Manichean terms in order to present a distorted vision of the future. The strategy of 'balance of power' has been applied by the United States since Truman and throughout the entire Cold War. Another policy is possible in Europe and the world as a whole, however, one that can prevent such lethal principles from being used. Such a policy can become possible as the rule of law develops in international relations.

19   *Ibid.*, pp. 43–4.
20   Karl Haushofer (1869–1946) was a founding father of the discipline of geopolitics, often identified with Nazi doctrines of world domination. His *Der Kontinentalblock: Mitteleuropa–Eurasien–Japan* (Munich, 1941) advocated a Eurasiatic great continental bloc. It was published in a French translation as *De la géopolitique* (Paris, 1986), pp. 113–54.
21   Kissinger, *Does America Need a Foreign Policy?*, p. 52.

Insofar as the national interests of Europeans coincide less and less with those of the United States, the political paradigm proposed by Kissinger presupposes attempts by the United States to fragment the European Union in order to weaken it until it falls apart.[22] In the contemporary history of the United States, however, an alternative does exist to the paradigmatic kind of 'out-law' that Kissinger has practised and continues to sponsor. Designed by Franklin D. Roosevelt to build peace following the defeat of the fascist countries, it involved leaving behind the traditional division of the world into areas of influence and developing instruments of international relations subordinate to the rule of law. Kissinger, by contrast, in promoting a sphere of influence for the United States and prohibiting other states from having one, is sowing the conceptual seeds of a new hegemonic confrontation:

> Russian membership in NATO would turn the Atlantic Alliance into a mini-United Nations type of security instrument or, alternatively, into an anti-Asian – especially anti-Chinese – alliance of the Western industrial democracies. Russian membership in the European Union, on the other hand, would split the two sides of the Atlantic. Such a move would inevitably drive Europe further toward seeking to define itself by its distinction from the US and would oblige Washington to conduct a comparable policy in the rest of the world.[23]

Kissinger's proposal for the future: a return to Metternich and his Holy Alliance

The reality underlying the strategic concepts developed by Metternich in Germany and followed by Kissinger is well-known, though no mention is made of the source: state absolutism as opposed to the republican ideals of 1776 (in the United States) and 1789 (in Europe) that Kissinger conceals by presenting them as 'militarism':

> At the end of the Napoleonic Wars (...) despite the fear of a resurgence of French militarism, Europe nevertheless succeeded in integrating France into the international system. The Quadruple Alliance – of Russia, Britain, Austria and Prussia – protected Europe against a militarily resurgent France. At the same time, France was made an equal participant with the members of the Quadruple Alliance (...). Some analogous solution is needed for the contemporary international order. NATO must be maintained as a hedge against a reimperializing Russia. Coincidentally, the industrial democracies should design a responsible system of co-operation with Russia.[24]

---

22 *Ibid.*, p. 54. Kissinger explains his opposition to a politically autonomous European military force with regard to NATO in pages 58 and 61.
23 *Ibid.*, p. 79.
24 *Ibid.*, pp. 79–80.

The important thing to note here is that the plan Kissinger puts forward rests on the premise that its implementation is above all international legal principles, and further, that it presupposes the struggle to distribute the world into areas of influence:[25] Thus, he argues, for example, that:

- the USA must turn implacable when the balance of power or America's national interest are, in fact, threatened;[26]
- if US troops leave the rim of Asia, an entirely new security, and above all political situation would arise all over the continent;[27]
- faced with a threat of hegemony in Asia – whatever the regime – the USA would resist as it did Japan's in the Second World War and the Soviet Union's in the Cold War.[28]

The practice of such a policy of blocs, of a policy of force, is outside international law and assumes the need to use war crimes and crimes against humanity, if deemed appropriate, as an instrument, as well as the necessity to carry out undercover operations in sequences of constant low or high intensity warfare, a state of war maintained indefinitely as a means of achieving discipline within one's own bloc and of harassing a (real or imaginary) rival.[29]

Resorting to systematic crime as a political instrument is also held to be a suitable remedy given the symptoms that are emerging from the social and economic situation within the United States' own sphere of influence, to which Kissinger alludes:

a permanent world-wide underclass is in danger of emerging, especially in developing countries, which will make it increasingly difficult to build the political consensus on which domestic stability, international peace, and globalization itself depend ...

the dark cloud that is hanging over globalization is the threat of a global unravelling of the free market system under political pressure ... the international economic system may come to face a crisis of legitimacy ...[30]

25　*Ibid.*, p. 95: he argues that both MERCOSUR, and the free trade agreement that it has with the countries of the European Union; 'are contrary to the US national interest'.

26　*Ibid.*, p. 118.

27　*Ibid.*, p. 134.

28　*Ibid.*, p. 137.

29　'America's first national interest in Asia is to prevent domination of the continent by any single power, especially an adversarial one,' *ibid*, p. 160.

30　Kissinger, *Does America Need a Foreign Policy?*, pp. 230–3.

International law, crimes against humanity and universal jurisdiction

Those who are in favour of subjecting international relations to the rules of the jungle, who have carried out clandestine operations in the domestic affairs of other states and who want to practise them in the future, dread the advance of the rule of international law. By limiting outside interventionism, the application of international law contributes to the strengthening of the domestic sovereignty of states. The expansion of universal jurisdiction over crimes against humanity and terrorism limits impunity and also makes it difficult for Kissinger's emulators to breed more Pinochets. The development of international law in accordance with the UN Charter favours democracy within state borders and reduces the use with impunity of crime as an instrument of power.

To those who believe in dividing the world up into areas of influence, one must point out that the principles of absolutism of 1648, the Holy Alliance after the French Revolution and the balance of power of the nineteenth and twentieth centuries cannot be the paradigm for either the present or the future of humanity. Their limitations in preventing the spiral of human catastrophes that have occurred on an increasingly horrendous and massive scale have all too clearly been shown. Those who postulate the principles of the Peace of Westphalia today are those who have made the greatest use of clandestine operations to subvert the stability of other states. Interventions like Kissinger's in Chile between 1968 and 1976 make a mockery of the sovereignty of states, of the UN Charter of 1945 and of international legality.

By contrast, the current regulations that establish universal jurisdiction over crimes against humanity assume that state rulers are subordinate to the double control of international law and local law that in both cases must be applied by independent judges.

Just as the rule of law can be made compatible within the national arena through the criteria of discretion and opportunity that are typical of political and governmental spheres, it must also be possible to achieve this in international relations. This compatibility is dreaded by those who favour the impunity of crime insofar as this is their instrument for imposing a particular view of the world. They do not want to hear about the fact that civilisation has generated the necessary principles of law, of *ius cogens* or of insurmountable limits such as the right to life and the free dignity of every nation and individual. They conceal their rejection of international law by caricaturing universal jurisdiction as 'substituting the tyranny of judges for that of governments; historically, the dictatorship of the virtuous has often led to inquisitions and even witch-hunts'.[31] Observe here that the law itself is absent in this caricature and that, in his

31 *Ibid.*, p. 273.

negation of justice and impartiality that are the purpose of law, Kissinger converts the judges into 'tyrants'.

The caricatures sketched by Kissinger do not stand up to the slightest analysis. Here are just a few:

> The doctrine of universal jurisdiction asserts that there are crimes so heinous that their perpetrators should not be able to escape justice by invoking doctrines of sovereignty or the sacrosanct nature of national frontiers.[32]

Kissinger's premise makes an amalgam of different political, legal and judicial concepts, with confusion the result. The principles of *sovereignty* and *non-intervention* in the domestic affairs of states form part of the Charter of the United Nations. The 'undercover' or 'indirect intervention' that Kissinger practised in various states, particularly Chile, to 'destabilise' the democratic socio-political system and make way for a dictatorship founded on crime is contrary to both of these. A different concept is that of 'crime against humanity', which has been developed in conventional terms beginning with the Charter of the Nuremberg Tribunal (1945), the Judgement of the Nuremberg Tribunal (1946) and the Principles of the Charter and Judgement of the Nuremberg Tribunal adopted by the general Assembly of the United Nations on 11 December 1946, which form part of customary international law.

The Member States of the United Nations are under voluntary obligation to prevent and punish these crimes, whether they are committed in times of peace or war, having ratified the Charter of the United Nations in 1945 and the successive Agreements drawn up by the UN such as those that penalise genocide (drawn up in 1948) and torture (adopted in 1984). Furthermore, the Geneva Conventions of 1949 and their Additional Protocols made it obligatory for states to try and punish 'war crimes' in accordance with the principle of universal jurisdiction.

Thus, contrary to what is claimed by Kissinger, application of the prevention and punishment of crimes against humanity and war crimes is perfectly legitimate and compatible with the rest of the United Nations' principles. They all form part of the same legal system. What is not compatible with international law since 1945 is the invocation of *sovereignty* as a protective umbrella for the impunity of individuals while they are committing such crimes and afterwards, to escape justice, even when the suspected criminal leaves the territory that has served as refuge for him. This is what Kissinger has done in the case of Pinochet since 11 September 1973 and again after Pinochet in October 1998 voluntarily travelled to the United Kingdom, where the courts, exercising their jurisdiction and their obligations in accordance with international treaties, obliged Pinochet

32 *Ibid.*, pp. 273–4.

to appear, with all guarantees of defence, to decide whether he would be tried in London or extradited to another country whose Courts had requested extradition in accordance with international and national law. The Bow Street Magistrates' Court finally ruled on extradition on 8 October 1999.[33]

'The very concept of universal jurisdiction is of recent vintage.'[34]

Kissinger's second premise ignores the origins in time of the extra-territorial persecution of certain crimes. The basic principle of extradition, *'aut dedere aut judicare'* (the person is either extradited to the country that wants to judge him or is subject to trial in the country where he or she is), has its origins in the beginnings of modern states and international law. The Spaniard Diego de Covarrubias[35] in the sixteenth century and the Dutchman Hugo Grotius[36] in the seventeenth century considered it intolerable for a criminal to benefit freely from crimes committed in another country, and they concluded that the alleged offender should be arrested in the place where he was at the time and either be judged there or extradited to the place where the crime was committed, if he was sought for trial there. Similarly, the principle of universal jurisdiction has been applied to pirates for centuries and was reaffirmed by the Geneva Convention on the Law of the Sea of 29 December 1958 and art. 105 of the Treaty of Montego Bay of 10 December 1982. The Conventions against Genocide (1948), the Geneva Convention of 1948 and the Convention against Torture (1984), among others, assume or affirm universal competence to persecute these crimes.

> It is unlikely that any of the signatories of the United Nations conventions thought it possible that national judges would use them as a basis for extradition requests regarding alleged crimes not committed in their jurisdiction.[37]

Kissinger's third premise denies the binding character, even where this is *self executing*, of the legal principles established in ratified international treaties and incorporated into internal legislative systems, thus making the application of these principles by the courts obligatory. The wording of the Conventions, or the *travaux préparatoires* for each one, makes clear Kissinger's sophistry. For example, article 5 of the Convention against Torture rules that:

---

33 Judgement in the Bow Street Magistrates' Court THE KINGDOM OF SPAIN v. AUGUSTO PINOCHET Mr Ronald David Bartle Metropolitan Magistrate 8 October 1999 (magist/magistfr.htm" http://www.lcd.gov.uk/magist/pinochet.pdf).

34 Kissinger, *Does America Need a Foreign Policy?*, p. 274.

35 Diego de Covarrubias y Leyva, *Practicarum quaestionum* (Salamanca, 1560) chapter II, No. 7. Covarrubias (1512–1577) was a minister under Philip II of Spain – President of the *Consejo de Castilla y de las Indias* – and also a lecturer at the University of Salamanca.

36 Hugo Grotius, *De Iure Belli ac Paci* (Paris, 1625) book II, chapter XXI, para. 4; book I, chapter V.

37 Kissinger, *Does America Need a Foreign Policy?*, p. 275.

1. Each State Party shall take such measures as may be necessary to establish its jurisdiction over the offences referred to in article 4 in the following cases:

   (a) When the offences are committed in any territory under its jurisdiction or on board a ship or aircraft registered in that State;

   (b) When the alleged offender is a national of that State;

   (c) When the victim is a national of that State if that State considers it appropriate.

2. Each State Party shall likewise take such measures as may be necessary to establish its jurisdiction over such offences in cases where the alleged offender is present in any territory under its jurisdiction and it does not extradite him pursuant to article 8 to any of the States mentioned in paragraph 1 of this article.

3. This Convention does not exclude any criminal jurisdiction exercised in accordance with internal law.

The British courts granted Pinochet's extradition to Spain on the basis of application of the provisions of article 5 of the Convention against Torture, with the jurisdiction of the Spanish courts being exercised by virtue of the provisions of article 23.4 of the Spanish Constitutional Law of Judicial Power (*Ley Orgánica del Poder Judicial*) of 1 July 1985.[38]

> It was never argued until very recently that the various UN declarations (sic) subjected past and future leaders to the possibility of prosecution by national magistrates of third countries without due process safeguards or institutional restraints.[39]

Kissinger's fourth premise is a confusion between what is a UN 'declaration' and a normative 'agreement'. He is unaware of the fact that compliance is obligatory when an Agreement is ratified by a state and incorporated into its internal law.

His fifth premise consists of another amalgam, between, on the one hand, extra-territorial jurisdiction (the basis of which in the Pinochet case consisted in international treaties freely ratified by Chile, Spain and the United Kingdom) and on the other hand, elements of the internal judicial system such as *due process* and *institutional restraint*, that must be respected in any case pursuant to the provisions of Conventions such as the International Pact of Civil and Political Rights of 19 December 1966 (arts. 14 and 15), that raise the customary principles contained in Declarations like the Universal Declaration of Human Rights of 10 December 1948 (arts. 10, 11 and 30) to conventional law.

---

38 Article 23.4 of the Spanish Constitutional Law of Judicial Power: '*4. Spanish jurisdiction is also competent for establishing offences committed by Spanish citizens and those of other countries outside of the national territory that can be classified, according to Spanish criminal law, as one of the following crimes:*

a) Genocide. b) Terrorism. c) Piracy and air piracy. d) Falsification of foreign currency. e) Crimes connected with prostitution. f) Illegal trafficking of psychotropic, poisonous and narcotic drugs. g) Any other that, according to international treaties and conventions, should be persecuted in Spain.'

39 Kissinger, *Does America Need a Foreign Policy?*, p. 275.

It is not surprising that from such premises Kissinger derives equally ill-founded affirmations. For example, his ignorance of:

- the fact that the Spanish courts which have investigated Pinochet since 1996 and which indicted him in 1998 are courts in a democratic system operating under the rule of law and in a time frame where the Cold War, which protected the continuity of the dictatorship – established in Spain with the help of the German Third Reich and fascist Italy – up until the death of Franco in 1975, had already come to an end.
- the difference, on the one hand, between judicial proceedings for the extradition of an alleged offender (which rest on the concurrence of the formal assumptions for extradition) and, on the other, trial in court on the basis of the alleged charges in the claiming State.[40]
- the request to extradite Pinochet, which Kissinger presents as '*seeking to try him for crimes committed against Spaniards on Chilean soil*', that is to say, a jurisdiction based on *passive national* jurisdiction.
- the fact that the aim of Spain's action was to try Pinochet for the crimes of which he is accused, whatever the nationality of the thousands of victims, as is typical of crimes against humanity and universal jurisdiction.[41]
- the fact that the extradition granted on 8 October 1999 by the British courts referred to alleged crimes of torture committed upon non-Spanish victims.

It would be ironic if a doctrine designed to transcend the political process turns into a means to pursue political enemies rather than universal justice (...) A universal standard of justice should not be based on the proposition that a just end justifies unjust means, or that political fashion trumps fair judicial procedures (...) universal jurisdiction may undermine the political will to sustain the humane norms of international behaviour so necessary to temper the violent times in which we live.[42]

The sixth premise of Kissinger's caricature ignores the judicial essence of universal jurisdiction and turns it into an instrument of lowly and ignoble political struggles. His ignorance of the meaning of international law and rule of law would appear to be boundless. Kissinger then takes the ingenious conceptual scaffolding that he has constructed and launches it like a missile against another UN treaty, signed in Rome in July 1998 by 120 states, which set up the International Criminal Court (ICC) with the authority to try crimes of genocide, crimes against humanity and war crimes. Kissinger attributes the ICC with the imaginary premises explained above and stretches them to even greater absurdity by presenting the ICC as

40 *Ibid.*, p. 278.
41 *Ibid.*, p. 275.
42 *Ibid.*, pp. 278–9, 282.

assigning the ultimate dilemmas of international politics to unelected jurists – and to an international judiciary – (...) the advocates of universal jurisdiction seek to place governments under the supervision of magistrates and the judicial system (...).[43]

Here Kissinger crosses the limits of intellectual dishonesty by supporting his thesis with fabrications that he attributes to unidentified persons: 'the advocates of universal jurisdiction argue that the state is the basic cause of war and cannot be trusted to deliver justice.'[44]

Such a peculiar postulate is alien to the doctrine and practice of universal jurisdiction applied by both state tribunals (from the Eichmann case in 1961 before the Jerusalem District Court and the High Court of Israel,[45] to the Pinochet case before the Courts of the United Kingdom, Spain and Belgium), and the International Tribunals created in 1945 for Germany and Japan, and in 1993 and 1995 for the former Yugoslavia and Rwanda. It is also alien to the Treaty of Rome of July 1998, which establishes the primacy of state tribunals to investigate and judge crimes over which the ICC has jurisdiction when the alleged criminal cannot be tried by the courts where the crime was committed or where he is a national citizen, or where they do not want to try him.

As opposed to the prosecution of war crimes, crimes against humanity and genocide by the International Criminal Court, or by the state tribunals that apply international conventions incorporated into their internal legislation, what proposal does Kissinger offer when the courts of the country in which the crimes have been committed are unable or unwilling to judge them, or where those of the state of which the alleged criminal is a national citizen are similarly unable or unwilling? His solution is that they can only be tried if the UN Security Council agrees to create an *ad hoc* tribunal, according to the model created for the former Yugoslavia and Rwanda.[46] In other words, bearing in mind that the Security Council is a political body in which, moreover, some states have the right of veto, international criminal law could only be effectively applied case by case insofar as, and according to the way in which this was authorised by the political power. Kissinger could not state more plainly that the 'rule of law' and the bodies for its jurisdictional control neither exist nor can exist permanently in international relations. Further, he insists that acts by states entailing crimes against humanity, genocide and war crimes are neither subordinate nor can be made uninterruptedly subordinate to international law, and

43 *Ibid.*, pages 279–81
44 *Ibid.*, p. 281.
45 Eichmann case, *I.L.R.*, 36, pp. 39–42, 45–8, 288, 295.
46 Kissinger, *Does America Need a Foreign Policy?*, p. 282.

that law that is applicable to and that penalises the above-mentioned serious crimes should be subordinated to the discretion and arbitration of political power.

Such conclusions reaffirm the absolutist and pre-modern foundations of Kissinger's way of thinking, rooted in a centuries-old practice quite contrary to the development of the democratic values that have succeeded one another since the social and political changes that occurred in 1688 in England, in 1776 and 1789 in the United States and France, and in 1945 in the whole world. For if the *ancien régime* established state law, then the democratic revolutions sought to establish the Law of Humanity, as Immanuel Kant explained so well.[47]

The system defended by Kissinger is incompatible with an international society governed by international law whose primacy over internal legislation is a principle recognised by the international community. For the former secretary of state of presidents Nixon and Ford, the development of the rule of law in relations between states, and within states, is an enemy to be beaten. In the world without common law that Kissinger defends, power without any other limit than force outside of the law, the inherent resorting to massive crime practised on countries and people, the continual impunity of the worst criminals, has been, is and will be the seed of violence between states. And this is also true within the borders of states, whatever their level of development, cultural identity and geographical location.

In today's world, a realistic approach is one that recognises that global needs cannot be countered by one nation, no matter how powerful, that repressive authoritarian regimes are a long term danger, even if in the short term they assure local or regional stability, and that the rule of law is vital to the success of economic progress and internal and international peace.

So far, the most important terrorist act carried out in the United States by agents in the service of a foreign country that has been judged before the courts, resulting in firm and definitive convictions, took place in Washington, DC, on 21 September 1976. On that day, a commando under the orders of the secret services of Kissinger's protégé used a bomb to blow up a car travelling along Embassy Row, killing a US citizen, Ronnie Moffit, and the man who had been Chilean Ambassador to the United States between November 1970 and June 1973, Orlando Letelier.[48] More recently, the case of the terrorist attack in New York and Washington on 11 September 2001 is, at the time of writing, judicially still open, although the US authorities maintained that it was organised with the direct or indirect support of the Taliban regime established in Afghanistan at

---

47 Immanuel Kant, *Perpetual Peace: A Philosophical Sketch* (Könisberg, 1795 and 1796).

48 See Taylor Branch and Eugene M. Propper, *Labyrinth* (New York, 1983); John Dinges and Saul Landau, *Assassination on Embassy Row* (New York, 1981). Joan Garcés and Saul Landau, *Orlando Letelier, testimonio y vindicación* (Madrid, 1996).

the end of the 1980s with the financial and military support of the Reagan Administration.[49]

Professor Georges Scelle taught in 1948 that 'seule la société internationale détient la souveraineté et l'inexistence présente d'organes internationaux supérieurs à l'État relève d'une "carence institutionnelle" à laquelle il est possible et nécessaire de remédier'.[50] International law has been, and must continue to be, an instrument of solidarity to democratise and humanise international life between individuals, people and states.

49 See Jean-Charles Brisard and Guillaume Dasquié, *Ben Laden. La verité interdite* (Paris, 2001).
50 Only international society possesses sovereignty, and the current absence of international organs superior to the state expresses an 'international inadaequacy' which it is possible and necessary to remedy. Georges Scelle, *Manuel de Droit International Public* (Paris, 1948).

CHAPTER 3

Constitutional and political foundations of impunity in Chile

Brian Loveman

The arrest in England in October 1998 of Chile's ex-dictator and president, Senator Augusto Pinochet Ugarte, raised numerous issues of international law and significantly complicated domestic politics in Chile, the UK and Spain. The Pinochet case, initiated in Spain in 1996 by the head prosecutor of the Superior Court of Valencia, joined together human rights activists and organisations from Argentina, Chile, the UK, the European Community and the United States. It quickly took on broad international implications due to the special circumstances of Spanish law, Chilean–Spanish bilateral treaties, and the judicial activism of Spanish judges, in particular of Manuel García Castellón and Baltasar Garzón Real.[1]

A central concern in the Pinochet case, for human rights organisations, for the prevailing system of international law and for domestic political actors in the affected countries was the extent of immunity and/or impunity that could be enjoyed by former national political leaders, or those currently claiming diplomatic or sovereign immunity under international norms, in cases involving international human rights law. The Pinochet case posed directly the question of whether Spain, or any other country, might exercise jurisdiction over crimes committed in foreign territory, by foreign civilian or military personnel, against a country's own citizens or citizens of other countries. It also raised the issue of universal jurisdiction for certain types of crimes under international law, particularly crimes against human rights as defined in the Geneva Conventions and subsequent human rights treaties, conventions and regional regimes, such as the Inter-American Commission on Human Rights.[2]

1 See Madeleine Davis, *The Pinochet Case* (London, 2000).
2 For a discussion of the applicability in Chile of the Universal Declaration of Human Rights, the Charter of the Organization of American States, and other international and regional treaties and conventions on human rights see Detzner, *Tribunales chilenos y derecho international de derechos humanos* (1988); Carlos López Dawson, *Justicia militar. Una nueva mirada* (Santiago, 1995)

Other chapters in this book address directly these issues of enormous significance for international politics. The present chapter considers several prior
questions, as a historical framework for understanding the politico-juridical
context of the Pinochet case in Latin America and Chile. In particular, it
examines, from a historical vantage, certain Spanish American and Brazilian
constitutional, legal and military traditions that erode civil liberties and rights
and make impunity for crimes committed by civilian and military government
officials routine rather than the exception. These include institutional traditions
that shield armed forces' personnel from judicial accountability for illegal
violence against citizens, including human rights violations; legal and military
traditions that subject civilians to military jurisdiction, thereby legally denying
'normal' due process and constitutional guarantees for 'political crimes'; and the
particular legal and institutional foundations of constitutional tyranny and
military impunity, *in place in Chile prior to 1973*, that impeded Chilean prosecution of military personnel guilty of human rights violations from 1973 to 1990.
The chapter also briefly considers changes (usually more severe and authoritarian 'reforms') to these legal and institutional foundations of impunity introduced by the military government after 1973. Finally, consideration is given to
changes since 1990 that alter the foundations of constitutional tyranny and
military impunity in Chile.

Internal security, the armed forces and military law in the Iberian tradition[3]

From the sixteenth century until the early eighteenth century Spanish rulers
were almost always at war, preparing for war or recovering from war. In addition to their external warfare roles, the officers and soldiers in Iberian military
forces were also responsible for law enforcement and maintenance of public
order. Riots in Madrid that spread throughout Spain in 1766 provoked military
reforms that further militarised Spanish politics and administration.[4] Having
fused civil and military authority, the king made Madrid a military department
(*plaza de armas*) and stationed fifteen thousand troops in the capital and envir-
ons. Political opponents were subjected to the jurisdiction of ad hoc tribunals
(*juzgados especiales*), and the government ordered secret executions and the
'disappearance' of enemies. Military forces were assigned many routine police

3 This section is based on material from Brian Loveman, *For la Patria: Politics and Armed
   Forces in Latin America* (Wilmington, DE, 1999) and Brian Loveman, 'Historical Foundations
   of Civil–Military Relations in Spanish America,' in David Pion-Berlin (ed.), *Civil–Military
   Relations in Latin America: New Analytical Perspectives* (Chapel Hill, 2001), pp. 246–74.
4 For details on causes of the riots and the political opposition to King Carlos III, see Laura
   Rodríguez, 'The Spanish Riots of 1766,' *Past and Present*, vol. 59, May 1973, pp. 117–46.12

functions and served as bailiffs in civil and military courts.

Further militarisation of internal administration followed. From 1774 to 1779 the government created new militia units to repress highwaymen, bandits, and vagrants. In 1781 regular army troops were stationed in Andalusia and Extremadura to fight contraband and banditry, with orders to act *as if they were in a state of war* (*como si lo executasen en guerra viva*). In 1784 a Royal Instruction ordered the captains-general to compile lists and information concerning bandits in their jurisdictions, and to share such information across jurisdictions, an internal intelligence function that, if taken literally, required a permanent political espionage system.[5] Deliberate confusion between 'bandits' and political adversaries became the rule in Spain (and, later, in Spanish America), since 'bandits' were typically subject to military tribunals, immediate execution, and 'ley fuga'.[6] By 1805 army officers presided over every territorial tribunal in Spain. These patterns for dealing with internal security and political opposition, to greater or less extent, were extended to Spanish America (see below) and were retained after independence.

Important provisions of the military regulations of 1768, and their language, survived the Spanish American independence struggles, along with the nation-building and constitution-writing in the nineteenth and twentieth centuries, to guide military behaviour until almost the end of the last century. What is striking is the resilience of these colonial regulations – the almost exact replication of the language and spirit of colonial military regulations in nineteenth and twentieth-century military codes. In particular, the language regarding obedience to orders and the responsibility of each officer to assure 'the precise fulfilment of the particular orders issued, and the more general provisions of the Regulations (*Ordenanzas*)'[7] as indicated by the italicised phrases below, survived from the Spanish regulations of 1768 to the Chilean regulations of 1839 (Chile's first post-colonial military regulations, reaffirmed in 1860), and to those of Argentina (1969) and Peru (1975).

Spain, 1768, Article 9:
Todo oficial en su puesto será responsable de la vigilancia de su Tropa en él; *del exacto cumplimiento de las órdenes particulares que tuviere, y de las generales que explica la Ordenanza*, como de tomar, en todos los accidentes y ocurrencias que

---

5 A more detailed discussion of these provisions may be found in Brian Loveman, *For la Patria*.

6 Article 288 of the 'liberal' Constitution of 1812 declared that if 'there is resistance [to arrest] or flight [*la fuga*] is feared, force may be used to secure (*asegurar*) the person. This language constitutionalised the practice of 'shot while attempting to escape'.

7 *Ordenanzas* were essentially Crown regulations or ordinances that governed spheres of administrative activity, for example, the militias, police, municipal government, regional government and finance (*ordenanzas de intendentes*).

no le estén prevenidas, el partido correspondiente a su situación, caso, y objeto, debiendo en los lances dudosos elegir el más digno de su espíritu y honor.

Chile, 1839, 1860, Ordenanza para el Rejimen, Disciplina, Subordinación i Servicio de los Ejércitos de la República, Titulo XXXII (9):
Todo Oficial en su puesto será responsable de la vigilancia de su tropa en *el exacto cumplimiento de las órdenes particulares que tuviere, i de las jenerales que esplica la Ordenanza*, como de tomar en todos los accidentes y ocurrencias que no le estén prevenidas, el partido correspondiente a su situación, caso i objeto, debiendo en los lances dudosos elejir el más digno de su espíritu i honor.

Argentina, Reglamento de Servicio Interno, 1969:
El que comandare una tropa será responsable de la vigilancia de ella, *del exacto cumplimiento de las órdenes particulares que tuviere y de las disposiciones contenidas en las leyes y reglamentos*, como de tomar, en todos los accidentes y ocurrencias que no estén previstos, el partido correspondiente a su situación, caso y objeto, debiendo en los lances dudosos eligir él que considere más digno de su espíritu y honor.

Perú, Reglamento General del Servicio Interior, 1975:
Todo oficial es responsable de la vigilancia de su tropa, *del exacto cumplimiento de las órdenes particulares que tuviere y de las prescripciones reglamentarias*, así como de tomar en todos los accidentes y ocurrencias que no estén prevenidos, la actitud correspondiente a su situación, caso y objeto, debiendo en los trances dudosos elegir el más digno de su espíritu y honor.[8]

These military regulations embedded the concept of 'due obedience' (*obediencia debida*) and its corollary, individual immunity for actions carried out *under orders*. The consequences of disobedience could be drastic. Chile's first post-independence military code, adopted in 1839 and reformed in 1860, stipulated: 'Any soldier, corporal or Sergeant, on active service, who fails to obey all and any Officers of the Army, will be sentenced to death' ('*será castigado con pena de la vida*').[9] The same penalty was prescribed for sergeants and corporals who did not obey their superiors, namely higher ranking non-commissioned officers.[10] Under these circumstances, it is easy to understand why 'due obedience' would be a legal defence for soldiers and officers. The military codes (unlike the British and then United States tradition of 'objecting' to illegal orders) did not recognise 'illegal orders' as a proper rationale for failure to obey orders.

---

8 Cited in Ministerio de Defensa Nacional, El Salvador, *Doctrina militar y relaciones ejército/ sociedad* (El Salvador, 1994), pp. 130–1.

9 *Ordenanza para el rejimen, disciplina, subordinación i servicio de los ejércitos de la República* (2nd edition Santiago, 1860), p. 72, Título LXXX (75).

10 *Ibid.*, pp. 28–9, Sección 2a 'De la Inobediencia'. Disobedience during active duty, but not 'in campaign or during war' brought lighter sentences: one to two years of prison, and forced labour in public works projects (Article 71).

Almost everywhere in Latin America this sort of language was retained in military codes during the twentieth century.[11] Use of the concept of 'due obedience' as a defence by military personnel in cases involving violation of human rights in the 1980s and 1990s is grounded in this pre-1948, pre-Nuremberg military doctrine. The events of the 1980s and 1990s in some respects reaffirmed this doctrine, whether by plebiscite in Uruguay (1989) or with the 'due obedience law' in Argentina (1987).[12] In the latter case, after a military rebellion in April 1987, the Argentine Congress passed legislation stipulating that all military personnel below the rank of colonel during the 'dirty war' could not be considered punishable for any crime committed as 'part of their military duties.' Such personnel were considered to have acted 'in a state of coercion, subordinated under superior authority, and in compliance with orders ...' In Uruguay, under military pressure, the citizenry reaffirmed by plebiscite an amnesty passed by congress in 1986, guaranteeing impunity to military personnel who had carried out their duties under the dictatorship, including torture and disappearances.

The military *fuero* and jurisdiction of military tribunals over civilians

The military *fuero* in Spain and colonial Spanish America is a complex topic both legally and historically.[13] The concept of 'fuero' refers to 'privileges and immunities' and also to 'jurisdiction'.[14] *Fueros* also existed for special groups in society – nobles, religious orders, guilds and the military. Priests and other religious pertaining to the ecclesiastical *fuero* enjoyed immunities from civil authority in certain stipulated cases and were subject to ecclesiastical courts.

11 An important exception was the *Ordenanza del Ejército de El Salvador* (1934): 'Las órdenes *legales* del superior deben cumplirse por los subordinados sin hacer observación ni reclamación alguna, sin vacilación y sin murmurar; pero *podrán reclamar si hubiera lugar a ello, después de haberlas cumplido*.' ('The *legal* orders of superiors must be obeyed by subordinates without making any comment or remonstrance, without vacillation and without murmur; *but they may object [to the order] if there is cause, after complying with it*.') Article 9, emphasis added.

12 On the 'due obedience law' in Argentina see J. Patrice McSherry, *Incomplete Transition: Military Power and Democracy in Argentina* (New York, 1997); Deborah Norden, *Military Rebellion in Argentina. Between Coups and Consolidation* (Lincoln, NE, 1996), pp. 103–4. In some countries, such as Bolivia (1994), Ecuador (1998) and Venezuela (1999) the 'due obedience' doctrine has been explicitly rejected in constitutional and statutory reforms of the 1990s.

13 See Lyle McAlister, *The 'Fuero Militar' in New Spain, 1764–1800* (Gainesville, 1957).

14 Medieval towns obtained *fueros*, a royal charter of privileges from the king. Such *fueros* were the basis for local government, a sort of medieval 'federalism' that was gradually eroded by the centralising encroachments of the developing European nation-state to the time of the French Revolution (1789).

This might mean 'protection' against civil authority or it might mean lack of protection against ecclesiastical law by appeal to the 'rights' of other subjects. This was also true for the guilds (*gremios*) and for military personnel.

Within the military *fuero*, officers acting as military judges might protect their personnel against civilian claims, both in civil and criminal cases, but might also impose the extremely harsh penalties stipulated in the military codes for everything from bigamy to bestiality. Thus the military *fuero* could be a mixed blessing, despite its use as an enticement to military service in both the militia and regular army, especially where recruits were offered exemption from taxes, from ordinary jurisdiction in civil litigation and enhanced social position. In Spanish America these privileges were especially attractive to the lower classes and 'people of colour' (*pardos*, *mulatos* and the various *castas*).

For purposes of understanding civil–military relations in Spain and Latin America, however, three main aspects of the *fuero* are essential. Firstly, military personnel were subject preferentially to military jurisdiction and tribunals in cases of alleged criminal behaviour, whether the alleged crimes were committed against civilians, against other military personnel, or against government authorities. Military officers acting as judges in courts martial (*consejos de guerra*) heard such cases, and had some incentive to find that military personnel had acted properly when accused of misdeeds – especially if they had acted under the orders of an officer. This aspect of the military *fuero* resulted in 'a withering respect for justice, [an] undermining of the prestige and credibility of local government, and the establishment of the military as a dominant force in the provinces [of Cartagena and Panama].'[15] In short, the *fuero* potentially implied impunity for military personnel for crimes or abuses committed against civilians; *in Chile the extent of military jurisdiction remained extraordinarily broad into the 1990s*. In practice, many tribunals dismissed human rights cases after 1990, and even before, often applying the controversial 1978 amnesty decree law 2.191.[16]

Secondly, in many instances, *civilians were subject to military jurisdiction*, especially for crimes in which military personnel jointly participated with civilians, when the crime committed was rebellion, sedition, tumult or other such crimes in which 'internal security' was threatened (as already exemplified in the case of bandits, vagrants and those who disseminated subversive writings).

Thirdly, military jurisdiction generally meant that 'normal' judicial protection and due process was not available to the accused. These patterns were maintained after independence in most of Spanish America, though the extent

---

15 Allan J. Kuethe, *Military Reform and Society in New Granada, 1773–1808* (Gainesville, 1978), p. 38.

16 For detail on Decree Law 2.191 see Brian Loveman and Elizabeth Lira, *Las ardientes cenizas del olvido: vía chilena de reconciliación política 1932–1994* (Santiago, 2000), pp. 451–64.

of military *fueros* and jurisdiction over civilians recurrently became a matter of political debate in the nineteenth century.[17]

While systematic study of the politics associated with elimination of military *fueros* in the nineteenth century remains to be done, it is clear that persistence of military *fueros* and military jurisdiction over civilians for certain criminal proceedings on the model established in the colonial period and retained in the nineteenth has significantly influenced civilian-military relations in Spain and much of Spanish America into the twenty-first century.[18] Indeed the jurisdiction of military tribunals over civilians and the application of military law 'in time of war' to civilians, for 'political crimes', was a crucial element in the human rights violations that characterised both military and civilian regimes in much of Spanish America from the 1960s until the 1990s.[19]

In Chile the nineteenth-century Military Code of Justice and its subsequent renditions in the twentieth century provided for extensive military jurisdiction over civilians for crimes ranging from sedition and rebellion to 'libel' and public insults (*injuria*). This remained the case in 1973, allowing the military government wide legal latitude in subjecting civilians to military tribunals.[20] Decrees of the military government assigned crimes defined as 'terrorist' to military jurisdiction.[21] Civilians continue to be prosecuted in military tribunals for a variety of

17 This issue is discussed in more detail, for each country in Spanish America, in Brian Loveman, *The Constitution of Tyranny: Regimes of Exception in Spanish America* (Pittsburgh, 1993).

18 Spain's *Código de Justicia Militar* (Madrid, 1906), pp. 250, Ley 23 de marzo de 1906, C.L. Núm. 66) assigned to military tribunals jurisdiction in cases in which military personnel or civilians 'openly or covertly' defamed or offended the Army or Navy: '*Los que de palabra ó escrito, por medio de la imprenta, grabado ú otro medio mecánico de publicación, en estampas, alegorías, caricaturas, emblemas, ó alusiones, injurien ú ofendan clara ó encubiertamente al Ejército ó á la Armada ó á instituciones, armas, clases ó cuerpos determinados del mismo, serán castigados con la pena de prisión correccional.*' ('Those who by word or in writing, in the press, by taped recording or other mechanical means of publicity, in stamps, allegories, caricatures, emblems or allusions, directly or indirectly defame or offend the Army, Navy or related institutions, arms, groups or units, will be punished with imprisonment.')

19 In many cases more specialised 'antiterrorism laws,' 'arms control laws,' and 'national security laws' specifically established military jurisdiction over civilians for 'political crimes'. In other cases the Military Code of Justice had already established military jurisdiction in cases of rebellion, sedition and related crimes. See, for extensive treatment of these issues, Alvaro del Barrio Reyna and José Julio León Reyes, *Terrorismo, ley antiterrorista y derechos humanos* (Santiago, 1991).

20 For a discussion of the history of military jurisdiction in Chile, with comparative references to European and other Latin American cases, see Renato Astrosa Herrera, *Código de Justicia Militar Comentado* (third edition Santiago, 1985). The *Código de Justicia Militar* in place in 1990, and little-reformed since then, stipulated the types of crimes to be assigned to military tribunals in 'peace time' (*tiempo de paz*) and war (*tiempo de guerra*).

21 Law 18.314 (1984) '*Determina conductas terroristas y fija su penalidad.*' ('Terrorist conduct defined and penalties established.')

'crimes', including 'insulting military officers' up to the present day. Thus, in a legal sense, application of military law to civilians after the 1973 coup, including detention, courts martial, and execution, did not *necessarily* imply human rights violations or even violations of the rule of law – though in practice even military regulations and military code law were frequently not respected.[22] In the 1973–1976 period, failures to follow even the procedures specified in military law were notorious, but the underlying authority of military officers in 'state of emergency zones' (*zonas en estado de emergencia*) had at least a putative legal foundation.[23]

Fusion of military and civilian authority

Related to the internal security role for the armed forces and application of military law to civilians, both in Spain and the colonies in the eighteenth century, there existed, for some purposes, a routine overlap and fusion of civil and military authority. The decrees regulating regional administration (for example, the *Ordenanza de Intendentes del Río de la Plata* (1782) and of Nueva España [Mexico], 1786,) gave viceroys, *intendentes*, and other *comandantes general* 'total authority' (*todo el lleno de la superior autoridad y omnímodas facultades*).[24] At the end of the eighteenth century civil and military authority often overlapped. Tensions frequently existed between civil and military authorities, especially at the local level (*cabildo*), but the 'special' status of the military was recognised in law and in practice. While the military was 'subordinate' to government authority, it was also immune from oversight and subject to separate channels of authority that went directly to the king or, after independence, the President of the new Latin American countries.

In Chile the 1844 Law of Internal Administration (*Lei sobre el Réjimen Interior*) assigned to the provincial *intendentes* the obligation to maintain internal order and to the military and police authority to suppress banditry and conspiracies. In many cases, the *intendentes* were appointed both as commander of the armed forces and *intendente* for their respective provinces (Arts. 42–49). In the twentieth century, this fusion of military and civilian authority eroded but under certain circumstances ranking military officers within a region declared in a 'state of 'assembly' or 'state of emergency' assumed full governmental

22   The 1839 *Ordenanza Jeneral del Ejército* (Santiago) defined military jurisdiction in Títulos LXXI-LXXXI.

23   Manuel Antonio Garretón, Roberto Garretón and Carmen Garretón Merino, *Por la fuerza sin la razón* (Santiago, 1998) discuss the unconstitutional and illegal actions taken by the military junta and the *consejos de guerra* in the immediate post-coup period.

24   The *intendente* was the highest ranking provincial administrator, appointed directly by the President.

authority, equivalent in most respects to martial law. In addition, in efforts to overcome political corruption and vote-buying, the Chilean congress in 1941 assigned to the armed forces responsibility for monitoring elections, essentially turning the country over to the armed forces to ensure fair electoral outcomes. Put another way, the politicians did not trust themselves to protect the most basic procedure of a democracy – elections.[25] A political decision, agreed to by the parties in congress, literally made 'protecting democracy' the function of the armed forces from 1941 to the present. With transition from the military government to the elected government of Patricio Aylwin in 1990, this basic feature of Chilean 'democracy' remained in place.[26] Chilean citizens are accustomed to seeing military personnel, fully-armed, at polling places. On election days, by law, the armed forces assume control of the country to guarantee the proper administration of national and local elections. This continues to be a routine feature of Chilean politics.

Nation-building, constitutions and the armed forces after independence

The independence wars (1809–1830) and the numerous regional and trans-national wars that eventually established the boundaries of the new nation-states became the benchmarks for Latin American military institutions. The region's armies claimed a tutelary, guardianship role, what they called a 'historical mission' to oversee the 'transcendental destiny and values' of *la patria*.

The desperate circumstances of the early nineteenth century in Latin America made reestablishing political stability and law enforcement a primordial task for nation-builders, whether they proclaimed themselves liberals or conservatives, republicans or monarchists, centralists or federalists. The traditional fusion of military and civil authority in territorial administration, the jurisdiction of military tribunals over 'bandits' and others who threatened public tranquillity, and the dual mission of armed forces – internal order and external defence – were constitutionalised and codified in most of the region after independence. Of 103 constitutions adopted from independence until 1900, slightly over 80 per cent defined the role of the armed forces *in the constitution*. Usually this definition included maintaining internal order, law enforcement, and protecting the constitutional order against usurpation. In a few cases the military even had a mandate to supervise elections (a function adopted in the twentieth century in

---

25 Ley General de Elecciones (Ley 6.834), amended in 1949 (Ley 9.334), 1958 (Ley 12.891), 1962 (Ley 14.852).
26 For a brief overview of the role of the armed forces in the Chilean political system before 1973 see Hugo Frühling, Carlos Portales, Augusto Varas, *Estado y fuerzas armadas* (Santiago, 1982).

more Latin American countries), to ensure proper presidential succession, and to prevent 'staying over' in office by presidents (*continuismo*).

Thus nineteenth-century Latin American constitutions frequently made the armed forces virtually a fourth branch of government, designated in constitutional language *as permanent institutions* of the various republics. Moreover, these constitutions rarely specified who would decide when 'disorder' warranted military intervention, when the actions of presidents, legislators, or local officials constituted threats to the 'constitutional order' or to republican institutions, or when 'internal commotion' (a common phrase in nineteenth-century constitutions) justified military action.

Regimes of exception

Latin American constitutions, from the first wartime charters adopted during the independence struggles, included clauses that allowed suspension of civil liberties and rights to meet all manner of emergencies: natural disasters; threats to constitutional order; insurgency; rebellion; 'internal commotion'; civil war and many other contingencies. Regimes of exception have different names and purposes from country to country and from time to time. Common regimes of exception are 'states of siege', 'internal war', martial law, and 'state of emergency'. In Chile, the 1839 military regulations (*Ordenanza General del Ejército*) created a further regime of exception, the *provincia de asamblea* (a province in a state of assembly) under which military authorities, 'in time of war' could issue *bandos* (edicts) – *essentially the scheme used by the Chilean military after the 1973 coup.*[27]

These names for regimes of exception do not imply similar political and legal meanings; thus 'state of siege' in Chile before 1874 implied virtual constitutional dictatorship but after 1874, with constitutional reform, was much more limited regarding the 'emergency powers' extended to the president. In all cases, however, regimes of exception are the result, in constitution-making, of a priori philosophical, moral and political decisions which held that, at times, civil liberties and rights, including basic 'human rights' must be subordinated to 'protecting *la patria*.'[28] Illustratively, Argentine General Adcel Vilas explained that, 'the offensive against subversion presupposes in the first place freedom of action in all areas ... a series of special procedures, an instantaneous response, a persecution to the death.'[29] And in Chile in 1973, the military junta declared that

27 Title LXVIII, Art. 2 – see Loveman (1993): 332–4.
28 The evolution and use of regimes of exception in Spanish American politics is the subject of Loveman, *The Constitution of Tyranny*.
29 Cited in Donald Hodges, *Argentina's 'Dirty War': An Intellectual Biography* (Austin, 1991), p. 125.

the state of siege that it imposed, in accord with well-established Chilean practice since 1925, implied a 'state of war' for legal and judicial purposes, as established in the Military Code of Justice.[30] Thus the debate over whether a state of war *really* existed in Chile in 1973 – that is, whether there was a 'real' civil war or insurrection – misses the point. The Military Code of Justice in place throughout most of the twentieth century explicitly stipulated that 'for the effect of this Code, a state of war or time of war is understood to exist not only when war or state of war has been officially declared, in accord with the respective laws, but also when, in fact, (*de hecho*) war exists or mobilisation for war has been decreed…'[31] When the military junta decreed a state of siege in 1973, understood as a 'state of war,' that act established the putative legal foundations (regime of exception) for extensive jurisdiction of military tribunals over civilians. Likewise, therefore, there should have been a presumption that the laws of war, including the Geneva Conventions ratified by Chile in 1951, were (and remain) applicable.

National security and military law

From the late nineteenth century most Latin American penal codes, like many codes in continental Europe, included special sections dealing with political crimes such as sedition, rebellion, and insurrection.[32] Chile's Penal Code (1874) had provisions regarding crimes and misdemeanours against the internal security of the state.[33] Laws regulating the press, censoring untoward comments on religion or the Catholic Church and prohibiting offensive publications, posters and speeches also sought to dampen opposition to incumbent governments.[34]

In some instances these penal codes overlapped with the military codes; in others certain crimes were automatically assigned to military courts. In still other cases crimes defined in penal codes or in special internal security laws, normally

---

30 This interpretation was reaffirmed in the navy's response to the Rettig Commission in 1991: 'Informe presentado ante el Consejo Nacional de Seguridad por el Comandante en Jefe de la Armada de Chile, Almirante Jorge Martínez Busch,' March 27, 1991.

31 *Código de Justicia Militar*, Título III, Art. 418 (1944) (Santiago, 1949).

32 The Latin American penal codes relied on European models, particularly Spain, France, Belgium and Germany. Laws to protect 'internal security' were common in Europe and were emulated as the Latin American countries replaced or modified Spanish colonial criminal law.

33 *Código Penal de la República de Chile*, esplicado por Pedro Javier Fernández, second edition (Santiago, 1899), pp. 254–63.

34 Interestingly, there were also provisions penalising government officials who illegally banished, detained, or arrested citizens, held prisoners 'incomunicado' or applied torture to prisoners, or any public officials who 'exercised judicial functions' and applied corporal or other punishment without proper judicial orders (*Código Penal de la República de Chile*, Arts. 148–52).

assigned to civilian courts (*fuero común*) were (and still are) assigned to military courts if committed when the country, or a region of the country, is under a declared regime of exception such as 'state of emergency', 'state of siege' or 'state of internal commotion'. These overlapping and mutually reinforcing constitutional, legal and military code provisions establish an ostensibly constitutional regime whose architecture *designs-in* military guardianship, restrictions on civil liberties and rights by civilian governments and, when necessary, by military institutions, and threatens civilians with military law and military tribunals if '*la patria* is threatened'.

More importantly, this permanent regime of 'protected democracy' came to be accepted as normal by many if not most civilians, indeed came to be viewed as an essential ingredient of constitutional 'democracy' in the Latin American context. As long as there is no immediate crisis, no threat of disorder, no significant political polarisation, such systems may operate as if they were democratic. But the cumulative effect of these colonial and nineteenth-century patterns of civil–military relations, reinforced by twentieth-century elaborations, was to fashion a political culture, or more accurately, national political cultures, with deeply embedded authoritarian and militarist political institutions and practices. Indeed these institutions and practices are so deeply embedded in the political mentality of the region that well-known civilian politicians, regarded as democrats, accept these authoritarian institutional underpinnings as natural. Illustratively, Chilean ex-president, Eduardo Frei Montalva, in an interview in Spain after the 1973 military coup in his country, declared: 'the military have saved Chile ... they were called on by the nation and they fulfilled their *legal* duty ... If a people has been so weakened and harassed (*acosado*) that it cannot rebel, ... then the Army substitutes its arms and does the work.'[35]

'Protected democracy' became a common foundation of Latin American politics, with important national variations and propensities for direct military intervention in the post-World War II years.[36] In Chile, there were no military coups or illegal changes in government from 1932 to 1973. Indeed, Chile was the only Latin American country that experienced no illegal government successions during this period. For that reason it was often held up, along with Uruguay, as the most democratic of Latin American nations. In some ways this was true, especially regarding the gradual expansion of the electorate, relatively open party competition, comparatively 'free' press, the significant role of the

35 Cited in Carlos Molina Johnson (Lt. Col.), *Algunas de las razones del quiebre de la institucionalidad política* (Santiago, 1987), pp. 91–2 (author's italics).

36 For details on variations in this system see Brian Loveman, '"Protected Democracies" and Military Guardianship: Political Transitions in Latin America, 1978–1993,' *Journal of InterAmerican Studies and World Affairs*, vol. 36, issue 2, 1994, pp. 105–89.

Table 1: Protecting Chilean 'Democracy' 1833–1972*

Constitution of 1833	1833	State of Siege (implemented by decree or Congress on various occasions from 1831–1861)** Emergency Powers (*Facultades Extraordinarias*) (Delegated various times from 1833–1861)
Press Laws	1812	Censorship Law
	1846	'Sobre abusos de la libertad de imprenta'
	1872	'Sobre abusos de la libertad de imprenta'
	1925	Decree Law 425
Ordenanza de Intendentes (Internal Administration)	1821	
Military Code (*Ordenanzas*)	1839	establishes military jurisdiction over civilians for stipulated crimes; role of military in internal administration; amended 1852
Law of Internal Administration (*Ley de Réjimen Interior*)	1844	Fusion of civil and military authority for internal administration; amended 1885
Penal Code	1874	*Libro Segundo:* Title I: Crimes against external security and sovereignty of the State; Title II: Crimes against the internal security of the State; Title III, Crimes that affect Constitutional Guarantees (civil liberties and rights)
Law of Rural Police	1881	
Constitution	1925	State of siege, emergency powers, etc.
Decree Law 425	1925	Press and media censorship
Decree with Force of Law 143	1931	Press and media censorship
Decree Law 50	1932	First Internal Security Law
Law 6.026	1937	Law for Internal Security of the State
Law 6.834	1941	Tasks armed forces with supervising elections
Law 7.200	1942	Establishes authority of President to declare 'emergency zones'
Military Code	1944	Reaffirms military jurisdiction over civilians; crimes against the flag, patriotic symbols. See especially Title III, Arts. 418–20 on meaning of '*estado de guerra*' and '*tiempo de guerra*'.
Law 8.987	1948	Law for 'Permanent Defence of Democracy' (Derogated 1958)
Law 12.927	1958	Law for Internal Security of the State
Law 13.959	1960	In case of public calamity the president may declare a 'state of emergency' for the affected zone during six months
Law 15.576	1964	Press and Media Censorship (nicknamed Ley 'Mordaza')
Law 17.798	1972	Arms Control Law

* For discussion of use of these constitutional and statutory provisions from 1932–1973 see Felipe González Morales, Jorge Mera Figueroa, and Juan Enrique Vargas Viancos, *Protección democrática de la seguridad del Estado, estados de excepción y derecho penal político* (Santiago, 1991).

** Chile was the first country in Latin America to include a 'state of siege' clause in its constitution (1833).

legislative branch of government, and routine *legal* government succession. Nevertheless, the constitutional and statutory underpinnings of protected democracy remained in place – constitutional regimes of exception (and their periodic application with states of siege and delegation of 'extraordinary authority' [*facultades extraordinarias*] to presidents to confront 'emergencies' or 'crisis'), laws on internal security, censorship laws and criminal sanctions against those who 'abused' freedom of the press or mass media, extensive jurisdiction of military tribunals over civilians in some circumstances, broad military *fueros* that impeded civilian jurisdiction over military personnel for what would be considered 'common crimes' in other countries, and a highly insulated and authoritarian judicial system.[37] Table 1 outlines benchmarks in the construction and accretion of the Chilean version of 'protected democracy.'[38]

Given this historically-rooted constitutional and statutory tradition of protected democracy, and its incorporation as a normal part of Chilean political culture in the 'democratic' era (1932–1973), it would be no coincidence that the military junta that took power in 1973 explicitly formulated many of its decree laws and military edicts (*bandos*) as 'modifications', reforms, or simple applications of existing legislation (see Table 1 above) or that an important, but neglected, book published in December 1973, shortly after the coup, was dedicated to the esoteric topic of jurisdiction of military tribunals over military personnel and civilians.[39]

Chile 1973–1990

The politico-juridical history of the Chilean military regime is fairly straightforward: overthrow of president Salvador Allende (1973); dictatorship under a

---

37 One of the few studies that anticipated the potential consequences of the persistence of protected democracy in Chile called for elimination or reform of the system of regimes of exception in the 1950s: Elena Caffarena de Jiles, *El recurso de amparo frente a los regímenes de emergencia* (Santiago: 1957). In one of those historical ironies that defy explanation, the prologue to this volume was written by Patricio Aylwin Azócar. Aylwin said that while he did not share Caffarena's Marxist inclinations and while he believed that human rights could only be protected in a system based on respect for natural law (divinely-inspired), the excessive use of regimes of exception in the country could only cause alarm for those who 'truly love liberty and justice, not as simple words, but as attributes inherent in the dignity of humanity and indispensable for the realisation of the common good' (p. 13).

38 This table is an extremely abbreviated version of the constitutional and legal foundations of protected democracy in Chile. For a documentary history with the original legal texts see Brian Loveman and Elizabeth Lira (eds.), *Arquitectura política y seguridad interior del Estado, 1811–1990* (Santiago, 2002).

39 See Renato Astrosa Herrera, *Jurisdicción Penal Militar* (Santiago, 1973); *Código de Justicia Militar Comentado*, third edition (Santiago, 1985).

military government (1973–1981); 'transition regime' as specified in the 1980 Constitution 'approved' by plebiscite (1981–1990). On 5 October 1988 a plebiscite rejected the continuation of General Pinochet's presidency for another eight years and another plebiscite in 1989 (30 July) approved constitutional reforms negotiated between the political opposition and the military regime, paving the way for presidential elections to take place on 14 December 1989. On March 11 1990 the first elected president and congress since 1973 took office. While the unamended version of the 1980 Constitution was in effect, 'transitory article' 24 assigned to the president (General Pinochet) special repressive authority; even without invoking this article, the country was governed under one or several simultaneous regimes of exception during fifteen years.

The military junta that took power in Chile in 1973 gradually refashioned the political system. Before adopting a new constitution in 1980, the junta explicitly tied its decrees, decree-laws, and 'constitutional acts' (1976) to existing statutes and regulations, defining their actions as amendments, modifications or 'applications' of existing law. Chile's authoritarian tradition, the regimes of exception in the 1925 Constitution, laws regarding censorship, national security, gun control, terrorism and the existing military code and regulations provided an elastic juridical foundation for dictatorship. Of course, sometimes the junta went well beyond any possible interpretation of existing law – but most often it sought to legitimate its actions, even retroactively, with decrees and decree- laws.

As indicated, the initial actions of the military took the form of *bandos* (edicts). *Bando* 5 justified the overthrow of the Allende government for having violated the constitution and promoted class conflict, and affirmed the legitimacy of the military junta and the moral and civic obligation of the citizenry to obey its orders.[40] The junta further advised that under the declared state of siege strict censorship would be applied, in accordance with *the existing censorship law* (*ley sobre abusos de la publicidad*), authorising publication only of *El Mercurio* and *La Tercera de la Hora* (*Bando* 15). Political propaganda would be punished under the *existing military code* for 'times of war' (*Bando* 32). Persons in possession of arms or explosives would be severely punished, 'in accord with the *existing military regulations and the arms control law* (*Bando* 17). Other *bandos* relied on the authority of the existing law on internal security or other repressive legislation.

In addition to the *bandos*, the military junta relied on decree-laws, that is legislation approved without the congress (with the junta assuming the legislative powers) – another little studied but important aspect of Chilean politics. Emblematic was Decree-Law 3, establishing a state of siege in the entire republic.[41]

---

40 Bando 5, 11 September 1973, is reproduced in Loveman and Lira, *Arquitectura política*, pp. 321–2.
41 Decree Law 3. 1973, published in 'Diario Oficial' NE28.653, 18 September 1973.

This state of siege relied ostensibly on the authority of Constitutional Article 72 (17) and Part I, Title III of the Code of Military Justice, the latter imposing military jurisdiction on civilians *as if in a state of internal war.* Under this authority, 'trials' by military courts and sentences of death or prison were *legal.* Appeals of sentences could, theoretically, be heard by military tribunals – in times of war. Decree Law 5 clarified these dispositions, reaffirmed that the country was, legally, 'in a state or time of war', and significantly modified existing legislation, among other actions, by expanding the jurisdiction of military tribunals. Important to note is the reliance again on existing legislation, in particular, the Military Code of Justice, Law 12.927 on Internal Security of the State (a law whose original language dated in part from Decree Law 50, 1932), and the Arms Control Law, adopted in 1972 under the Allende government, as a foundation for the repressive decrees of the military junta, in particular Decree Law 5,1973.[42] The text of Decree Law 5 also emphasised the putatively legal foundations of the military junta's decrees.[43]

This pattern of relying on, or modifying, existing legislation continued throughout the 1973–1990 period, with periodic adjustments, refinements, and tightening of the legal screws on opposition politicians, media, and movements.[44] It is critical to note the persistent efforts made by the Chilean military junta to legitimate itself and to 'act legally' in public during the dictatorship. Acting 'legally' creates immunity from prosecution by definition; the amnesty decree law of 1978 (Decree Law 2.191) was part of this effort, as was the manipulated plebiscite that approved the Pinochet regime's constitution in 1980.[46] Table 2 illustrates, without being exhaustive, the basic 'legal' foundations of military rule from 1973–1980.

42 'Declara que el estado de sitio decretado por conmoción interna, en las circunstancias que vive el país, debe entenderse "estado o tiempo de guerra" para los efectos de lo dispuesto en tales casos por el Código de Justicia Militar y demás leyes penales; modifica el Código de Justicia Militar, la Ley 12.927 sobre Seguridad Interior del Estado y la Ley 17.798 sobre Control de Armas.' ('It is hereby decreed that the state of siege, promulgated due to internal commotion, in the present circumstances, should be understood as a "state or time of war" for the effects and the dispositions of such circumstances as established in the Code of Military Justice and other criminal laws; [the present decree] modifies the Code of Military Justice, Law 12.927 on Internal Security of the State and Law 17.798 on Arms Control.')

43 Decree Law 5, published in 'Diario Oficial' No. 28.657, 22 September 1973, is reproduced in Loveman and Lira, *Arquitectura política*, pp. 337–41.

44 For details see Brian Loveman, *Chile. The Legacy of Hispanic Capitalism*, third edition (New York, 2001), Table 10–11 (pp. 273–4), lists the 'legal' foundations of military rule from 1973 to 1987.

46 The 1978 amnesty law in Chile was one of many adopted by the Latin American military governments from the 1970s into the 1990s. Brazil (1979), Argentina (1983, 1986, 1987, 1989), Uruguay (1986, reaffirmed in plebiscite, 1989), Guatemala (1986), Honduras (1987), El Salvador (1987 and 1992, 1993), Peru (1995).

Table 2: 'Legal' Foundations of Military Rule, 1973–1980[45]

Decree Law (DL) 3	11 September, 1973	State of siege, defined initially as 'state of internal war'
DL 4		state of emergency in provinces and regions
DL 5		Interpretive decree regarding Military Code of Justice, affirming the existence of a 'state of war'
DL 8		Delegation to military authorities of power to rule through military edicts (*bandos militares*) and to exercise judicial authority over civilians
DL 81	6 November, 1973	Authority to expel (banish) persons from the country during the state of siege (which lasted until 1978 and was reimposed several times after that)
DL 521	14 June 1974	Official creation of the DINA (secret police, accountable to Pinochet, which already functioned extra-officially in late 1973)
DL 527	17 June 1974	Charter of the Military Junta (*Estatuto de la Junta de Gobierno*)
DL 604	10 August 1974	Prohibits entry into country of persons who spread or support doctrines that threaten national security or who are known to be 'agitators or activists'
DL 640	2 September 1974	Regulations defining the various 'regimes of exception'
DL 788	4 December 1974	Provides that 'decree laws' of the military government have the effect of amending the 1925 Constitution
DL 922	11 March 1975	State of Siege decree
DL 1.008 and 1.009	8 May 1975	Increases period during which detainees may be held 'incomunicado' in cases involving crimes against security of the state (detainees cannot see lawyers or obtain habeas corpus writs)
Supreme Decree 890 (Minister of Interior)	26 August 1975	Modifies the Law of State Security; greatly restricts civil rights and liberties (*garantías constitucionales*)
DL 1.281	11 December 1975	Authorises military commanders to censure or suspend publication of up to six editions of magazines, newspapers, and other media

45 This table is adapted from Loveman, *Chile. The Legacy of Hispanic Capitalism*, pp. 273–4.

'Constitutional Acts'

DL 1.319, 1.551-53	9 January/ 11 September 1976	Amends 1925 Constitution regarding 'essential foundations of Chileanism', regimes of exception, constitutional rights and duties
DL1.877	13 August 1977	Modifies Law 12.927 (Internal Security Law); increases presidential authority during states of emergency
DL1.878	13 August 1977	Creates CNI (new secret police to replace DINA) and details its authority
Decree 400 (Ministry of Defence)	6 December 1977	Modifies arms control law and assigns administration of provisions to Minister of Defence
	19 April 1978	State of Siege ends; country remains in 'state of emergency'
DL 3.168	6 February 1980	Authorises internal exile (*relegación*) for up to three months, for persons who alter or seek to alter public order (modifies DL 81 and DL 1.877)
Plebiscite for new Constitution	11 September 1980	Occurs under 'state of emergency'. Constitution adds a new regime of exception, 'state of perturbation of internal peace,' with special powers for president when such circumstances exist

Immunity, impunity and the Pinochet case: hope for the future?

The survival of these constitutional, legal and institutional legacies of authoritarianism and of the military dictatorship remains, at the beginning of the twenty-first century, a challenge for more than superficial democratisation in Chile. So does the legacy of fear and the continuing operation of clandestine networks of ex security personnel, sometimes in association with politicians, administrative personnel, and military officers of the Pinochet regime. The arrest of Pinochet in London, a result of the resistance to impunity of Chilean human rights activists, lawyers, families of victims, a small number of judges and political leaders, as well as the collaboration of international human rights organisations, non-governmental organisations, activists and judges in the Americas and in Europe, challenges this history of immunity and impunity. Since 1998 an increasing number of ex military and security personnel have been brought to court on charges of human rights violations during the dictatorship. Some have been tried and incarcerated – an outcome that few would have predicted in 1990.[47]

47 A running list of persons charged and prosecuted for human rights violations during the dictatorship can be found at the Internet website of the Fundación de Ayuda Social de las Iglesias Cristianas (FASIC): ⟨http://www.fasic.org/juri/nomina.htm⟩.

Looking into the future, there can hardly be 'redemocratisation', in Chile or elsewhere, where constitutional democracy with general respect for civil liberties and rights and the rule of law (not merely elections and civilian government) previously did not exist, or, at best, existed conditionally. The historical patterns of civil–military relations described in this article are 'living legacies' of colonial, post-colonial and twentieth-century development. Their modification or elimination requires changes in embedded cultural patterns, enduring institutional arrangements, political practices of centuries past, and the more recent institutional handiwork of the military dictatorship. This task goes well beyond the restoration of an idealised 'democratic' past. It also requires further development of international human rights law and a redefinition of the meaning of 'sovereignty' compatible with the Universal Declaration of Human Rights and a commitment to universal jurisdiction for certain crimes to better protect the world's peoples against state terrorism.

A case from Africa suggests that to some extent the Pinochet case provides inspiration for this effort in Chile and elsewhere. *The New York Times* reported in March 2001 that 'even as British courts ponder whether the former Chilean dictator Augusto Pinochet should be excused from trial in Spain on human rights charges because he is medically unfit, the enduring legacy of his case has been demonstrated on another continent. Last week a Senegalese court indicted the exiled former dictator of Chad, Hissène Habré, on torture charges. It was the first time that a former African head of state had been charged with human rights violations by a court in another country, and it opens a welcome new chapter in the evolution of international criminal law.'[48] Apparently the Senegalese citizen who initiated this case, a torture victim himself, had decided to oppose impunity, inspired by the Pinochet case:[49]

---

48 'Editorial: An African Pinochet,' *New York Times* available at http://www.remember-chile.org.uk/comment/00-02-11nyt.htm. Despite rejection of jurisdiction by the Senegalese Court of Cassation, Amnesty International's Annual Report for 2002 reported that at the end of 2001 '40 individual and two collective complaints were under investigation. The complaints had been lodged by the ... Chadian Association of Victims of Political Repression and Crime against members of the ... Directorate of Documentation and Security, a security service that was answerable directly to former President Hissein Habré. The complaints related to "crimes of torture, murder and enforced disappearance". In May the N'Djaména Constitutional Court had ruled that, although a special court to try Hissene Habré and his collaborators, provided for in a 1993 law, had never been established, the ordinary courts had jurisdiction over the cases.' See (http://web.amnesty.org/web/ar2002.nsf/afr/chad!Open).

49 For a more detailed overview of the influence of the Pinochet case in the Senegal prosecution see the report by Human Rights Watch, 'The Pinochet Case – A Wake-up Call to Tyrants and Victims Alike,' http://www.hrw.org/campaigns/chile98/precedent.htm.

One year after his release, with the improving rights situation, Mr Guengueng and others founded the Association of Victims of Political Repression and Crime. With an accountant's meticulousness, he then began gathering testimony from victims, widows and orphans. 'We interviewed more than a thousand people, but we had 712 very good files, with testimony and photos,' he said. 'Because we are all created in God's image, should all these people created in his image be silenced, forgotten? Was there not something that we could do for the victims and their relatives to regain their honor?

... Then, last year, in a case inspired by the one against the Chilean dictator Augusto Pinochet, several rights groups led by Human Rights Watch filed suit against Mr. Habré in Senegal — arguing that he could be tried anywhere for crimes against humanity and that former heads of state were not immune.

... When the case was thrown out this month in Senegal, whose courts ultimately were not independent enough, Human Rights Watch and other groups said their new strategy would be to get an arrest warrant and extradition request from Belgium (one of Chad's victims is now a Belgian citizen) and put Mr Habré on trial there.[50]

This could be done under the precedent set by the Pinochet case. If they succeeded – still a big if – other African despots might then think twice about abusing citizens at home and taking their shopping trips abroad in Paris and New York.[51]

Thus the Pinochet case may be not only a potential sea change for the course of impunity in Chile and Latin America, but for impunity around the globe as international human rights law and traditional notions of sovereignty come into conflict. This outcome, of course, is in no way certain; the strength of commitment to sovereignty and the nation-state as an organising principle of the international system may be under duress but it has certainly not been discarded. Nevertheless, though it is too soon to assess the long-term impact of Pinochet's detention, it is not too soon to notice that policy makers and ex policy makers around the globe, from military officers in Latin America to ex-leaders of Serbia and Bosnia and ex-US Secretary of State, Henry Kissinger, have altered travel plans on the chance that the Pinochet precedent might be applied to them.

---

50 Charges were filed against Habré before Judge Daniel Fransen of the Brussels district court, even before the Senegalese courts dismissed the case. The Senegalese president agreed to hold Habré pending an extradition request. For background and progress see http://www.hrw.org/justice/habre/intro_web2.htm

51 See 'He bore up under torture. Now he bears witness,' by Normitusu Onishi, *New York Times* at http://www.hrw.org/french/themes/habre-NYtimes-SG.html

CHAPTER 4

The Pinochet factor
in Chilean politics

Alan Angell

What do we mean by the Pinochet factor in Chilean politics? It is more than the personal influence wielded by one man. It has a broader meaning. It refers to the political attitudes and behaviour that changed the Chilean military's generally non-interventionist stance to one of active involvement in political matters, justified by the doctrine that the military was the guarantor of the new institutional structure, and of the national interest against self-seeking politicians. The Pinochet factor has civilian aspects too. It refers to the development of a political movement, combining party political components (above all the Unión Democrática Independente – UDI) and entrepreneurial associations, which firmly believes that certain parts of the Pinochet project are sacrosanct, that the institutional structure reflected in the 1980 Constitution is the right one, and that the neoliberal economic framework is part of a national project which may be altered in detail but never questioned in fundamentals. This is surely the most permanent and important inheritance of the Pinochet years. There is widespread consensus from left to right that the balance between state and market is the right one in Chile, and that social equity is achieved not by interfering with the model but by increasing welfare expenditures on the poor and investing more in education and health.

There are cultural aspects to the Pinochet legacy. One need not accept all of Tomás Moulián's (empirically unsubstantiated) critique of present-day consumerist Chile to recognise that there has been a shift in values to a greater emphasis on individualism, to an acceptance of inequalities, and to a lessening of the ties of community that, despite the extent to which they have been

The author would like to thank the following for their comments and criticisms: José Miguel Benavente, Eda Cleary, Lisa Hilbink, Carlos Huneeus, Kirsten Sehnbruch, Rachel Sieder, Alejandro San Francisco and, especially, Samuel Valenzuela.

exaggerated, were stronger in earlier times.[1] (That the intellectual conversion to these values has been stronger at the elite than the popular level is one of the sources of political and social tension at present.) Finally the Pinochet factor represents a way of re-writing the history of Chile to laud the selflessness of the military in its struggle against the sinister forces of international Marxism, and to present a vision of Pinochet as the O'Higgins and Portales of the late twentieth century – both soldier and statesman.[2] This may be hotly contested, but it is no less hotly defended by many Chileans.

Pinochet became a marginal figure after he retired from active command of the army and even more so after his return to Chile following his arrest in London. Yet he exerted a powerful influence during the democratic presidencies of Patricio Aylwin (1990–1994) and of Eduardo Frei (1994–2000). But more than his personal authority, the changes he brought about in Chilean society, politics and the economy persist in many respects to the present. This chapter examines four major public areas, and assesses the extent to which they have changed after thirteen years of democracy. These areas are: the institutional structure created by the Pinochet government; the nature of civil–military relations; the role of the judiciary; and the extent of civil support for the Pinochet system and for Pinochet in his hour of need. The chapter will not examine the economic model, if only because this has been exhaustively analysed elsewhere.[3] Neither does it address the extent of cultural changes because the author is not sure how to assess them, because most of the writing in this area consists of essays which, intelligent as they are, raise the question of empirical verification, and because it is difficult to separate out the Pinochet factor from the effects of economic growth and globalisation.[4]

My argument is that the democratic governments have seen, and helped to bring about, a gradual erosion of the Pinochet legacy, that this erosion weakened

1 See Tomás Moulián, *Chile actual. Anatomía de un mito* (Santiago, 1997). This first sustained critique of the Pinochet model, and of the acceptance of most of it by the new democratic government, became a best-seller for weeks. Paley, *Marketing Democracy: Power and Social Movements in Post-Dictatorship Chile* (2001), p. 168 makes an interesting point in her discussion of social movements after 1990 when she argues that 'the conversion of social organizations into micro-enterprises had political implications. Now grassroots groups would be dedicated towards developing technical skills, not building consciousness or extending political *formación* … Microenterprises would inculcate an entrepreneurial spirit appropriate to a neoliberal economy'.

2 Bernardo O'Higgins is regarded as the liberator of Chile from Spanish domination and Diego Portales as the architect of the long-lived 1833 Constitution which put an end to a period of anarchy.

3 The latest amongst many interpretations is by Felipe Larraín and Rodrigo Vergara, *La transformación económica de Chile* (Santiago, 2000).

4 See, for example, the essays in Paul Drake and Iván Jaksić (eds.), *El modelo chileno. Democracia y desarrollo en los noventa* (Santiago, 1999).

the personal authority of Pinochet himself, and that this process was far advanced by the time of his arrest in London. Hence the arrest of Pinochet was not the precipitating factor in the decline of Pinochet and *pinochetismo*, but one additional if crucial step in a longer and deeper process.

The Pinochet project

The Chilean transition to democracy was unusual in that the military government was not discredited by economic and political failure as had happened in Argentina or Brazil. The military government, headed by General Pinochet, enjoyed considerable public and political support and was in a strong position to negotiate a return to democracy on terms favourable to the military. Indeed, it is probably more accurate to describe the transition as an imposition of the military – both of the economic system and the political structure – rather than as a genuine pact between the military and the democratic forces. As Felipe Agüero argues, a real pact would have produced a constitution agreed upon by all parties – that is not the case in Chile, where apart from the reforms of 1989, Pinochet's Constitution of 1980 remains basically intact despite the efforts of the democratic governing alliance, the Concertación, to reform it.[5]

It is unusual for a military regime to leave power with its reputation still relatively high, not least after having governed for seventeen years. The longevity and strength of the Chilean dictatorship was based upon hierarchical and disciplined armed forces utterly loyal to Pinochet. Central to the power of the regime was the extensive and greatly feared apparatus of repression and control, the DINA (later renamed the CNI). Chile became a police state with Pinochet enjoying almost uncontested power.[6]

Pinochet used the military to administer his rule but not to share in making policy or to deliberate on political or economic matters. The military was the basis upon which Pinochet founded his regime, but it was obedient to him and was the instrument of his rule. The military occupied more offices of state than in other comparable regimes. Of the 133 cabinet ministers during the Pinochet

---

5 Felipe Agüero, 'Transición Pactada?,' *El Mercurio*, 20 November 1998. Samuel Valenzuela, 'La Constitución de 1980 y el inicio de la redemocratización en Chile', in Torcuato Di Tella (ed.), *Crisis de representatividad y sistemas de partidos políticos* (Buenos Aires, 1998) refers to the Concertación's acceptance of the Constitution of 1980 as a necessary concession in the creation of a general political consensus but not a formal pact.

6 The best overall academic study of the Pinochet government is Carlos Huneeus, 'Technocrats and Politicians in an Authoritarian Regime; the "ODEPLAN Boys" and the "Gremialists" in Pinochet's Chile', *Journal of Latin American Studies*, vol. 32, issue 2, May 2000, pp. 461–501. An excellent account by a team of investigative journalists is Cavallo, Salazar and Sepúlveda, *La historia oculta del régimen militar* (Santiago, 1989)

regime, 67 were from the military (37 from the army). As late as 1988 the chief positions in the ministry of economy were in the hands of military men – as was the major state copper company, CODELCO, the development agency CORFO and the Central Bank.[7] Civilian ministers rotated frequently to prevent any one of them acquiring too much power, and military advisers shadowed them. Pinochet made the rules, could change them with a minimum of consultation, and found the courts willing allies.

This structure of authority and obedience persisted after the return to democracy in 1990. The army remained loyal to Pinochet and supported him in acts of defiance against the government. Most of the entrepreneurial sector and the political right would accept no criticism of the general, and defended the structure of the Pinochet system – not simply for ideological reasons but also because it served their interests, at least until 1998.

Pinochet's economic model enjoyed total support from the right and acceptance by the new government. This was a powerful underpinning for the authority and influence that Pinochet continued to exercise long after he left the presidency. The model was never quite as neoliberal as portrayed – there was a massive state presence in copper, bail-outs of the ailing banking sector, a first wave of privatisations that obeyed a political rather than an economic logic and, after 1985, considerable subsidies to certain economic sectors. But eventually the system did produce sustained growth and certainly produced enormous gains to the economically powerful.

Creating the new institutional and constitutional structure

The core of the Pinochet project was the creation of an institutional and constitutional structure to embody his ideas, values and policies. The constitution of 1980 embodies his ideas of a state with a limited role, but with authoritarian controls over democratic processes. It gives the president excessive powers – except over the military, which in the original version was given a tutelary role over the political system. It limits the ability of congress to perform an adequate regulatory and monitoring role over the executive. It provides for nine designated senators in the Senate, four of whom are nominated directly by the military. Its normative elements enshrine the virtues of the free-market economy. The constitution safeguards private property rights against the state, and gives the courts extra powers to ensure that the free-market economy remains intact. The constitution is difficult to reform.[8] During the first eight years after the return to

---

7 Huneeus, 'Technocrats and Politicians in an Authoritarian Regime', p. 189
8 The *leyes orgánicas constitucionales* need the support of four sevenths of the congress. These laws govern the Central Bank, the armed forces, and the laws regulating the party system

democracy the right enjoyed a virtual veto power over legislation through a combination of *pinochetista* designated senators, and an electoral system that bene-fited the right not least in the way that the electoral boundaries were drawn.

Pinochet intended that when the constitution came into force in the 1990s it would have an additional safeguard – himself as president (now elected) until 1997. The constitution contained a clause allowing the representative of the armed forces to stand in a plebiscite, which, if it gave its approval, would elect that candidate to the presidency for an eight-year term of office. But in a plebiscite held in October 1988 Pinochet lost by 55 per cent votes against his continuation in office to 43 per cent in favour, and this forced him to call for a free election for the presidency to be held in December 1989. Nevertheless, the 43 per cent of the vote that he obtained was testimony to the extent of support that he still enjoyed, even if part of that vote is discounted because of the fear of some voters of the consequences of voting against him.

Pinochet's strategy after the plebiscite defeat was to safeguard his own position by insisting upon his constitutional right to remain as commander-in-chief of the army whoever won the forthcoming elections in 1989. His aim was a military free of civil interference in internal matters such as promotions, and enjoying a privileged budgetary position for equipment, salaries and pensions. The military budget could not be reduced below its 1989 level in real terms, and the obligatory 10 per cent of the share of copper sales of the state corporation CODELCO assured it a considerable sum for arms purchases. Expenditure on the military during the Pinochet regime according to one calculation was the highest in Latin America (outside Cuba) as a percentage of GDP and continued to be so during the democratic governments – though in Chile the police was included in the military budget as were the generous military pensions paid by the only part of the pension system that remained in state hands. The government lacked the power to make cuts.[9] Pinochet also sought to make impossible any trials of members of the armed forces for human rights abuses.

---

and the electoral law. Constitutional reform needs the support of three-fifths of congress. The *reformas a las bases institucionales* need the support of two thirds of congress. These laws relate to basic ways of reforming the constitution itself, to relations between the civil and military powers, and to the role of the National Security Council.

9 Figures of military expenditures are very difficult to calculate because many items appear in the budgets of other ministries – military hospitals under those of the Health Ministry, subsidies for defence industries under economic development and so on. These figures are drawn from Eugenio Lahera and Marcelo Ortúzar, 'Military Expenditures and Development in Latin America,' *CEPAL Review*, no. 65, Aug. 1998, pp. 15–30.

However, the loss of the plebiscite did necessitate limited negotiation with the opposition.[10] The National Security Council established by the 1980 constitution lost the military majority in its membership and became equally balanced between civilians and military. It became a consultative institution rather than one with the right to inform the president of its opinion – in the original version it had the right to represent (*representar*) its opinion but in the amended version it had the lesser right to make known (*hacer presente*) its views.[11] Article 8 of the Constitution which outlawed 'subversive' opinions was repealed. The president lost his power to dissolve the lower house of congress. The number of elected senators was increased from 26 to 38, reducing the influence of the nine nominated senators. Civil control over the designation, promotion, and retirement of armed forces personnel and police officers was increased, although the executive still lacked the power to remove the commanders-in-chief of the four armed forces (the police remained part of the military establishment).   .

If there were concessions on the one hand, on the other laws were passed (known in Chile as the *leyes de amarre* – the binding laws) restricting future governments. For example, one law granted security of tenure in the public sector, so that the incoming government had few posts at its discretion. Another prohibited the incoming congress from investigating the activities of the Pinochet government: the right to present constitutional accusations against state functionaries (Article 48 No 2), was limited by the Organic Law of Congress which ruled that such investigations could only relate to activities that took place after 11 March 1990 (Article 3).[12] Members of the Supreme Court were offered handsome payments to retire to make way for equally conservative, but considerably younger judges. The Pinochet government even tied up state funds to deprive the Aylwin government of freedom of action. An estimated US $2 billion in the Copper Stabilisation Fund, on which the Aylwin government was counting as a cushion against likely future falls in copper prices, was spent by the Pinochet government to repay the bad debts accumulated by the Central Bank when it bailed out the private banking sector after the collapse of 1982–3.

10 A good account of the changes is contained in the Americas Watch Report, *Human Rights since the Plebiscite* (New York, 1989), pp. 51–8.

11 J. Samuel Valenzuela, 'La Constitución de 1980 y el inicio de la redemocratización en Chile,' in Torcuato Di Tella (ed.), *Crisis de representatividad y sistemas de partidos políticos* (Buenos Aires, 1998), p. 179

12 Carlos Huneeus, 'Technocrats and Politicians in an Authoritarian Regime', pp. 461–501, p. 606.

Democratising the Pinochet structure

Many commentators in 1990 saw the structure inherited by the Aylwin government as a straitjacket from which it would be difficult to escape. Lira and Loveman, for example, argue that the government's acceptance of the institutional
structure made it almost impossible to create the rupture with the past that an
active human rights policy would imply.[13] Yet despite both the new government's acceptance of continuity and the restrictions imposed by the Pinochet
government, there have been changes.

The initial starting point for democratic rule in Chile was unfavourable. Yet
the story since then has been of strengthening those aspects of the institutional
structure that favour democracy, and of the gradual reduction of those features
that entrench authoritarianism. There has been slow but steady erosion of the
Pinochet system. Constitutionalism has been strengthened at the expense of
authoritarianism. This is partly a matter of legislative change. One major constitutional reform was the restoration of democratic elections for local mayors
and councillors. The eight-year term of the presidency has been reduced to six.
The nine designated senators are no longer all *pinochetistas* since the government has been able to appoint three of them after the 1997 congressional
elections. But perhaps more significant than such reforms has been the development of conventions of constitutional and legislative behaviour that embody the
spirit of democracy.

Formal constitutional rules are not necessarily a guide to the real power of
particular institutions – constitutional conventions can alter the spirit if not the
letter of the constitution. There has been a strengthening of the legitimacy of
the democratic government and of the democratic process, as government and
opposition have bargained over issues comparable to those in many other
democracies – how to reform the health system, what should be the appropriate
level of taxation, and how to deal with crime. As early as 1990, there was
political agreement between the government and opposition on a major tax
reform to take a modest amount from the immodest gains of the business sector
and use it for social purposes. There was agreement about a labour reform
which, though far short of the aspirations of the labour movement, was an
improvement on the Pinochet reforms. There was agreement about the way
Congress and its committee system should operate.

The process of 'normalisation' of political life was assisted by a high degree
of internal unity within the governing coalition and by the relative lack of substantive disagreement with the opposition. The governments of Aylwin and Frei

---

13 Elizabeth Lira and Brian Loveman, *Las ardientes cenizas del olvido: vía chilena de reconciliación política 1932–1994* (Santiago, 2000), p. 351.

oversaw economic growth and control over inflation without precedent in recent Chilean development and only very recently has attention shifted to the limitations of the economic model. The fears of the right that the new government would be unable to manage the economy proved unfounded. The democratic governments have also restored the legitimacy of Chile in the international arena, and have been successful in creating a more stable international environment for Chile by such actions as the (almost complete) resolution of border disputes with Argentina, and by signing or ratifying international conventions safeguarding human rights. Resolving the internal question of human rights abuses committed by the Pinochet government has been more difficult and is discussed later, but the government did re-establish the rule of law. By the end of the Aylwin presidency in 1994 all political prisoners had been released – even those committed for the attempted assassination of Pinochet in 1986.[14]

There was also the positive experience of frequent – perhaps too many – elections in which the vast majority participated, in which very few votes went to anti-system parties, and in which abstention was low. Failure to register and abstention (and spoiled ballot papers) did rise alarmingly in 1997 so that only 53.4 per cent of the total eligible population voted compared with 81.4 per cent in 1989 and 73.7 per cent in 1993. But 1997 was the first time that congressional elections took place separately from presidential elections. When there were presidential elections again in 1999, the level of valid votes cast was 68.2 per cent, which compares very favourably with the rate in most developed democracies (though in the congressional elections in 2001 the level of participation fell to a rate similar to 1997).[15]

As the practices and conventions of democracy became entrenched, and as it became clear that the left was no threat to the democratic system and that the right would work within it, some of the fundamental underpinnings of the Pinochet system started to unravel, and with them support for Pinochet himself. As the left and right converged in democratic competition, and in acceptance of the basic rules of capitalism, the space for an authoritarian alternative reduced. The continuation of *pinochetismo* depended upon antagonism and mutual mistrust between government and opposition. In practice, as an unintended consequence of the electoral system, antagonism and mistrust is much stronger

---

14 However Anthony Pereira and Jorge Zaverucha, 'The Protected Step-child: Military Justice in Chile,' unpubl. Paper, LASA Conference, Washington, DC, 2001, argues that this involved a trade-off with the right which left the system of military justice still with extensive powers beyond those normally accepted in democracies.

15 Alan Angell and Benny Pollack, 'The Chilean Presidential Elections of 1999–2000 and Democratic Consolidation,' *Bulletin of Latin American Research*, vol. 19, no. 2, 2000, pp. 357–78.

between the two parties of the right than it is on many issues between government and opposition. Samuel Valenzuela writes that, 'If the continuity of the 1980 Constitution has not been broken, the transformations have been significant, and the recreation of previous institutional practices has been so extensive, that one can say that there has been a transition, not yet finished, towards the recreation of a fundamental legal framework for the practice of democracy.'[16]

Civil–military relations

The Aylwin presidency was punctuated by episodes of tension between the government and the military. In October 1990 the Chamber of Deputies started to investigate the way in which the army had made a considerable profit during the military government by purchasing a well-functioning defence company for very little money, including a large payment made to Pinochet's son (even though public officials are forbidden to conduct business with relatives of the president). After tense meetings between Pinochet and members of the Aylwin government, the army withdrew to barracks, in their words, in an 'exercise of security, readiness and coordination'. Congress agreed to exclude the activities of Pinochet, father and son, from their investigations, and it was thought that the affair would become buried in a complicated legal maze. However, when the matter resurfaced in 1993 (at a time when there was increased tension about human rights issues) the army this time took to the streets dressed in camouflage fatigues.[17] The government made it clear that it was harmful to civil–military relations to proceed, and the judge in charge duly declared that the case was outside his jurisdiction.

These episodes indicated that the army was not prepared to accept any investigations into possible misdemeanours – it put itself above the rule of law

16 Valenzuela, 'La Constitución de 1980,' p. 195.
17 The military also objected to Defence Minister Patricio Rojas' refusal to authorise the promotion of military officers suspected of human rights violations. Samuel Valenzuela, personal communication. There appear to have been about sixty such cases. The military showed its control over the murky world of intelligence in a case involving the interception and taping of a mobile telephone conversation between a Senator of *Renovación Nacional*, Sebastián Piñera, and a businessman. The tape, played in Piñera's presence on a TV programme, consisted of abusive comments about another RN politician, and possible presidential candidate of the right, Deputy Evelyn Matthei. As a result of judicial investigations an army captain from the telecommunications unit was placed under military arrest, and later, the General in charge of Santiago telecommunications unit, Ricardo Contreras, requested early retirement. See Alan Angell, 'What Remains of Pinochet's Chile?,' Occasional Paper No. 3, Institute of Latin American Studies, University of London, 1993.

and above the democratically elected representative government.[18] There seemed
to be two parallel systems of power in Chile: one democratic, controlling the
economy and most aspects of the political system; and another, a carry-over
from an authoritarian past posing a veiled threat to the civilian authorities – in
Pinochet's words, a sleeping lion.

Yet what is perhaps surprising is that these episodes of conflict did not
develop wider political significance. They were seen as incidents in which the
military was defending its own interests rather than trying to influence broader
political issues. In the absence of widespread social conflict there were no
conditions for legitimising another military coup. Between the president and the
head of the army, General Pinochet, there developed a 'working relationship'.
In most matters Pinochet accepted that the military was subordinate to civil
authority as he was to the president (though he resisted having to go through
the minister of defence to have access to Aylwin).[19] Moreover, the military
knew it could count upon the support of most of the political and economic
right, even if some politicians on the right would have been happy to see
Pinochet step down (on the grounds that this would lead to a more professional
less political military). Politicians of the left, as much as they condemned the
historical record of Pinochet, had little influence over the balance of military
power either inside the institution or between it and the civil order.

While civil–military relations were at their most tense during the Aylwin
government, there were similar episodes of tension during that of President Frei –
notably the long time that elapsed before the government was able to apprehend and
imprison General Manuel Contreras after he had been convicted of complicity
in the assassination of Orlando Letelier in Washington, DC in 1976. Yet what
might have been expected to provoke the greatest unrest in the military – the arrest
of Pinochet in 1998 in London – did not, in fact, do so. Indeed, the army behaved
with greater moderation than did a considerable number of politicians of the right.

The changing attitudes of the military

One notable development since 1998 has been the gradual distancing of the
military from Pinochet's belief in its political role, and from the ideological

---

18   Details of these complicated affairs can be found in Ascanio Cavallo, Manuel Salazar and Oscar
     Sepúlveda, *La historia oculta del régimen militar* (Santiago, 1989) and in Weeks, *The Military
     and Chilean Democracy*, unpublished paper: Latin American Studies Association Conference,
     Chicago, 1998.

19   In an interview President Aylwin told the author that when he asked Pinochet for his
     resignation at the outset of his government, Pinochet's reply was that if he went then those
     who took over would be far less respectful of the government. And, according to Aylwin
     that indeed was the case. Interview March 1997.

tenets of geo-politics and other Cold War doctrines. In public no serving and few retired officers would breathe a word of criticism of the general. But military support for Pinochet through the trials and tribulations that followed his arrest appeared to be a formal gesture, and certainly came nowhere near to threatening the constitutional or political order as politicians on the right had alleged would be the case. What explains this gradual distancing and the reversion to a more typical professional and non-interventionist role?

It is partly a question of generational change. The generals closest to Pinochet have all retired. His successor in the army, General Ricardo Izurieta, removed from the military those officers suspected, with good reason, of involvement in cases of human rights abuses. In the first round of promotions under his control over 200 officers associated with hard-line attitudes were forced into retirement. General Pinochet himself partly contributed to this distancing by his decision to enter the Senate. Under his constitution, all presidents who had served for six or more years may become senators for life. For a man who publicly expressed his contempt for politicians, to become one himself was a massive contradiction. No doubt one motive was to acquire parliamentary immunity from trial, but his departure from active command to political involvement inevitably eroded his authority in the military.[20]

There is little doubt that General Izurieta wanted to look to the future rather than to the past.[21] This is not necessarily because he was more democratically inclined than his predecessor. The logic of military development in the Southern Cone is one of integration with other militaries of the region. Even the unthinkable has happened – joint military manoeuvres in the late 1990s with the old enemy Argentina. The Chilean military is conforming to the regional norm. Lira and Loveman point out that it is quite possible that reconciliation over the human rights issue could become acceptable to the military 'if only for pragmatic reasons so as to be able to function normally in the international community'.[22] Samuel Valenzuela advances several reasons to explain gradual changes in civil–military relations. Governments since 1990 have developed expertise in the area of security and defence, so that military matters are no longer exclusively the prerogative of the armed forces. Secondly, the military depends upon the government being willing to purchase the new technology

20 According to Samuel Valenzuela, based on an interview with the Defence Minister's chief advisor, Izurieta did not consult with Pinochet on institutional matters once Pinochet left active command. Personal communication.

21 Though in one salute to the constitutional rather than the dictatorial past of the government he named the new Military Barracks of La Reina in Santiago after General René Schneider, who was assassinated in 1970 by the extreme right with CIA support. *¿Qué Pasa?* 3 December 2000.

22 Lira and Loveman, *Las ardientes cenizas del olvido*, p. 332.

constantly being developed in the area of security. Thirdly, the government has extended its influence through the appointment of civilian ministers and vice-ministers for all branches of the armed forces. Finally, by exercising its right not to approve the promotion of military officers, the government has enforced the resignation of a considerable number of officers suspected of human rights abuses or of lack of respect towards the civil authorities. This provoked the public indignation of Pinochet but his protest fell on deaf ears in the ministry of defence.[23]

The military has even moved a little towards acknowledging responsibility for human rights abuses. Participation in a *Mesa de Diálogo* with representatives of the government and of some human rights groups (not all would participate) produced relatively few concrete results. There was no agreed version of the past (could there ever be?), and the information given by the military on the whereabouts of those who disappeared was both very restricted in terms of the number of individuals it admitted knowledge of, and misleading as to details. Still, it does represent an advance in terms of a closer civil–military relationship. The military in effect admitted that there had been a campaign of disappearances, though it denied that there was any 'institutional responsibility'. Opinion about the value of the *Mesa* differs even amongst those who participated. One participant writes,

> For the army to accept and recognise what happened, and even more to admit the horror of it, was as far as it could go. It was, above all, recognition and they fully accepted that. It was also an intelligent move on the part of Izurieta because what he wanted was to distance himself from the past, though without a total break and a public apology as he knew he did not have the institutional power to do that. The *Mesa* marked an important change in breaking the inevitable sequence that went from explanation of what happened to automatic justification.[24]

The opinions of another member of the *Mesa*, Roberto Garretón, a human rights lawyer, in the weekly *¿Qué Pasa?* bear the heading, *La Mesa de Diálogo ha sido un Fracaso* ('the *Mesa de Diálogo* has been a failure'). In fact the opinions expressed are more balanced. On the positive side he stresses that there was dialogue, and that the human rights representatives were able to confront the military with the scale and nature of the human rights abuses. If as a result of the process, the military says 'never again' then that would be worth the effort. But the failure so far has been that of not producing information about the remains of most of those who disappeared.

23 J. Samuel Valenzuela, 'Los escollos de la redemocratización chilena,' *Boletín SAAP*, vol. 5, no. 9, Spring 1999, pp. 122–3.

24 Sol Serrano, member of the Mesa, personal communication 5 October 2001. In interviews in the press, General Izurieta has referred to the human rights abuses as atrocious acts.

In the same way that the constitutional and institutional system evolved so as to diminish the importance of the Pinochet factor in politics, the evolution of the military moved in the same direction. The most recent and dramatic example of this was the appointment in January 2002 of Michelle Bachelet as minister of defence. Not only is she the first woman to occupy this post, she is also the daughter of a former army general who died under torture in 1974. Yet the army reacted calmly to the appointment and even welcomed it as a way of making atonement for the death of General Bachelet. But what of that unquestioning redoubt of Pinochet during his rule – the Supreme Court?

The Supreme Court and the role of the judiciary

The Supreme Court did little to impede the construction of an authoritarian system and had a lamentable record in human rights. Lisa Hilbink writes that 'during most of the 1990s, the Chilean judiciary threw its symbolic weight behind illiberal political principles and authoritarian institutions ... The Supreme Court generally endorsed the institutional edifice constructed by the leaders of the authoritarian regime and left largely unchallenged the principles and values embodied therein'.[25] Jorge Correa points out that there was no need for the military to put pressure on the courts – they fully accepted the claims of the military, and in return the military treated the courts with respect, and left them unreformed.[26]

During the last few months of his government Pinochet appointed nine of the seventeen members of the Supreme Court, leaving a court that was conservative and influential. On the Constitutional Tribunal three of the seven members are nominated by the Supreme Court. Two more are nominated by the National Security Council, five of the eight members of which are either judges or military officers. Moreover, the Supreme Court nominates three of the nine designated senators. The Supreme Court also resisted as far as it could

---

25 See Lisa Hilbink, 'Un Estado de Derecho no liberal,' in Paul Drake and Iván Jaksic (eds.), *El modelo chileno. Democracia y desarrollo en los noventa* (Santiago, 1999), p. 325; and by the same author, 'An Exception to Chilean Exceptionalism? The Historical Role of Chile's Judiciary,' in Susan Eva Eckstein and Timothy P. Wickham-Crowley (eds.), *What Justice? Whose Justice? Fighting for Fairness in Latin America* (Berkeley, 2003), where she writes that 'the long-standing institutional structure and ideology of the judiciary, namely tight hierarchical control by the Supreme Court over judicial careers and a strict, positivist-inspired distinction between law and politics served to reproduce conformity and conservatism in the judicial ranks'.

26 Jorge Correa, 'Cinderella stays at the party. Judicial power in Chile in the nineties,' in Paul Drake and Iván Jaksić (eds.), *El modelo chileno.*, p. 301.

any reforms of the judicial system. Government proposals to modernise the judiciary through the creation of a Judicial Council to oversee the appointment, training and behaviour of judges were opposed. The Court lapsed into its traditional complacent conservative corporatism.

After the return to democracy the judiciary – with a few notable exceptions – continued to accept the binding nature of the amnesty of 1978. The Supreme Court refused to accept allegations of complicity in covering up cases of human rights abuses. It condemned the Rettig report (the official government enquiry into deaths and disappearances during the military regime) for being 'impassioned, ill-considered, tendentious, the product of an irregular investigation, and of probable political bias'. [27]

However, the Supreme Court became the subject of political controversy, and faced increasing pressure from other branches of government. President Aylwin, himself a distinguished lawyer, accused the court of a lack of 'moral courage'. In December 1992 a group of deputies presented a constitutional accusation against three members of the Court accusing them of a 'notable abandonment of their duties' in failing to take action in cases of human rights abuses, and of unjustly passing a case from the civil to the military courts. Only one judge was removed – and that was because members of the right accused him, though not publicly, of involvement in corrupt activities. The political message was clear. The legislature would not accept indifference to cases of human rights abuses, and the members of the court would not enjoy immunity for their actions simply by virtue of being members of the court. The courts were criticised not just by the left but also by the right, for traditional, slow methods of procedure and for failure to adapt to the new neoliberal order. Thus the Supreme Court in the 1990s was in the worst of circumstances – it possessed neither democratic legitimacy nor claims to modernity, and was under attack from both right and left. [28]

The increasing pressure on the Supreme Court eventually led to some convictions in human rights cases. The most notorious criminal convicted was the former head of the secret police (DINA) General Manuel Contreras, along with his associate in crime Colonel Fernández Larrios, partly in response to US pressure over the assassination of Orlando Letelier and a North American colleague in Washington in 1976. Other prosecutions related to equally gory crimes committed in Chile – three human rights activists were brutally murdered in 1985 by a special unit of the Carabineros in a case known as *los degollados*. The investigation of this episode was successful because rivalry between the various intelligence units of the police and the army led to information being passed to

27 Hilbink, 'Un Estado de Derecho no liberal,' p. 332.
28 *Ibid.*

the judicial authorities. Judge Juica handed down sentences on 15 members of the Carabineros, the most severe of which were two of 18 years and one of 15. However, the amnesty law did not apply to these cases as they occurred after the period covered by that law.

The process of judicial activism began slowly and with reverses. In 1994 two chambers of the appellate court ruled that since the Pinochet government claimed that Chile had been in a state of war in 1974, the country was bound by the terms of the Geneva Conventions. But this was overruled by the Supreme Court. In September 1998 the criminal chamber of the Supreme Court reopened some human rights cases covered by the 1978 amnesty law, arguing that Chile was bound by international humanitarian law. This too was overturned – with two dissenters – a few weeks later when the composition of the criminal chamber had changed. Two new interpretations of the amnesty law began to circulate and gain acceptance – though not on a major scale until the arrest of Pinochet in October 1998. One was that before an amnesty could be applied the case had to be investigated to establish the truth – something that President Aylwin had sustained as early as 1990. Effectively the details of the crime and those who committed it had to be established before amnesty could be applied. Even more useful for those pursuing justice was the reinterpretation of the amnesty law to designate unsolved disappearances as 'aggravated kidnappings' which escape the limits of that law – in this interpretation the crime is still being committed. This was crucial in the Supreme Court judgement on the case of five senior military officers accused of participating in the Caravan of Death, and has implication for hundreds of other cases.[29]

In addition to the new interpretations, a number of courageous judges began prosecution. By 1997 there were more than 200 cases in the courts relating to instances of disappearance, and over 400 military officers had been called to give evidence.[30] By 1999 five former army generals were facing human rights charges – two for the *Operación Albania* in 1987 when a number of suspected leftists were murdered, one for involvement in the Caravan of Death, and two for complicity in the assassination of trade union leader Tucapel Jiménez in 1982.

In the most dramatic of all cases, the Supreme Court lifted the parliamentary immunity of Senator Pinochet. An investigating magistrate, Judge Guzmán, had assembled overwhelming evidence of Pinochet's involvement in, and authorisation of, the infamous Caravan of Death murders, and a series of hearings came to a halt in 2001 only when a narrow majority accepted medical evidence that the general was not fit to stand trial. Lifting parliamentary

---

29 Davis, *The Pinochet Case*, p. 20.
30 Valenzuela, 'La Constitución de 1980 y el inicio de la redemocratización en Chile,' p. 192.

immunity in Chile requires powerful evidence of guilt – more than the standard of proof required for a similar charge in the USA. Moreover Guzmán had started his investigation in January 1998 – before the arrest of Pinochet.

What explains this change in the attitude of the judiciary? After years of resisting reform, the courts finally accepted a package of reform measures enacted in 1997 – in part because mounting accusations of corruption were affecting its standing. The Supreme Court was increased from seventeen to twenty-one members; there was retirement for judges over seventy-five; Senate approval of Supreme Court appointees was introduced; and five posts were reserved for lawyers outside the judicial hierarchy. In the end, the 1990s had proved to be a decade of change in the legal system. Only four of the seventeen Pinochet appointees remained in place by the end of the decade. The system of appointment of judges changed for the first time in a hundred years; the Supreme Court was divided into specialised chambers and became a real court of final appeal. At the end of the decade after a long struggle a *Ministerio Público* (Attorney General) was established and the penal procedural code was changed in an initial limited experiment from the traditional inquisitorial one to an oral adversarial one.[31]

The Supreme Court was responding mostly to domestic pressures but also to international ones following the arrest of Pinochet in London. Judges are not immune from changing political and social attitudes, both at home and abroad, as any survey of the US Supreme Court would show. In Chile the rather insular Supreme Court took notice when the British law lords showed that a judiciary normally considered as conservative and traditional could nevertheless respond positively to accusations of human rights abuses. Within Chile there was increasing pressure from some sectors to follow the example of the law lords. The tireless human rights groups, human rights lawyers and a number of investigative journalists kept the issue alive and on the political agenda.[32] Recognising that Pinochet was a lost cause, the Supreme Court sought to restore its tarnished reputation – both at home and abroad – by embracing the cause of human rights.

Whatever the motives, the sight of the Chilean judiciary deciding that there was *prima facie* evidence of the former dictator being complicit in human rights abuses both symbolised and hastened the marginalisation of Pinochet.

---

31 The Supreme Court elected its first ever woman member in October 2001.
32 Notably the writings of Patricia Verdugo whose book, *Los zarpazos del puma* (Santiago, 1989), telling the story of the brutal reprisals of the military in the north of Chile not long after the coup, had an immense impact on public opinion.

Pinochet, the civilian right and public opinion

Pinochetismo was central to the policies and beliefs of one of the two major parties of the right, and central to important, though not all, factions of the other party. Two parties dominate the right. The Unión Demócrata Independiente (UDI), a combination of traditional Catholicism and neoliberal economics, has grown in cohesion and strength even after the assassination of its founder and ideologue of the Pinochet regime, Jaime Guzmán, in 1991. Receiving lavish support from the business community, it also practices a grass-roots politics unusual in contemporary Chile. Many of the local mayors nominated by Pinochet were from the UDI, and the party used its local presence to establish a variety of grass-roots organisations providing health care, and help with education and housing. It is a young party with most of its voters under the age of 50. It has gradually improved its electoral performance – increasing its share of the vote for the Chamber of Deputies from 9.8 per cent in 1989 to 14.4 per cent in 1997, and in 2001 becoming the largest party in Chile with 25.2 per cent of the vote.

Renovación Nacional (RN), the other main party of the right, is an uneasy coalition of members of the old nationalist right, the traditional liberal right and modernising politicians. Although initially more popular than the UDI, its internal differences and its uneasy relationship with the business world has damaged its image, standing and support. It has been marked by continuous internal squabbling and dissent. The modernising democratic wing of the party suffered a severe loss when its dynamic president, Andrés Allamand, lost to the UDI candidate in the 1997 senatorial contest.[33] It received 18.3 per cent of the vote for the Chamber in 1989 but was down to 16.8 per cent in 1997; and fell further to 13.7 per cent in 2001.[34]

An important bloc of the electorate cast their support for parties born or reborn in the Pinochet period, with the expressed intention of defending his legacy. A substantial sector of public opinion as late as 1996 had a positive view of his rule. Asked whether the Pinochet government was one of the best governments of the twentieth century in Chile, 27 per cent agreed, and 59 per cent disagreed, with 13 per cent not answering or holding no opinion. But amongst UDI voters 67 per cent thought it was one of the best – and amongst socialist voters 81 per cent thought that it was not. (In response to another

33 For a fascinating account of the politics of the right see Alland, Denis and Ferrand, Frédérique, 'Jurisprudence Française en matière de Droit International Public,' *Revue Générale de Droit International*, vol. 102, no. 3, 1998, p. 828.

34 It is difficult to calculate exact support for the parties because the nature of coalition making means that not all parties present candidates in all constituencies, and in 1989 many independents, associated with but not yet members of either party, also ran and were in some cases elected.

question 65 per cent of UDI voters thought that his government was not a dictatorship, while 86 per cent of socialist voters thought that it was.)[35] The parties of the right enjoyed another major advantage. In the absence of any regulations on campaign finance in Chile, they received generous funding from the business sectors committed to the continuation of *pinochetismo* – which after all had seen them become very wealthy.

The problem for the political right was how to move from a strong if minority position in Congress to mount a credible campaign for the presidency. In 1989 and 1993 the presidential candidates of the right were so clearly going to lose, that they were abandoned by the congressional candidates of the right to concentrate on their own congressional campaigns. A major change took place with the right's choice of candidate for the presidential elections of 1999–2000 – a consummate and proven politician who decided to break with the past and project himself and his campaign towards the future. Joaquín Lavín, a founder member of the UDI, made his name as a successful mayor of the prosperous suburb of Las Condes in Santiago. Confident of the support of the parties of the right, he presented himself as above parties, appealing widely as a successful administrator rather than as an ambitious politician. His campaign slogan of the need for change could be interpreted as a reference to the need for change from the governing coalition, but also to the need to break away from the legacy of *pinochetismo*.

The arrest of Pinochet proved marginal to the campaign. The two major candidates avoided the issue and it was not an important factor for the voters. Lavín was fortunate that Pinochet was facing trial in London and not in Santiago. His emphasis on the future would have been less convincing with the general facing a controversial trial in Chile. Lavín was careful to distance himself from Pinochet and made few references to the past. He paid only one visit to Pinochet in London, presented as a humanitarian rather than a political gesture. In his campaign Lavín made progressive gestures on the human rights issue – he rejected imitating the *punto final* of Argentina, criticised UDI proposals to extend the amnesty law beyond 1978, visited families of the disappeared, and supported the right of the courts to investigate human rights violations. And the result was a stunning achievement for Lavín with only a handful of votes separating him on the first ballot from the coalition candidate, Ricardo Lagos. Lagos won 47.95 per cent of the vote to 47.51 per cent for Lavín, although Lagos gained enough votes in the second round to emerge the narrow victor. Lavín secured his place as the unchallenged leader of the right and the architect of a policy that distanced the right in general from aspects of the Pinochet past other

---

35 Carlos Huneeus, 'Las elecciones en Chile después del autoritarismo,' in Silvia Dutrenit (ed.), *Huellas de las transiciones políticas* (Mexico, 1998), p. 157.

than the economic policy and certain key parts of the 1980 constitution (relating more to the economic than the political arrangements).

The campaign strategy of Lavín was heavily influenced by the public response to the Pinochet affair. A MORI poll in mid-November 1998 asked if the detention of Pinochet 'had any effect on you and your family?' The responses were – no effect at all, 71 per cent, it made me happy, 6 per cent; and it made me angry 7 per cent. Asked if as a result of the arrest, democracy was in danger, 66 per cent replied that it was not, and 27 per cent that it was. Asked if it was good or bad that he was arrested, 44 per cent said good, and 45 per cent said bad. Asked if they thought Pinochet was guilty, 63 per cent said yes, and 16 per cent said no.[36] A CERC poll published in March 1999 asked if the future of Chile depended on the outcome of the Pinochet case; 78 per cent disagreed and only 16 per cent agreed – though if the poll is disaggregated by political preference, 40 per cent of UDI supporters agreed though even so 57 per cent did not. Another CERC poll published in July 1999 asked if Pinochet should return to Chile. 51 per cent said that he should and 38 per cent said that he should not.[37] Following the detention of a number of other officers for possible participation in human rights abuses, including an ex-director of the CNI, General Gordon, as many as 71 per cent thought that the detention was just and only 14 per cent that it was not. Even amongst those who declared their support for Lavín, 51 per cent agreed with the detention and only 31 per cent did not.

After the return of Pinochet to Chile a poll in July 2000 asked respondents if they thought that the Supreme Court should lift the congressional immunity of the General; 52 per cent were in favour and 35 per cent against. However, asked if the government should continue with its policy of trying to solve the human rights issue, 47 per cent agreed that it should, and 44 per cent that it should not (rising to 82 per cent amongst UDI voters). Asked if the problem of the disappeared was important or not, 67 per cent said that it was, and 27 per cent that it was not important. In December 2000 asked if they agreed with Judge Guzmán in ordering the detention of Pinochet for complicity in the Caravan of Death murders, 50 per cent agreed, and 33 per cent disagreed.

How can we interpret this data? Opinion divided along predictable lines, but there were interesting differences. Supporters of the government were more convinced of Pinochet's guilt than his supporters were convinced of his innocence. Most people had an opinion on the issue but it was not a central concern and much less so than issues of unemployment, health, security and

36 MORI poll taken between mid and late November. The figures do not add up to 100 per cent as those not replying or having no opinion have been omitted.
37 The figures in this and the next two paragraphs are taken from the polls conducted by the polling agency CERC. They are available on their website, www.cerc.cl

education – the four most quoted items when voters were asked about their major concerns. Any intelligent political strategist of the right would draw the lesson that while support for the general should not be abandoned, given its low salience for most people, neither should any campaign treat it as a prominent issue. Which was exactly the lesson that Lavín learnt – much to the reported disgust of Pinochet and his family.

Politically the impact of the Pinochet case was paradoxical. It encouraged the right – erstwhile unconditional supporters of Pinochet – to move away from him and his legacy. It had the effect on the governing coalition – once die-hard opponents of the general – of dividing them over issues of justice versus political expediency. The expected aggressive response from the military never came. Business protested, but assured Spanish and British investors that their investments were safe in Chile. The public in general was concerned, but not enough to take to the streets to protest – the size of demonstrations, either for or against, was tiny compared with protest movements in the past. But it would be wrong to write off the case as a political damp squib. The fact that the Pinochet case did not feature much in the campaign should not diminish its overall political significance. As Madeleine Davis writes, 'The symbolic and expressive significance of the case has been tremendous, not least because the enormous world interest has enabled victims to tell their stories on a world stage and moreover in a context which is about pursuing not only truth but retribution and justice – hitherto largely impossible in Chile itself.'[38] While broadly true, this underestimates the way in which there was progress towards justice before the Pinochet case, and this progress explains both why the case had a national favourable context for its symbolic importance and also why it did not generate the expected level of internal political discord.[39]

Conclusion

Chilean democracy has many admirable qualities. The state is reasonably efficient and honest. The judiciary in contrast to many Latin American countries is independent. Electoral participation is high. The overall context – economic and social – is stable. Nonetheless, many commentators point to a general malaise. Alex Wilde writes about public life exhibiting a 'certain muffled quality reflective of what might be called a "conspiracy of consensus" originating among the political elite but permeating the whole society. Within the citizenry there appears to be a widespread aversion to open conflict, related to low levels

38 Davis, *The Pinochet Case*, p. 19.
39 There was also justice in the payment of reparations to the families of those who disappeared or were murdered.

of social trust'. He adds that 'politicians practice a cautious politics of elite consensus building – almost a kind of political engineering – with few channels to organised society or citizens' discontent'.[40] This accounts for excessive caution in the area of human rights. 'After the early years of the Aylwin government, 'human rights' became an issue identified exclusively with its most serious victims, rather than a guiding principle on which to found a new national politics.'[41]

Lechner and Guell explain this *'desencanto'* as a response to years of such trauma that the people are averse to conflict and prefer a *'democracia de los acuerdos'* (democracy of agreements). They claim that after the Rettig report the government refused to elaborate its version of the past. As a result *'nos hemos quedado sin historia'* ('we have been left without history') both at the level of the individual and of society as a whole. Though as an alternative interpretation they posit that Chileans have a 'memory of silence' rather than a 'memory of forgetting'. They cite a United Nations Development Programme report which shows lack of expectation about the future, a discourse of hopelessness, and a high level of disenchantment. The report indicates a high level of lack of confidence in interpersonal relations, and a high level of insecurity.[42]

Persuasively presented as these arguments are, they need to be treated with caution. The trends described are not dissimilar from those found, for example, in the pages of Robert Putnam's *Bowling Alone* based on the USA.[43] Disenchantment with politicians and parties appears to be an almost universal trend. Perceptions of increased insecurity need not just be psychological but could reflect real trends in criminality. Chileans may express disenchantment not so much because of a failure to resolve the devils of the past but as a reflection of gross inequalities of wealth and income. The contrast with the 'good old days' is difficult to sustain in the absence of empirical evidence to demonstrate how good they were in practice and not just in the imagination of the analyst. But cautious scepticism aside, it is unarguable that the recent memory of the dictatorship is bound to leave deep scars on society and to influence personal behaviour. In this sense, the trial of Pinochet – even if it never reached the final concluding stage – could have the effect of unlocking the past, of releasing a real debate about what happened, and of moving towards a reconciliation based upon acceptance of responsibilities and not simply upon an agreement to forget.

40 Alex Wilde, 'Irruptions of Memory: Expressive Politics in Chile's Transition to Democracy,' in *Journal of Latin American Studies*, vol. 31, no. 2, 1999, p. 476.

41 *Ibid.* p. 494

42 Norbert Lechner and Pedro Guell, 'Construcción social de las memorias de la transición chilena,' in Amparo Menéndez and Alfredo Joignant (eds.), *La caja de Pandora* (Santiago, 2000), p. 194.

43 Robert D. Putnam, *Bowling Alone: The Collapse and Revival of American Community* (New York, 2000).

But that will only happen if this case is seen as one amongst many others. Pinochet was not the only abuser of human rights in Chile. Responsibility goes much further, and justice is far from achieved by the disgrace and marginalisation of one man. The courts, the politicians and the people have a long way to go but this case surely marks a decisive step.

PART 2
Legal progress

CHAPTER 5

The progress of Pinochet through the UK extradition procedure: an analysis of the legal challenges and judicial decisions

Diana Woodhouse

In October 1998 the UK authorities received two international warrants from Judge Baltasar Garzón of the Central Court of Criminal Proceedings in Madrid for the arrest of Senator (formally General) Augusto Pinochet Ugarte. This resulted in provisional warrants being issued, the first on 16 October by Mr Nicholas Evans and the second on 22 October by Mr Ronald Bartle, both stipendiary magistrates, and in Pinochet being detained at the private London hospital where he was receiving treatment. So began a chain of events which placed the Home Secretary, Jack Straw, and the Appellate Committee of the House of Lords at the centre of the international stage. The issues to be decided by the Home Secretary were whether to initiate extradition proceedings and subsequently, whether there were factors which militated against extradition. Although these issues were located in the political arena, they were tempered by considerations laid down by the Extradition Act and susceptible to challenge in the courts.[1] Moreover, in the charged atmosphere surrounding Pinochet, such challenges were inevitable. Hence the decisions of the courts were crucial to the progress of the senator through the extradition procedure.

However, before the Home Secretary could make a formal decision on the initiation of extradition proceedings, the courts were asked to decide whether a former head of state had sovereign immunity which protected him from criminal proceedings and thus from the extradition process, and, if he were not so protected, whether his alleged crimes were extraditable crimes under the Extradition Act 1989. These were issues which required the judges to move beyond the familiar territory of statutory interpretation and the common law and engage with the substance and spirit of international law. In all fifteen judges were involved in this process, three in the Divisional Court and twelve in the House of Lords.[2]

---

1 Through the common law and via section 12 of the Extradition Act.
2 Five in *Pinochet 1* and seven in *Pinochet 3*.

Inevitably, some judges rose to the challenge better than others. There were those, notably Lords Slynn, Lloyd and Goff, whose rulings were cautious and conservative, and those, such as Lords Nicholls, Steyn and Millett, who were prepared to move the law forward in a way which accorded with the prevailing political and moral climate. Yet to categorise the judges in this way is to underplay the diversity in judicial reasoning which was a feature of the Pinochet case and which not only obfuscated the final decision, but also raised broader questions about the suitability of the House of Lords as a final court of appeal in constitutional and political cases. It was not alone in doing so. A further issue was the composition of the bench or panel chosen to hear *Pinochet 1*, which was challenged in *Pinochet 2* on the grounds of bias and resulted in the need for the case to be reheard – hence *Pinochet 3*.

The Pinochet case (or cases) therefore had implications for national and international law and for the reputation of the House of Lords as a judicial institution. Not only were its decisions subject to international scrutiny, any defects in its operation were also there for all to see.

Pinochet challenges the validity of the warrants (*Pinochet 1*)

The arrest and detention of Pinochet on 16 October was headline news and brought a response of outrage from his supporters and delight from his detractors. It also resulted in his lawyers making two applications, the first to the Home Secretary, seeking to persuade him not to issue the necessary authority for the extradition proceeding to begin, and the second to the Divisional Court, requesting an order of *habeas corpus* and leave to apply for judicial review for the warrant to be quashed. Their argument was that the crimes listed in the warrant did not accord with the definition of 'extradition crime' given in the Extradition Act.[3] This requires the offence to have been committed in the country seeking extradition, or the accused to be a citizen of that country, or the offence to be one over which the United Kingdom courts have jurisdiction. None of these requirements was satisfied, the basis for the warrant being that there was evidence that between 11 September 1973 and 31 December 1983 Pinochet had murdered Spanish citizens in Chile. The offences had not been committed in Spain, they had not been committed by a Spanish citizen and they were not within the jurisdiction of the United Kingdom courts which can only try cases of murder committed outside the United Kingdom, if committed by British citizens.[4] The fact that under Spanish law Pinochet could be tried in Spain was not sufficient. The charges failed to satisfy the double criminality requirement

3 Section 2.
4 Section 9 of the Offences Against the Person Act 1861 (24 and 25 Vict. c. 100), as amended.

for extra-territorial crimes, that is, that the offence is a crime both in the country seeking extradition and in the UK.

Pinochet's lawyers also sought judicial review of the second warrant, which had been issued by Mr Ronald Bartle. This alleged that there was evidence that 'between 1 January 1988 and December 1992 being a public official [Pinochet] intentionally inflicted severe pain or suffering on another in the performance or purported performance of his official duties within the jurisdiction of the Government of Spain' and that, within the same period, he 'conspired with persons unknown to intentionally inflict severe pain or suffering on others in the performance or purported performance of his official duties'.[5] He was, in addition, accused of detaining and conspiring to detain individuals and of threatening those detained with death, injury and further detention in order to compel them to act as their captors required. The dates for these other offences were January 1982 to January 1992 and January 1976 and December 1992, respectively. The warrant also alleged conspiracy to commit murder.

Unlike the first warrant, this one contained offences which could be tried in the United Kingdom, namely, torture, under the Criminal Justice Act 1988, and hostage taking, under the Hostage Taking Act 1982. The basis of Pinochet's challenge was therefore different, the grounds being that, as a former head of state, he had immunity under the State Immunity Act 1978[6] and, as a consequence, could not be subject to extradition proceedings.

The two applications for judicial review were heard on 26 October by the Lord Chief Justice, Lord Bingham, accompanied by Mr Justice Collins and Mr Justice Richards. Two days later they quashed the decisions of both magistrates to issue warrants.[7] The first warrant was held to be 'plainly bad in law', the murder of Spanish citizens in Chile not being an extraditable offence between the UK and Spain. As to the second warrant, while the offences were accepted as valid extradition crimes,[8] Pinochet, as a former head of state, was held to be entitled to sovereign immunity. According to the Lord Chief Justice, the State Immunity Act,[9] read in conjunction with the 1961 Vienna Convention of Diplomatic Relations,[10] conferred a lifelong immunity on a former head of state

5   *R v. Bow Street Metropolitan stipendiary Magistrate and Others, Ex parte Pinochet Ugarte (Amnesty International and others intervening) (No. 1)* [1998] 4 All ER 897 at 901.
6   Part 1.
7   *Re Pinochet Ugarte* (1998) 38 ILM 68.
8   Through Criminal Justice Act 1988 (Section 134), Taking of Hostages Act 1982 (Section 1), Suppression of Terrorism Act 1978 (Section 4).
9   Section 20 (1) which extends the Diplomatic Privileges Act 1964 to heads of state, subject to 'any necessary modifications'.
10 This is incorporated through the Diplomatic Privileges Act 1964 and includes immunity for former diplomats in respect of acts performed in the exercise of their functions.

for acts done while he held that position. This immunity was not, in his opinion, affected by UK legislation on genocide, hostage taking and torture, as the relevant statutes[11] did not contain provisions removing it for these offences.

It followed from the reasoning of the Divisional Court that Pinochet was immune from civil and criminal proceedings in the English court and, consequently, from extradition proceedings. However, despite the court's ruling, Pinochet was not released, the quashing of the second decision to issue a warrant being stayed, pending an appeal from the Crown Prosecution Service (on behalf of Spain) to the House of Lords on 'a point of law of general public importance …, namely the proper interpretation and scope of immunity enjoyed by a former head of state from arrest and extradition proceedings in the United Kingdom in respect of acts committed while he was head of state.'[12] Pinochet therefore remained subject to the restrictions of bail.

On 3 November a formal request for Pinochet's extradition was received from Spain and, coincidentally, the next day the House of Lords began to hear the appeal from the Divisional Court. The great interest in the case, evident outside the court in the demonstrations from those seeking Pinochet's extradition, was recognised by the House of Lords in its decision to grant leave to intervene to Amnesty International and others representing victims of the alleged activities.[13] Exceptionally, intervention by these parties was allowed not just in the form of written submissions but also through oral contributions. Written submissions were also accepted from other interveners[14] while the court itself sought the assistance of an *amicus curiae* or legal adviser.[15]

The House of Lords gave its decision on 25 November and by a 3:2 majority allowed the appeal.[16] The dissenting judges were Lords Slynn and Lloyd. Lord Slynn reiterated the view of the Lord Chief Justice in the Divisional Court that a former head of state was entitled to immunity in respect of official acts carried out as head of state and that 'the acts relied on were done as part of his functions' in that capacity.[17] Moreover, he considered that there was nothing in the relevant international treaties or any general consensus concerning crimes against international law which removed this immunity. Thus Pinochet could not be

---

11 Genocide Act 1969, Taking of Hostages Act 1982, Criminal Justice Act 1988.

12 *Pinochet (No. 1)* [1998] 4 All ER 897 at 899.

13 These were the Medical Foundation for the Care of Victims of Torture, the Redress Trust, Mary Ann Beausire, Juana Francisco Beausire and Sheila Cassidy. Professor Brownlie appeared on behalf of the interveners.

14 Human Rights Watch, Nicole Drouilly, representing the Association of the Relatives of the Disappeared Detainees, and Marco Antonio Enríquez Espinoza.

15 Mr David Lloyd Jones.

16 *Pinochet (No. 1)* [1998] 4 All ER 897.

17 At 908.

subject to extradition proceedings. Lord Slynn accepted that 'international law does not recognise that it is one of the specific functions of a head of State to commit torture or genocide but', he continued:

> the fact that in carrying out other functions, a Head of State commits an illegal act does not mean that he is no longer to be regarded as carrying out one of his functions. If it did, the immunity in respect of criminal acts would be deprived of much of its content.

In this Lord Slynn was correct; immunity would 'be deprived of much of its content'. However, when the illegal acts constitute crimes against humanity, this is surely the point. No one, including a head of state, should be immune from prosecution.

Lord Lloyd, in his opinion, went even further, arguing that Pinochet was not only acting in his sovereign capacity, but that the acts relied upon were acts of state and, as such, were not attributable to him personally. It followed therefore that while Pinochet could be tried in Chile or, when established, by an international criminal court, he could not be tried in the municipal courts of another state unless Chile waived its sovereign immunity. Such an interpretation, which relied on authorities from the nineteenth and early twentieth century, seemed to ignore developments in international law which sought to promote the concept of individual criminal responsibility. They were not, however, ignored by the majority (Lords Nicholls, Steyn and Hoffmann), who took a more robust line.[18]

In his judgment Lord Steyn set out the three central issues as being, first, 'the nature of the charges brought by Spain against Senator Pinochet', second, 'whether he is entitled to former Head of State immunity under the applicable statutory provisions' and, third, 'if he is not entitled to such immunity, ... whether under the common law act of state doctrine the House ought to declare that the matters involved are not justiciable in our courts.'[19] As far as the first issue was concerned, Lord Steyn noted that the court was 'not required to examine the correctness of the allegations', but rather to assume their correctness 'as a backcloth of the questions of law' which arose.[20] This moved him on to the second issue on which he held that 'the statutory immunity [under Section 20 of the State Immunity Act] in favour of a former Head of State is not absolute'[21] but relates only to official acts performed in the exercise of his

---

18 Lords Nicholls and Steyn both gave separate Judgements; Lord Hoffmann did not give his own Judgement, simply agreeing with his two colleagues.

19 at 942.

20 at 943.

21 at 944.

functions as Head of State. This raised the question of whether the crimes of which Pinochet was accused 'should be classified as acts performed in the exercise of the functions of a Head of State', a question which Lord Steyn answered in the negative, being satisfied that 'as a matter of construction of the relevant statutory provisions the charges brought by Spain against Senator Pinochet are properly to be classified as conduct falling beyond the scope of his functions as head of state.'[22] Moreover, he was critical of the Divisional Court's conclusion that there 'was no justification for reading any limitation based on the nature of the crimes committed into the immunity that exists,' noting; 'It is inherent in this stark conclusion that there is no line to be drawn. It follows that when Hitler ordered the 'final solution' his act must be regarded as an official act deriving from the exercise of his functions as Head of State. That is where the reasoning of the Divisional Court inexorably leads.' It was a lead he was not prepared to follow.

He also refused to recognise any wider immunity under international law and, on his third issue, stated that no question could arise of the court declining jurisdiction on grounds of the common law doctrine of act of state, as the Taking of Hostages Act 1982 and the Criminal Justice Act 1988 made express provision for such jurisdiction. Lord Nicholls' judgement similarly repudiated the arguments put forward by Pinochet's lawyers. In his view, 'international law has made plain that certain types of conduct, including torture and hostage taking, are not acceptable conduct on the part of anyone. This applies as much to heads of state, or even more so, as it does to anyone else; the contrary conclusion would make a mockery of international law.'[23] Lord Hoffmann gave no separate opinion, but concurred with Lord Nicholls.

Thus, by a majority, their lordships held that the applicant's status, as former head of state, did not confer immunity from extradition proceedings in respect of the crimes of which he was charged. They therefore ruled that as Pinochet had no claim to immunity and there were no grounds for a declaration of non-justiciability, the decision to issue the second warrant was a valid decision and should be restored. As a consequence, Pinochet was required to remain in Britain and await the decision of the Home Secretary whether to authorise the continuation of the proceedings for his extradition.[24]

The decision of the House of Lords that Pinochet could face extradition proceedings was without precedent, for while a former head of state had been subject to criminal proceedings in the municipal courts of another state once before, the circumstances were fundamentally different. The occasion in question

22 at 946.
23 at 939–40.
24 Under Section 7(1) of the Extradition Act.

was the prosecution by the United States of General Noriega, ex-dictator of Panama, for drug trafficking and racketeering, criminal activities which, the prosecuting authorities claimed, affected the United States.[25] The United States had therefore had a direct interest in the prosecution. This was not the case with Pinochet where the United Kingdom clearly had no such interest. It was this that made the House of Lords' decision exceptional. The decision was also remarkable, at least as far as the British legal establishment was concerned, in its 'surprising willingness to apply, with municipal law effect, customary international law, with little regard to its source, status or date of coming into force.'[26] The House of Lords accepted that, where crimes against humanity were concerned, it had extra-territorial jurisdiction. Moreover, while both Lords Nicholls and Steyn were at pains to point out that this jurisdiction had a statutory basis, they were not constrained by the traditional approach taken by the courts, whereby the provisions of treaties are only recognised as having effect in the United Kingdom when they have been enacted by Parliament, and customary rules of international law are seldom applied directly. Rather, they sought to give effect to the spirit of international law and to the belief that those who commit crimes against humanity should be brought to justice.

Pinochet 1 can therefore be seen as a triumph for justice, in that it sent a message to former heads of state, accused of crimes against humanity, that they could 'no longer expect to escape justice simply by avoiding those states with an avowed interest in prosecuting them.'[27] It is not, of course, known whether a different panel of the House of Lords would have reached the same decision, although it is interesting to speculate. Neither is it known whether the same decision would have been reached had a Conservative government still been in power. The political atmosphere would, no doubt, have been different and, given the uneasy relationship in the 1990s between judges and some Conservative ministers, notably the Home Secretary, the House of Lords might have felt it expedient to be more cautious. It would certainly not have been on the verge of assuming a new constitutional role, that of giving direct effect to the European Convention on Human Rights, through the Human Rights Act 1998, which would require judges routinely to look to other jurisdictions and to developments in international law. The majority in the House of Lords might therefore have been anticipating an approach which was more principled and purposive than the one to which many United Kingdom judges were accustomed.

---

25 See *United States v. Noriega* (1990) 746 F Sup 1506.

26 Hazel Fox, 'The First Pinochet Case: Immunity of a former Head of State,' *International and Comparative Law Quarterly*, vol. 48, part 1, Jan. 1999.

27 D. Turns, 'Pinochet's Fallout: Jurisdiction and Immunity for Criminal Violations of International law,' *Legal Studies*, vol. 20, no. 4, 2000, p. 579.

The Home Secretary exercises his discretion

The decision of the House of Lords meant that attention, and political pressure, switched from the courts to the Home Secretary, who, under the Extradition Act, is empowered 'to issue an authority to proceed unless it appears to him that an order for the return of the person concerned could not lawfully be made, or would not in fact be made, in accordance with the provisions of this Act.'[28] The Home Secretary, Jack Straw, therefore had to satisfy himself that the request for extradition had been made by an authority which had that function and that the basis for the request and the evidence furnished with it were in accordance with the requirements of the Act. This presented little problem as Spain is a party to the European Convention on Extradition 1957 and thus comes within the ambit of the Extradition Act, the Criminal Division of the Spanish National Court had, on 5 November, confirmed Spain's jurisdiction to try the alleged crimes, and the decision of the House of Lords had made clear that the alleged offences were extraditable.

However, representations from interested parties sought to persuade the Home Secretary to take other factors into account. The pro-Pinochet camp argued that he should consider the effect of Pinochet's prosecution outside Chile on the country's rehabilitation as a democratic nation, urging him to return Pinochet home and leave his fate to the Chileans. They also argued that the extradition of Pinochet would damage diplomatic and trading relations with Chile and was therefore not in Britain's national interest, and that it would provide a dangerous precedent which would have far-reaching national and international implications. Further, they contended that the circumstances of Pinochet's arrest whilst under medical supervision and recovering from an operation, together with his age and general state of health, militated against extradition.

Those seeking Pinochet's extradition conversely argued that, at this stage, the Home Secretary should limit his considerations to those of a quasi-judicial nature. They emphasised Britain's moral and legal obligations to the international community, arguing that crimes against humanity should always be prosecuted and that it was important for Britain's international reputation for it to be seen to be supporting this stance. However, there were fears from some in the anti-Pinochet camp that, with a Chilean jet standing by to take Pinochet home, Jack Straw would not issue an authority to proceed but would decide that Pinochet was too old and ill to face legal proceedings.

With this in mind, and concerned that the senator could be out of the country before they could challenge the Home Secretary's decision, Amnesty Inter-

28 Section 7(4).

national made a 'just in case' application to the courts on 9 December, the day
the decision was due but prior to its announcement. They sought leave to apply
for judicial review of the pending decision and the way in which it had been
made, on the basis that the Convention against Torture,[29] which requires a
person alleged to have committed torture to be extradited or, failing that,
prosecuted by the competent authorities, had the effect of turning the discretion
of the Home Secretary to issue authority to proceed into a duty. This meant,
according to Amnesty, that providing the Home Secretary was satisfied the
extradition request was lawfully made, he was obliged to authorise extradition
proceedings. Amnesty also requested an injunction or a stay in proceedings to
prevent any cancellation of the warrant and the discharge of the senator.

The application came before Lord Justice Simon Brown who thought it
'novel' for the court to be asked for interim relief in relation to a decision which
had yet to be taken but might, in fact, have been taken by the time he was
speaking, and which the applicant might, or might not, wish to challenge. He
was particularly concerned that to give effect to the injunction sought would
mean imposing physical restraints on a person on bail in advance of a decision
which was yet to be made and which, when made, was challengeable. This, he
considered, 'would not be appropriate, right or just'.[30] He therefore refused the
application, a refusal that was hardly surprising given the reluctance of the
courts to consider hypothetical situations.

In the event, Amnesty's fears were unfounded, the Home Secretary announc-
ing later that day that he had decided to issue an authority to proceed. Mindful
no doubt of the possibility of further legal challenges, he gave full reasons for
his decision, although there was no statutory requirement for him to do so.[31] He
said that he had satisfied himself that the extradition request was lawfully made
and that, having been advised that his discretion under the Act[32] was very wide,
he had taken a range of factors into account. These included: representations
made by, amongst others, Pinochet's lawyers, the Spanish Government, the
Chilean Government and the legal representatives of the 'interveners' before
the House of Lords; requests from the Swiss and French governments for extradition; and the UK's international obligation under the European Convention
on Extradition 1957 to extradite Pinochet to Spain.

29 Article 7.
30 'Ex parte Amnesty International,' *The Times*, 11 December 1998.
31 Section 7(5) simply states the authority to proceed 'shall specify the offence or offences
    under the law of the United Kingdom which it appears to the Secretary of State would be
    constituted by equivalent conduct in the United Kingdom'.
32 Section 7(4), together with his residual general discretion under Section 12.

He also said that he considered the crimes of which Pinochet was accused to be extradition crimes and that he had proceeded on the basis, first, that, at this stage, he was entitled to treat the Spanish request as well founded in Spanish law and, second, that Pinochet did not have immunity. He further stated that he was satisfied that the offences charged were not political offences, the request was made in good faith and was not a punishment for political opinions, there were no time bars to prosecution, the passage of time would not make prosecution unjust or oppressive, and Pinochet was not unfit to stand trial. He had also decided that the UK's obligation to extradite Pinochet to Spain was not outweighed by the possibility of a trial in Chile, the possible effect of extradition on Chile's stability and democracy, and, or, the possible consequences for the United Kingdom's national interest.

Straw was clearly intent on giving Pinochet's lawyers no grounds to argue that he had failed to take relevant factors into account, although questions of whether there are humanitarian, political or national interest factors which outweigh extradition would seem to relate to the final decision to extradite,[33] rather than to his decision at this stage. However, their consideration at this stage had the effect of denying Pinochet any possible grounds for judicial review, while there was no danger of those who sought extradition challenging the process by which the decision they wanted had been made. In any case, it may not necessarily be wrong to consider these factors at this point, providing they are reconsidered later. Straw indicated that this would be the case, stressing that if, subsequent to the extradition hearing, he was required to decide whether to return Pinochet, he would consider the extradition request afresh. This would include listening to further representations.

Pinochet challenges the House of Lords decision (*Pinochet 2*)

One factor specifically dismissed by the Home Secretary as being relevant to his decision was the charge of bias made by Pinochet's lawyers against the House of Lords. This, as he indicated, was not a matter for him, or indeed any Home Secretary, but for the Lords themselves. The accusation of bias, or rather of the appearance of bias, centred upon Lord Hoffmann's link with Amnesty International. Lord Hoffmann had not given a separate opinion in *Pinochet 1* but his concurrence with Lords Steyn and Nicholls had resulted in the decision going against Pinochet. After the House of Lords had handed down its opinion, it emerged that not only was Lord Hoffmann's wife employed by Amnesty International in an administrative position, but that Lord Hoffmann was a director and chairperson of Amnesty International Charity Limited, a trust

33 Section 12.

which undertook the charitable aspects of Amnesty's work in the UK. Lord Hoffmann was not paid for his work nor was he a member of Amnesty International itself. Moreover, as Amnesty's solicitors were at pains to point out, he had not been consulted nor had any role in Amnesty's intervention in the Pinochet litigation. Nevertheless, Pinochet's lawyers argued that given Amnesty's status as intervener and its representation by counsel at the appeal hearing, Lord Hoffmann should have disclosed his directorship prior to the case being heard and his failure to do so gave the appearance of bias.

On 10 December they therefore made an application to the House of Lords that its decision be set aside and the appeal reheard by a differently constituted panel. Such an application was unprecedented. The House of Lords had never before been asked to set aside its own previous decision and there was some initial doubt as to whether it had the jurisdiction to do so. The application did not delay the formal start of extradition proceedings, scheduled for the following day, which required Pinochet's appearance at Belmarsh Magistrates Court. It did, however, ensure that public attention remained focused on the House of Lords and, on 15 December, it began to hear the application.[34] Just as the challenge itself was unprecedented, so was the amount of media coverage given to those hearing it. The panel was composed of Lord Browne-Wilkinson, the senior law lord, Lords Hutton and Hope of Craighead, Lords of Appeal in Ordinary, and Lords Nolan and Goff of Chieveley, who were brought out of retirement. The previous decisions of the law lords, along with views as to their ideological inclinations – Browne-Wilkinson, liberal; Hutton, conservative; and Hope, centrist – were used by the media as a means of classifying them across the political spectrum and of predicting the likely outcome of the appeal, a foretaste of the scrutiny judges have come to expect since the Human Rights Act 1998 took effect.

Two days later, having accepted that it had an inherent jurisdiction to correct an injustice caused by its own previous decision,[35] the House of Lords found in Pinochet's favour that, although there was no suggestion of actual bias or that Lord Hoffmann actually held any personal views as to whether Pinochet should be extradited, his links with Amnesty International gave him a particular interest in the case and meant that he was automatically disqualified from hearing it.[36] The decision in *Pinochet 1* was therefore set aside on the grounds

34 *R v. Bow Street Metropolitan Stipendiary Magistrate and others, ex parte Pinochet Ugarte (Amnesty International and others intervening (No. 2)* [1999] 1 All ER 577

35 However, this jurisdiction was limited to instances of unfair procedure and did not extend to substance or the merits of the case.

36 For a full discussion see E. Grant, 'The Questions of Jurisdiction and Bias,' in D. Woodhouse (ed.), *The Pinochet Case: A Legal and Constitutional Analysis* (Oxford, 2000).

that the court had not been properly constituted. The finding of automatic disqualification, until then confined to financial and propriety interests, extended the application of the principle to 'the promotion of a cause' and seemed to suggest that, in future, judges would be unable to sit in any case where a charity they supported was involved. This was not, however, the intention, at least of Lord Browne-Wilkinson, who stated; 'Only in cases where a judge is taking an active role as trustee or director of a charity which is closely allied to and acting with a party to the litigation should a judge normally be concerned either to recuse himself or disclose the position to the parties.'[37] Indeed, all the opinions saw the essential ingredients for automatic disqualification as being a close relationship between the judge and one of the parties and an interest in the outcome of the case which could be imputed to the judge because of that relationship. Nevertheless, post *Pinochet 2* the courts received an array of challenges relating to the interests of particular judges with claims that these meant automatic disqualification.[38]

The finding of the House of Lords in *Pinochet 2* did little for its reputation. As the Lord Chancellor, Lord Irvine, said, the need to reopen the decision was 'in the highest degree unfortunate, particularly when the eyes of the world are upon us'.[39] It suggested that the final court of appeal was naive and unprofessional. Lord Hoffmann should have realised that his connection with Amnesty International made it inappropriate for him to hear the case and his failure to do so suggested carelessness or, worse, arrogance. He, no doubt, had complete confidence that his judgement would not be affected by his relationship with the charity. However, he should have realised that, in the political atmosphere surrounding the case, this was not sufficient. His confidence had to be shared by others and it was therefore essential that he, like the rest of the panel, was not only impartial but was seen to be so.

However, blame for the debacle cannot all be laid at the door of Lord Hoffmann. The House of Lords' decision to set aside its own ruling was an indictment of its own processes, hence the Lord Chancellor's instructions to the law lords to put procedures in place 'to ensure that this does not happen again.' It also brought into focus questions already being raised in the context of the pending Human Rights Act, about the suitability of the House of Lords as the final appeal court for cases of a political or constitutional nature.[40] These included the appropriateness of judges from a chancery or criminal law background

---

37 *Pinochet (No. 2)* [1999] 1 All ER 577 at 589
38 see *Locobail (UK) Ltd. v. Bayfield Properties Ltd.* [2000] QB 451.
39 Interview with J. Rozenburg, BBC Radio 4, 25 March 1999.
40 See, for instance, R. Brazier, *Constitutional Reform* (2nd edn., Oxford, 1998); Robert Hazell (ed.), *Constitutional Futures: A History of the Next Ten Years* (Oxford, 1999).

hearing such cases and the ad hoc nature of the selection of judicial panels. In the context of Pinochet, particularly pertinent were the questions; who decided, or by what process was it decided, that Lords Slynn, Lloyd, Steyn, Nicholls and Hoffmann should hear the case, and why did the panel consist of only five judges, rather than seven, as is usual when a case is legally or politically contentious? Had the law lords failed to recognise the constitutional, legal and political significance of Pinochet?

Pinochet 2 did, of course, give hope to the Pinochet camp for it meant that the appeal from the Divisional Court had to be reheard. So far arguments against him being subject to extradition proceedings had been considered by eight judges (three in the Divisional Court and five in the House of Lords) and although he had lost in the House of Lords, five of the eight judges had actually found for him. It was possible that the majority in a differently constituted House of Lords panel might do likewise.

The House of Lords rehears the appeal (*Pinochet 3*)

At the beginning of 1999 a panel of seven law lords,[41] none of whom had sat in the first appeal, was convened to rehear the case. The pressure of other judicial business, together, no doubt, with the need for careful consideration of the issues, meant that judgement was not given until 24 March. However, this delay did not diminish public interest in the outcome of the case and, in recognition of this interest and 'given the obscurity of the judgements' which meant that they were 'incapable of being understood without some explanation', Lord Browne-Wilkinson broke with tradition and gave a layperson's summary to peers in the House of Lords.[42] This innovation was welcomed, although it was a comment on the communication skills of the judges that their judgements needed to be translated and explained.

By a majority of 6 to 1, Lord Goff dissenting, their lordships ruled that Pinochet had no immunity from prosecution and thus could be made subject to extradition proceedings. To this extent, the ruling therefore followed the previous panel. However, it was much narrower. Moreover, the crimes for which Pinochet could be extradited were dramatically reduced to instances of torture and conspiracy to torture which were alleged to have been committed after 8 December 1988. Giving the leading judgement, Lord Browne-Wilkinson reasoned that the Extradition Act 1989 not only required the alleged conduct, for which extradition was sought, to constitute a criminal offence in the law of

41 Lords Browne-Wilkinson, Goff of Chieveley, Hope of Craighead, Hutton, Saville of Newdigate, Millett and Phillips of Worth Matravers.
42 Broadcast by Radio 4, 24 March 1999.

both the requesting and the requested state, but also required it to have been a criminal offence at the time it was committed. It was therefore the conduct date, not the request date, which was relevant. This interpretation of the Act was based on his reading of Schedule 1 of the 1870 Extradition Act. This had been replaced by the 1989 Act but, Lord Browne-Wilkinson noted, there was no evidence of any parliamentary intent to change the date of criminality and he thought it 'impossible that the legislature can have intended to change the date from one which had applied for over a hundred years under the 1870 Act (i.e. the conduct date) by a side wind and without investigation.'[43]

Lord Browne-Wilkinson's reasoning meant that Pinochet could not be extradited for alleged instances of torture and conspiracy to torture prior to 29 September 1988, the date at which such conduct became a crime through section 134 of the Criminal Justice Act 1988. Moreover, the period when Pinochet's conduct could be considered for extradition purposes was reduced still further by Lord Browne-Wilkinson's view of the immunity which attached to official acts. He accepted that the notion of immunity was inconsistent when it applied to conduct which had the status of an international crime. However, he had doubts as to whether torture had such a status prior to the coming into force of the Torture Convention, reasoning that 'not until there was some form of universal jurisdiction for the punishment of the crime of torture could it really be talked about as a fully constituted international crime.'[44] His conclusion was therefore that Pinochet only lost his immunity in relation to the organisation and authorisation of torture after 8 December 1988, the date on which the UK ratified the convention.

As far as the allegations of conspiracy to take hostages were concerned, Lord Browne-Wilkinson considered that these did not accord with the definition of hostage-taking given in Section 1 of the Taking of Hostages Act 1982, which sets the offence in the context of compelling a state, international organisation or person to do, or abstain from doing, something. The allegations of conspiracy against Pinochet were that he conspired to subject those who were already detained to threats that others would also be taken and similarly tortured. The charges were therefore 'bad and [did] not constitute extradition crimes'.[45]

The rest of their lordships, with the exception of Lords Goff and Millett, broadly supported Lord Browne-Wilkinson. Goff and Millett took opposing positions. Lord Goff believed there were no crimes for which Pinochet could be extradited. His conclusion that Pinochet's immunity was intact was closely allied

---

43 *R v. Bow Street Stipendiary Magistrate and Others, ex parte Pinochet Ugarte (Amnesty International and others intervening) (No. 3)* [1999] 2 All ER at 97.

44 At 114.

45 At 107.

to that of Lord Slynn in *Pinochet 1*. He seems also to have been influenced by the implication for other former heads of state and public officials if immunity were denied in this case, giving as an example the plight of 'a responsible Minister of the Crown, or even a more humble public official such as a police inspector' if a state, sympathetic to the IRA, should seek extradition from another nation 'on the grounds that he or she has acquiesced in a single act of physical or mental torture in Northern Ireland.'[46] He did not indicate whether it would have made a difference to him if acquiescence had been on a larger scale or where he would draw the line.

Lord Millett, in common with Lord Browne-Wilkinson, accepted that immunity could not co-exist with conduct which had the status of an international crime and that Pinochet could not therefore claim immunity for those offences judged to be extradition crimes. Where he differed was in his conclusion that torture was subject to universal jurisdiction as a matter of customary international law and that the exercise of that jurisdiction by the UK courts was not dependent on the Torture Convention. He argued; 'The jurisdiction of the English criminal courts is usually statutory, but it is supplemented by the common law. Customary international law is part of the common law, and accordingly I consider that the English courts have always had extra-territorial criminal jurisdiction in respect of crimes of universal jurisdiction under customary international law.'[47] Thus, when it came to such crimes, the courts were not dependent on the will of Parliament. The dates at which the various pieces of legislation took effect were therefore irrelevant and, as far as Lord Millett was concerned, all the charges against Pinochet were extradition crimes.

The remainder of the House of Lords followed the line taken by Lord Browne-Wilkinson. Like him, Lord Hope set the date at 8 December, similarly arguing that it was the obligation under the Torture Convention to prosecute the crime of torture that overrode any claim of immunity and the signing of the Convention by Chile meant that it forfeited any right to make such a claim. Lords Saville and Phillips agreed, both on the issue of what constituted an extraditable crime and on the date at which Pinochet lost his immunity, and Lord Hutton was in agreement on the first issue, although preferring 29 September 1988, the date the Criminal Justice Act came into force, as the date on which Pinochet's immunity ceased, arguing that torture had long been an international crime and thus it did not require the Torture Convention to make it such.

The basis for the decision in *Pinochet 3* was, therefore, different from that in *Pinochet 1*. This difference was justified by the House of Lords' panel on the

46 At 128.
47 At 177.

grounds that the point had not previously been argued, a justification which raised fundamental questions about the operation of the court and its dependence on counsel[48] and which was considered by Lord Donaldson, a previous master of the rolls, to be 'surprising'.[49] The decision was inevitably subject to considerable analysis, both informed and uninformed. On the positive side its apparent upholding of a universal jurisdiction for torture and its denial of sovereign immunity to an ex-head of state for the committal of such crimes, during the time he was head of state, provided an 'awesome' precedent.[50] Indeed, some human rights organisations argued that, in establishing the principle that former dictators do not have immunity for international crimes, it was the most important precedent since Nuremberg.[51] It was also important in the national context in that, like *Pinochet 1*, it unusually concerned the direct application of international law. Moreover, it was evident that some of the law lords, most notably Lord Millett, were prepared to apply the norms of customary international law over and above UK law. Such a development clearly has implications for the future and is perhaps indicative of a greater willingness on the part of some UK judges to move away from the narrow confines of the common law. It was also significant that, with the exception of Lord Goff, the law lords did not seek to invoke the national interest in the possible damage to Anglo-Chilean relations or to use Chile's emergence as a democratic nation as a reason for not extraditing Pinochet. Rather they used the need to enforce international criminal law effectively as a basis for their decisions.

On the negative side, the restrictive interpretation of the double criminality rule by the majority in *Pinochet 3* may have been to the letter, but was hardly in the spirit, of international law. Moreover, it impugned an intention to Parliament, when it ratified the Torture Convention, which would seem unsustainable, for the reasoning of Lord Browne-Wilkinson and his colleagues implied that where there had been a sustained campaign of torture, it was Parliament's intention that only those acts of torture committed after ratification should be considered as crimes for the purposes of the Extradition Act. Thus any dictator who ceased to be head of state on or before 7 December 1988 could not, on their lordships reasoning, be subject to extradition proceedings on the basis of allegations of torture, no matter how numerous and convincing the allegations. This seems unlikely to have been the intention of Parliament when it ratified the convention but, even if it had been, the fact that it was not expressly stated gave

48 For discussion of this see D. Robertson, 'The House of Lords as a Political and Constitutional Court,' in Woodhouse, *The Pinochet Case*.

49 Interview with J. Rozenburg, Radio 4, 25 March 1999.

50 Turns, 'Pinochet's fallout,' p. 588.

51 See Davis, *The Pinochet Case*, p. 17.

the House of Lords the opportunity to interpret the statute otherwise, something they are adept at doing when it suits them.

The analysis of *Pinochet 3* was not confined to the decision itself but, as with *Pinochet 2*, was extended by the press to a consideration of the personalities, interests and politics of the judges concerned. Lord Browne-Wilkinson was described as 'humane, liberal and charming', Lord Hope as 'quiet [with a] meticulous style [and] middle of the road politics', Lord Hutton as the 'most right-leaning of the panel', Lord Saville as 'friendly, affable and sporty', Lord Millett as 'the highest ranking Freemason in the judiciary; very clever, popular with lawyers – a favourite on the bench', Lord Phillips as 'liberal' and Lord Goff as 'known for intelligence and moderation'.[52] In addition, to aid identification, *The Times* took the unusual step of including photographs of the judges alongside the report of the case, which it published the following day.

The effect of the ruling of the House of Lords was to remove Pinochet's immunity from extradition proceedings while at the same time drastically reducing the number of extraditable charges from 31 to three, one of torture and two of conspiracy to torture. Moreover, it was evident that their lordships saw this reduction as possibly having an effect on the Home Secretary's decision to issue authority to proceed, believing that, in the words of Lord Hope, it was 'incumbent on the Home Secretary to reconsider the matter in the light of the very different circumstances which now prevail.'[53]

The case returns to the Home Secretary

Some took the recommendation that the Home Secretary should reconsider his decision as a strong hint to him that he should return Pinochet to Chile.[54] A better interpretation of the requirement may be that the House of Lords was simply confirming that, while the courts could rule on the process, in the end the decision whether or not to extradite was political. They were therefore returning the matter to its rightful place.

Whatever the intention of the House of Lords, on 15 April the Home Secretary announced that, having looked at the matter afresh, he was issuing a new authority to proceed. This replaced his previous decision, thus making the challenge to it, for which leave to apply for judicial review had already been granted, redundant. Straw stated that, as before, he had concluded that Pinochet was accused of extraditable crimes for which he had no immunity and that, even though the number of charges had reduced, they were still serious and had not

52 *The Times*, 25 March 1999.
53 *Pinochet (No. 3)* [1999] 2 All ER 97.
54 Such as J. Rozenburg, BBC Radio 4, 25 March 1999.

been committed so long ago as to make it unjust or oppressive for Pinochet to stand trial for them. As with his previous decision, the Home Secretary stated that he had taken account of claims that the general could face trial in Chile and the possible effect of proceedings on the stability of Chile and its relationship with Britain, but had given 'particular weight' to the UK's obligation, under the European Convention on Extradition, to extradite Senator Pinochet to Spain.

Straw's decision meant the extradition process continued, although it was, predictably, interrupted yet again by a legal challenge to the High Court, this time on the grounds that the Home Secretary had acted irrationally in authorising proceedings after the House of Lords had drastically reduced the number of offences. However, leave to apply for judicial review was refused by Mr Justice Ognall, who stated that it would 'needlessly disrupt the extradition process and postpone the machinery which will afford General Pinochet every proper opportunity to advance his case and protect his position'.[55] This opportunity came on 27 September when the formal extradition hearing began at Bow Street Magistrates Court before Ronald Bartle, who had issued the second warrant for Pinochet's arrest. By this time Judge Garzón, the instigator of the international warrants for Pinochet's detention, had added further offences to the list of charges. Thus having been reduced to one of torture and two of conspiracy to torture by the House of Lords, when the charges were read out in the magistrates court they had risen to 34 of torture and one of conspiracy to torture. During the four day hearing, Pinochet's lawyers argued that the court should only consider those charges detailed in the original extradition request and that others added since should be struck out. They also argued that Pinochet should not be held responsible for the actions of others and that the extradition request was politically motivated and thus should not be processed. Even more controversially, they argued that many of the alleged charges did not amount to torture, as legally defined, but were rather instances of police brutality and that torture could not be claimed where death was instantaneous.

On 8 October, in the absence of Pinochet, who was excused from attending on health grounds, Bartle gave his ruling. He found, first, that the court could consider the charges added since 14 April; second, that the double criminality rule, whereby the alleged offence must constitute a crime in both countries, was satisfied; third, that Pinochet could be extradited for the alleged crimes committed after 8 December 1988; and, fourth, that he should be committed to await the decision of the Home Secretary. Given the history of the legal proceedings to date, it came as little surprise when Pinochet's lawyers challenged Bartle's decision, seeking permission from the High Court to apply for a

55 *Guardian*, 27 May 1999

writ of habeas corpus. The hearing was set for 20 March 2000, but in the event was not necessary, as Pinochet had by then already been released. An indication of this release came as early as 11 January when, in a statement, the Home Secretary said that having received reports on Pinochet's medical condition, he was minded to halt the extradition process. However, it was to be a further seven weeks before release became a reality, during which time the Home Secretary was subjected to political pressure and yet another challenge in the courts, this time from human rights organisations and Belgium. The Spanish government had decided that, given the nature of the Home Secretary's discretion, a legal challenge was futile and, in terms of securing a successful outcome, they were right, for while the High Court held that fairness required Straw to release the medical report on Pinochet on a confidential basis to governments with an interest in the case, which now included Belgium, Switzerland and France, as well as Spain, it refused Belgium's request to order further medical examinations of the general. This, in effect, was the end of the road for those seeking extradition. They could, and did, make further representations to the Home Secretary but there was no basis on which to make a further legal challenge and on 2 March Straw announced he had decided that Pinochet was unfit to stand trial. He was satisfied that the condition of Senator Pinochet was such that a trial in any country would breach his right under Article 6 of the European Convention on Human Rights to a fair trial. Pinochet was therefore allowed to board the waiting plane and return to Chile.

Conclusion

The saga in the UK courts thus came to an end. It was a saga which had involved the magistrates court, the divisional court and most notably, the House of Lords, and the constitutional and legal implications were far-reaching. In the domestic arena, *Pinochet 2* raised questions about the suitability of the House of Lords as a final court of appeal for high profile constitutional and political cases. These were particularly pertinent given the new role the judges would acquire when the Human Rights Act 1998 came into operation in October 2000. Its procedures, the way it was constituted – as panels rather than sitting 'en banc' – and its reliance on counsel were all issues brought to the fore by the Pinochet cases. The cases also provided a foretaste of the public scrutiny judges would face when considering controversial human rights issues and, in so doing, drew attention to the shortcomings of the judicial appointments system, the need for greater openness and for judges to be more accountable.

However, it was the decisions in *Pinochet 1* and *Pinochet 3* which had the greatest impact and the criticisms of the judicial reasoning in *Pinochet 3* should not detract from their importance. They not only sent a warning message to other former heads of state but contributed to international jurisprudence concerning crimes against humanity and to discussions about the need for a coherent system of international criminal justice. Yet it needs to be remembered that it took a formal request from another state, namely Spain, to bring this about. If it had not been for that request, Pinochet would not have been arrested, despite the fact that, as was evident from the House of Lords judgements, there were statutory offences with which he could have been charged in the UK courts. Rather, it seems likely that Pinochet would have continued to come to and go from the UK as he pleased. The prosecution of Pinochet in the UK was not on the agenda, and while the solicitor general might have been forced to take some action if extradition proceedings had been halted because Straw considered that Pinochet was unfit to travel, the Home Secretary's decision, that the senator was medically unfit to stand trial in any country, let him off the hook.[56] Pinochet's future therefore now depended on the authorities in Chile.

---

56 See *H.C. Debs.*, 2 March 2000, cols. 589–92 for statement by Solicitor General.

CHAPTER 6

The Pinochet case
in the Chilean courts

Francisco Bravo López

Pinochet's legal ordeal did not end when he returned to Chile. An application was made by Judge Juan Guzmán Tapía to lift the immunity from prosecution enjoyed by Pinochet as a life-senator, in order to allow his trial on charges that had increased rapidly in number during his detention in London. Charges had been filed against him and other military personnel long before his detention, but few of these cases had prospered. This chapter examines the progress of the Pinochet case in Chile in the context of a survey of the obstacles to successful investigations and trials, in place both during the dictatorship and after the return to democratic rule, and assesses the extent to which these have been overcome, either as a result of or alongside the attempt to put Pinochet on trial.

Preliminary issues

The course of Chilean justice[1]

Both before and during the Pinochet era, the two fundamental instruments available to the Chilean judiciary for preventing or suppressing human rights violations were *recursos de amparo* (actions for infringement of fundamental rights and freedoms – habeas corpus) and the punishment of those responsible. In both principles the idea of prevention is important. The purpose of habeas corpus, of course, is to put a stop to illegal arrest and to ensure the well-being of a person under arrest. Had it been pursued, the punishment of those responsible, following judicial investigations, would also have led to a serious clampdown on any continuing occurrences of human rights violations. Both these avenues were pursued by the families of victims of repression from the start of the dictatorship, throughout its duration and subsequently. That their efforts

1 This section is based upon material from the *Informe de la Comisión Nacional de Verdad y Reconciliación* (Rettig Report), Santiago, 1991.

were largely ineffectual throughout this period had grave consequences, since in the relatively short lifetime of post-Independence Chile it was precisely then that this was most necessary, given that at various times from 1973 to 1988 the country was put under several 'states of exception' in which fundamental rights were restricted.

The inefficacy of the *recursos de amparo* was due to the subservience of the Chilean courts to political forces and also, in part, to the inadequacy of relevant legislation. Nevertheless, the legislation that was in force, although unsatisfactory, did provide the courts with some leeway to safeguard those affected by repression. Use was not generally made of this limited freedom of manoeuvre, however, and individuals were often left defenceless, without legal recourse, in violation of judicial regulations. Such infringements of the regulations included:

(1) non-application of the principle of 'immediacy'

This principle was enshrined in the 1925 Constitution (in force until the 1980 Constitution brought in by Pinochet) and again in the 1980 Constitution itself and article 308 of the Criminal Procedure Code, which set a time limit of 24 hours for compliance with a petition for habeas corpus. Neither was the judicial decree of 1932 enforced. This required that such petitions must be answered prior either to any injustice caused through wrongful imprisonment reaching serious proportions, or to the full sentence being served. There are records of cases where habeas corpus petitions were delayed by 55 days, 57 days and 70 days before being resolved. In such cases, the slowness of the administrative authorities does not exonerate the judges, both because the latter were authorised to dispense with the former's reports, and because they rarely pressed for or set deadlines for the submission of the relevant reports.

(2) arrests made without an arrest warrant were countenanced

According to the 1925 Constitution, the authority to order arrests during states of siege rests exclusively with the President of the Republic, who is not authorised to delegate such powers. Decree Law No. 228 of 3 January 1974 gave the Minister of the Interior authority to order arrests under the clause 'by order of the governing junta', thus enabling the Contraloría (Office of the Comptroller – the body revising the legality of the actions of the State administration) to dispense with the pertinent constitutional procedure. As a matter of routine, the courts delayed the settlement of the appeals until the Ministry of the Interior produced the warrants, with the loss of freedom then being declared as being in accordance with the law. In many cases, arrest warrants not issued by the Ministry of the Interior were accepted as valid. Furthermore, the courts refused appeals against arrests ordered by the DINA and later the CNI (the dictatorship's secret police). From the time the CNI was set up in 1977, many *recursos de amparo* disputed its authority to make arrests, an issue on which the courts routinely failed to rule, rather delaying so doing until the person under arrest was released, brought up in front of some tribunal or expelled from the country, at which point the courts would reject the appeal by virtue of the new situation that had developed. When, exceptionally, the Court of Appeal in Santiago did rule that the CNI had no power to carry out arrests and accepted an appeal following a hearing of *recurso de amparo*, Law No. 18.314, which expressly enabled the CNI to carry out detentions in cases where the law on terrorist conduct was being broken, was enacted.

(3) compliance with legal restrictions regarding places of detention was not enforced

The courts did not enforce the application of the constitutional provision whereby an individual cannot be arrested, subjected to preventive detention or imprisoned unless it is in his or her home or in public places assigned for this purpose.

During 'states of exception', arrests ordered under the relevant powers could not be carried out in prisons or other places assigned for the imprisonment of common offenders. Moreover, secret detention centres to which officials of the judiciary did not have access were in existence for years. Although it was impossible for the courts to be unaware of the existence of detention centres such as the National Stadium, the Chile Stadium, the Air Force War Academy, Villa Grimaldi, José Domingo Cañas 1367, Londres 38 and numerous other places in Santiago and the provinces, including, during the initial period, military compounds where those arrested were held and where torture was common practice, nothing effective was done to put a stop to these unlawful acts nor to report them, in spite of the continuous protests made in *recursos de amparo*.

(4) the courts did not oversee correct compliance with regulations relating to solitary confinement

Solitary confinement is a strict judicial measure of short duration laid down by law, which judges may only order when the success of investigations depends upon it. During the dictatorship, procedural solitary confinement was widely imposed as a form of punishment. Between 1973 and 1980, cases of solitary confinement of 109 days, 179 days, 300 days and even 330 days were recorded. There were even rulings that accepted the validity of procedural solitary confinement. In a ruling dated 30 July 1974, in a *recurso de amparo* filed precisely to petition a case of illegal solitary confinement, the Supreme Court pointed out that 'both arrest itself and its duration (in a state of siege) depend on the exclusive criterion of the executive authorities, just as it is also logical that the manner in which it is carried out depends on the same authority'. Another ruling was made by the Supreme Court on 3 December 1981, confirming a decision by the Santiago Court of Appeals on 23 November 1981 to uphold the use of procedural solitary confinement as legitimate in cases of terrorism where there is an *Estado de Peligro de Perturbación de la Paz Interior* (state of danger of disturbance of internal peace).

These infringements had serious consequences. If the courts had respected the constitutional order to act immediately; or complied with the legal mandate to come to a ruling within 24 hours; or exercised the legal power that forms the essence of the petition, namely having the person detained brought in person before a court (habeas corpus); or, in the end, complied with the requirement to issue a ruling before wrongful detention could assume serious proportions, then many cases of death, disappearance and torture could have been prevented. Further, the wrongdoers would have been notified that their actions had been rejected by at least one power of state and that, for this, they could eventually receive punishment.

(5) Other factors

There were a number of other factors, in addition to those described above, that contributed to the ineffectiveness of *recursos de amparo*. The lack of effective collaboration by the police authorities in investigating the fate of people on whose behalf appeals were made was crucial. From 1978 onward some lower court judges and some Courts of Appeal began to show signs of adopting a more active stance towards the protection of those exposed to possible human rights violations. However, lack of police collaboration prevented any such initiatives from effectively safeguarding victims' rights. Also crucial was the broad credence extended by many judges to the information provided by the executive with regard to people on whose behalf *recursos de amparo* were being filed. Many *recursos de amparo* were dismissed because judges accepted the assertion that the individuals concerned were not being detained or imprisoned by the authority being summoned. This was recently recognised by the President of the Supreme Court, Hernán Alvarez.

The number of fatal victims of human rights violations attributed to state agents during the Pinochet era stands at some 3,197, of whom the majority were victims of the political repression. Apart from a few very exceptional cases, the facts of these violations were not investigated by the courts, and nor did their perpetrators receive prison sentences. The courts dismissed cases on the basis of the amnesty granted in Decree Law No. 2191 of 19 April 1978 whenever uniformed personnel appeared to be linked with a case under the jurisdiction of this law, by resorting to the thesis that the application of the amnesty law prevented investigation of actions covered by the law. This thesis overruled the argument originating in article 413 of the Criminal Procedure Code that stipulates 'definitive dismissal of a case can only be ordered when the investigation to prove the corpus delicti ['*el cuerpo del delito*'] and to establish the identity of the offender has been exhausted'. Apart from those directly affected, this practice also created a problem for uniformed personnel who were wrongly or unjustly named before the public as having been involved in actions that constituted human rights violations, and whose situation also required clarification.

In judgements of 13 November 1973 and 21 August 1974, amongst others, the Supreme Court officially declared that military courts in times of war are not subject to its authority, overruling strong lines of argument to the contrary. Its failure to exercise the authority given by the 1925 Constitution over military courts in times of war meant that the Supreme Court could not effectively control the way that these courts complied with the regulations governing Criminal Proceeding in Times of War as laid down by the Code of Military Justice.

As of 2002 military justice (with its wide-ranging powers) was dealing with around 50 law suits which had been definitively closed through the application of amnesty and/or the statute of limitations. These resolutions were appealed against on grounds that were initially rejected by the Supreme Court early in the democratic transition (1990–1997) and which left the cases firmly closed. The Supreme Court has since readmitted them and ordered that investigations continue until events have been completely clarified and those responsible for crimes identified.

Justice in the democratic transition

One of the peculiarities of the Chilean military dictatorship was that it managed to institutionalise itself. The best demonstration of this is the establishment of the 1980 Political Constitution which established a regime of 'protected democracy', inspired by the Doctrine of National Security, that still remains in force today. A fundamental aspect of this regime is the role ascribed to the military as guarantors of institutionality ('*garantes de la institucionalidad*'), a role entailing military involvement in many of the country's institutions. There are, as Brian Loveman amply demonstrates in chapter 3, important constitutional foundations for impunity.

The 1980 Constitution was burdened by a plethora of complex rules and regulations that made it impossible for the new democratic regime to judge or review the conduct of the dictatorship, including human rights violations. Pinochet's own continuation as commander in chief of the army until 1998 and then senator for life (as ex-President of the Republic) is only one manifestation of this. Thus, the nature of the Chilean transition to democracy should be borne in mind when attempting to understand the judicial dynamic in trials for human rights violations – this was a pacted transition made more or less to measure for the dictatorship. This is why there was no immediate change in legal doctrines with the change in government.

During the initial phase of the democratic transition (1990–1996), the rulings of the courts tended to favour impunity and those Supreme Court judges who had been appointed by Pinochet remained in their posts. It was only from 1996 onwards, as a result of new laws, that the composition of the Supreme Court began to change. Several judges appointed by Pinochet stood down from their posts, encouraged by substantial compensation. This led to the arrival in the Supreme Court of new judges from Courts of Appeal and academic circles. New laws also introduced specialisation into the chambers of the Supreme Court, with criminal matters becoming the remit of the Second Chamber. The Second Chamber that now dealt with criminal affairs was made up of judges who were inclined towards, or 'sensitive' to, proceedings for human rights violations. This explains the legal shift that occurred in the Supreme Court and that eventually resulted in the ruling to deprive General Pinochet of his immunity from prosecution, analysed below.

Pinochet's trial

In January 1998 the Secretary General of the Chilean Communist Party filed a criminal suit against the then senator for life Augusto Pinochet Ugarte for abduction, first-degree murder, unlawful association and other crimes. The accusation denounced a series of unlawful actions committed during the Senator's dictatorship that comprised the practice of enforced disappearance, extrajudicial or summary execution and torture.[2]

The case was filed with the Santiago Court of Appeal,[3] which named Minister of Law Juan Guzmán Tapia as the examining judge in the light of the defendant's status as Senator of the Republic as enshrined in the constitution. Judge Juan Guzmán allowed the processing of the case and began summary proceedings. Other cases immediately followed, including those of the Agrupaciones de Familiares de Detenidos Desaparecidos y Ejecutados Políticos (AFDD

---

2 At the time of the events, Chilean criminal legislation did not specify the type of torture and the legal term used was 'apremios ilegítimos' (unlawful constraint).

3 The structure of the Chilean judiciary is pyramidal. The base is made up of the courts of first instance (preliminary investigations), immediately above which are the Courts of Appeal (seventeen in total). At the apex of the pyramid is the Supreme Court, which is made up of twenty-one judges and is the Court of Appeal and, in specific cases such as habeas corpus, a court of second instance. It operates through four specialised chambers.

– Group of Families of the Detained–Disappeared), professional associations, student federations and individual relatives of victims. All in all, the number of cases by mid 2002 stood at around 300.

Because of the large number of judicial actions and events to be investigated, Judge Guzmán began to form investigation 'chapters' and 'episodes'; for example, 'Operation Condor', 'DINA',[4] *Comando Conjunto*',[5] 'Villa Grimaldi',[6] 'Villa Baviera',[7] 'Pisagua',[8] 'Paine',[9] and 'La Moneda'.[10] The so-called 'Caravan of Death', which involved some 75 victims, was one of these episodes, carried out in October 1973 by an army unit (*Comitiva*) organised by Pinochet and covering most of the country. This unit possessed broad powers in its ostensible purpose to 'unify procedural criteria' and 'to speed up' legal proceedings conducted by the Councils of War set up after 11 September 1973 to try political dissidents of Salvador Allende's deposed government. Led by then General Sergio Arellano Starck, it scoured various Chilean cities. Horrendous killings ensued in each place, leaving a total of more than 75 dead, with the bodies in some cases being dynamited and made to disappear. Judge Guzmán had then General Sergio Arellano Starck brought to trial, along with the other officers who formed part of the army unit, for their participation in crimes of kidnapping and first degree murder. This resolution was a landmark in the investigation and raised hopes

4 The National Intelligence Administration (Dirección de Inteligencia Nacional), formally set up in June 1974 by Decree Law 521 but operative in events from November 1973, was the military government's main organ of repression and its operational director was the then army colonel Manuel Contreras Sepúlveda.

5 Organ of repression made up of members of the different branches of the armed forces and uniformed police (*Carabineros*) that operated between 1975 and 1977. Its objective was to persecute the Communist Party, especially the Young Communists (Juventudes Comunistas).

6 The DINA's main compound for confinement and torture. It operated between 1974 and 1977. A large house located in the east side of Santiago, it was demolished during the 1990s and today it is the site of the Peace Park (Parque por la Paz) and a memorial listing the name of all the detainees who were brought there and subsequently disappeared.

7 Name given to the country property where the so-called Dignity Colony Charitable Organisation (Sociedad Benefactora Colonia Dignidad) operated, which was set up in the 1960s by Paul Schaeffer and other fugitive Germans accused of collaborating with the Nazis. Judicial investigations have established links that show that the Colonia Dignidad and the DINA collaborated together in the case of the disappeared detainee Alvaro Vallejos Villagrán, a case opened by Judge Juan Guzmán and headed by the author.

8 A coastal location in northern Chile where one of the government's largest concentration and execution camps operated. A mass grave was discovered there in 1990 with the remains of 20 victims of human rights violations.

9 A small semi-rural town to the south of Santiago that, in proportional terms according to the number of inhabitants, was most affected by the repression, with around 70 people being executed or 'disappeared'.

10 This refers to the victims abducted on 11 September in the Palacio de Gobierno, La Moneda, who numbered around 20.

that these crimes would in fact be punished. It was contested by the accused through *recursos de amparo* filed at the Santiago Court of Appeals. These appeals were rejected in a decision that was confirmed by the Second Chamber of the Supreme Court of Justice in July 1999, which stipulated that the appropriate legal term for events in cases of murder where no body is found is 'abduction' (*secuestro*). This ruling was highly important in that the Supreme Court of Justice had established a legal criterion whereby, for want of a body, no murder had been committed, even though there might be other forms of proof, such as witnesses or confession. The importance of such a ruling was that the accused could not claim any grounds for the dismissal of criminal responsibility, such as the statute of limitations and/or amnesty to their own advantage, in view of the fact that abduction is a permanent crime, the investigation of which cannot come to an end until the whereabouts of the victim have been established.

Several months after the first charges against him had been filed in Chile, life senator Augusto Pinochet was arrested in London on the orders of Spanish Judge Baltazar Garzón. He was released on humanitarian grounds after a stay of more than a year in the UK by decision of the then British Home Secretary Jack Straw. This followed requests by the Chilean government, which at the beginning of the extradition process had initially insisted on the principle of the 'territoriality' of criminal law (in contrast to the arguments of human rights organisations upholding the universal character of jurisdiction) before finally resorting to the 'humanitarian' line of argument. Pinochet's return to Chile raised the question of whether he would in fact be judged in Chile, an imponderable dependent more on his political influence than on legal grounds.

In 2000 Judge Guzmán petitioned the Santiago Court of Appeal to deprive the lifetime senator of his congressional immunity, claiming that there were sufficient grounds to presume Pinochet's criminal involvement in the Caravan of Death events. The former general's defence counsel responded with a powerful gambit to prevent him from being tried, arguing that his health was too poor for him to instruct his defence, and that the proceedings violated his right to due process. After hearing the arguments of both parties, a plenary session of the Santiago Court of Appeal accepted the petition made by Guzmán and the plaintiffs and, by allowing a case to be brought against the senator, opened the way to deprive Pinochet of his congressional immunity. Pinochet's defence counsel then appealed to the Supreme Court. In August 2000 the Court confirmed the ruling by fourteen votes for and six against. Pinochet was deprived of immunity from prosecution and Judge Guzmán empowered to begin his judicial prosecution.

The lifting of Pinochet's immunity

A number of legal issues were discussed during the steps leading up to the lifting of Pinochet's immunity. As noted above, the counsel for the defence had insisted beforehand that Pinochet should not be put on trial because his health was too poor for him to instruct his defence, and that the proceedings violated his right to due process. This approach was rejected by the Court of Appeals, which held that the lifting of parliamentary immunity was not in itself a judgement but a simple preliminary procedure for authorising the criminal prosecution of someone who had previously had privileged status. After several other delaying tactics, such as the filing of appeals, the lifting of parliamentary immunity was conceded, and this in turn led to the oral hearings. These defence hearings raised various legal issues which are reviewed below.

The legal doctrine of the Supreme Court concerning the lifting of congressional immunity

The first part of the Supreme Court ruling upholding the decision to deprive Pinochet of his immunity discussed certain preliminary issues, such as the nature and purpose of the lifting of congressional immunity, and established the characteristics not of a trial as such but of a merely preliminary proceeding. For this reason, it pointed out, the guarantees of a fair trial (due process) for the senator were under no threat and he would be able to exercise them in any criminal proceedings as such. In order to give substance to these statements, the Supreme Court even resorted to the historical development of parliamentary immunity in Chilean constitutional law and an analysis of the institutional mechanisms for depriving immunity from a member of Congress. Lastly, though still in this first part of the ruling, the defence argument that a political trial was a prerequisite for the criminal prosecution of a former president of the republic with congressional privilege was heard and rejected, a decision based on the different nature and object of these cases.

As regards the substantive issues in the case, there would be some debate over whether the events being investigated could actually be classified as crimes and whether there was any well-founded suspicion as to Pinochet's criminal involvement in those events.

What is important here is that the highest court's ruling supported the position maintained by the Penal Chamber of the Supreme Court in various resolutions from 1997 on. These are set out below.[11]

---

11 The Chilean national legal system is based on the tradition of continental law, according to which the sole source of binding law for judges is statute law. Circuit judges are not therefore obliged to follow jurisprudence or legal precedents.

(1) Abduction: a permanent crime

The enforced disappearance of people is defined in the Chilean legislation under abduction and unlawful arrest.[12] This was confirmed by the Supreme Court, along with their definition as permanent crimes not subject to any statute of limitations.

In the specific instance of the prosecutions of General Arellano Starck's army unit for the aggravated abduction of nineteen people in the towns of Calama, Copiapó and Cauquenes, the Supreme Court upheld the view that these were abductions and not cases of homicide, in view of the fact that there was no evidential proof (body remains) of the fate of the victims. It is worth adding that homicide can only be verified in accordance with the provisions laid down in article 121 and subsequent articles of the Criminal Procedure Code that stipulate an examination of the body by means of judicial autopsy. As mentioned earlier, this was particularly important in establishing the possible existence of grounds for the judicial dismissal of criminal responsibility by amnesty or the statute of limitations.

(2) Amnesty as described in Decree Law 2191 and the statute of limitations

Although the Supreme Court stated that the debate as to whether to apply the amnesty or the statute of limitations was a matter for the judges of courts of first and second instance (who were leading the investigation) to resolve, it did make a pronouncement concerning the exact moment that the grounds for the dismissal of criminal responsibility, where appropriate, should apply, that is, not until the investigation had been exhausted, in keeping with the terms of reference of article 413 of the Criminal Procedure Code.

In any case, the Supreme Court was referring to the effects of amnesty and reasserting its subjective nature (as being conferred on the person and not the events), the result of which is to eliminate the sentence and its effects *but not the crime*. The Supreme Court based its position on the wording of article 93 no. 3 of the Criminal Code and the solid grounds underpinning this position, in stark contrast to the position maintained by the Supreme Court prior to 1997.[13]

This was important in that, once the investigation had been exhausted, amnesty would eventually have to be applied, a line of reasoning that could also be applied to the statute of limitations. This in turn meant that evidence for the

12 The difference between one criminal model and the other is that in abduction the active subject of the crime is an individual whereas in unlawful arrest it is a public employee. The difference is important for the accused in that firstly, in the case of unlawful arrest, jurisdiction comes under Military Justice and, secondly, because the sentence for unlawful arrest is much less severe than for abduction.

13 This is explained in part by the change in the makeup of the Supreme Court in 1996, with the retirement of various judges appointed by the military government and their replacement by others designated by President Eduardo Frei's government and the Chilean Senate.

event under prosecution must be established beforehand, and the identity of those who participated in the crimes verified in a process of indictment.

The court did not give its opinion on other aspects connected with these issues, such as the Former Criminal Adjudication (*Cosa Juzgada Penal*).[14] Nevertheless, it could logically be assumed from the Supreme Court's approach that cases definitively closed as a result of amnesty or the statute of limitations, where nobody has been brought to trial, could perfectly well be reopened, and events have subsequently shown this to be the case.

(3) International Human Rights Law

During the last four years progressive jurisprudential advances have been made at the level of the Supreme Court to the effect that the kinds of cases discussed above must remain open as long as investigations have not been exhausted, which involves establishing the identity of those responsible for crimes and, in the case of the disappeared, their whereabouts.

Despite this progress, save in one case,[15] the Supreme Court has hardly made any reference to the applicability of international human rights law or international humanitarian law. Prior to 1998 the only references made to international treaties, such as the American Convention for Human Rights, the Civil and Political Rights Pact and the Geneva Conventions, were to deny their applicability.[16] In some cases, this was due to their having been ratified by Chile subsequent to the occurrence of the relevant events; in others because, according to the rulings, there were no de facto assumptions allowing for the application of international laws (Geneva), or in others because international laws were considered to be subordinate to national constitutional or judicial regulations, including the most important of all, the Decree Law 2191 of 1978. Recent

14 Recent rulings by the Penal Chamber of the Supreme Court have upheld that the Former Criminal Adjudication (*Cosa Juzgada Penal*), as grounds for the dismissal of criminal responsibility, only proceeds when two connecting prerequisites coexist between two or more judicial proceedings, for example, the real nature of the crime and the identity of those responsible. The non-concurrence of either of these two prerequisites would not give rise to former adjudication. This was the ruling in the case of the two disappeared detainees Alvaro Barrios Duque and Sergio Cabezas Quijada.

15 The case of the abduction of Pedro Poblete Córdova. In a ruling on an appeal for annulment in September 1998, the Penal Chamber of the Supreme Court declared that Decree Law 2191 on amnesty and the statute of limitations was non-applicable with regard to the period of the events. Chile had been in a state of war and, accordingly, preference should be given to the applicability of the Geneva Agreements, which came into force in Chile from April 1951 onwards. The existence of the state of war was based on the legislation passed by the military government itself, especially decree laws nos. 1, 3 and 5 of 1973.

16 As in the case of the Spanish diplomat Carmelo Soria, and that of Lumi Videla Moya, who was abducted and murdered by the DINA, and dumped in the grounds of the Italian Embassy in 1974.

jurisprudence in the Supreme Court, apart from in the single case already mentioned, has not pronounced on the applicability of international law, and has neither accepted nor negated it.

Despite the wording of the ruling lifting Pinochet's congressional immunity, the perspicacity of Judge José Benquis (dissenting opinion) stands out. He queried whether an amnesty or the statute of limitation would necessarily be conceded, even with the investigation brought to the point of exhaustion because, at the time of the relevant events, the country was in legal terms in a state of war and, as far as the Geneva Conventions was concerned, military penal legislation would have been applicable. This would imply that it was the responsibility of the High Contracting Parties criminally to prosecute those responsible for crimes referred to in these agreements. According to this line of argument, an amnesty and the statute of limitation would not apply, as stated by the Penal Chamber of the Supreme Court in the appeal for annulment presented by the defence in relation to the disappearance of Pedro Poblete Córdova. (see note 15)

(4) Pinochet's involvement

With regard to the allegations concerning Pinochet's involvement in the Caravan of Death murders, key declarations were made by Sergio Arellano Starck himself, who acknowledged having been designated 'personal representative' of the commander in chief in the missions carried out in the various towns that the *Comitiva* army unit had passed through, and by the Chiefs of the Army Divisions[17] who all stated that Arellano Starck had gone over their heads. This evidence gave a basis for well-founded suspicions of Pinochet's involvement in the crimes concerned.

In their dissenting opinion, six judges of the Supreme Court considered that the material facts of the events must be qualified as homicide and not abduction, which according to the judges would mean that the Decree Law 2191 on amnesty would apply. Furthermore, the dissenting voices pointed out that that there were no signs of any antecedents giving rise to well-founded suspicions concerning the involvement of Pinochet. They also claimed that the right to due process had not been respected, in that the senator's state of health should have been taken into consideration. This meant, they concluded, that the nature of the lifting of congressional immunity was in fact that of a trial or prosecution and not a mere pre-trial formality, as the plaintiffs and the majority vote claimed.

---

17 The army is divided up on a territorial basis into six divisions under the command of an officer with the rank of major general.

Events following the lifting of congressional immunity

Successive attempts to take an investigatory statement from senator Pinochet were at first impeded by the refusal of his defence counsel on the basis of his precarious state of health, but in early 2001 Judge Guzmán finally managed to interrogate him. One of the formalities called for by Chilean law to bring a person to trial was hereby complied with,[18] and thus Judge Guzmán brought General Pinochet to trial as the *autor* (culprit) for the abduction and killing of seventy-five people. This was appealed against by Pinochet's defence counsel, who ultimately managed to get the legal qualification of *autor* changed to simply *encubridor* (abettor).

The defence counsel then requested that the case be dismissed on the grounds that Pinochet's health had deteriorated. In response Judge Guzmán ordered a series of neurological and psychiatric examinations, carried out by Chilean state doctors (of the *Servicio Médico Legal* – legal medical service), with both parties also designating an associate specialist.[19] The examination diagnosis showed 'moderate subcortical dementia'. For Pinochet's defence counsel, this diagnosis was sufficient for the case against the senator for life to be closed; for the plaintiffs, it was insufficient. At the same time, Pinochet's counsel for the defence requested that the Judge overturn the indictment that hung over the former dictator. Both requests were refused by Guzmán. Pinochet's counsel for the defence appealed these rulings.

The closing of the case against Pinochet

With regard to Judge Guzmán's refusal to suspend the case temporarily on health grounds, Pinochet's appeal was allowed by a Chamber of the Santiago Court of Appeals, but not as the defence counsel had planned. Among the grounds laid down in Chilean legislation for temporarily closing a case, there are none that temporarily free an accused person from being tried on account of physical or organic health reasons or even for humanitarian reasons. Pinochet's defence counsel was thus forced to recognise in its arguments that the grounds for closing the case against him were 'dementia' or 'insanity', which was problematic for Pinochet in terms of his person and image (particularly political). Two of the three judges admitted the grounds presented by Pinochet's defence and temporarily

---

18 Article 274 of the Criminal Procedure Code indicates the prerequisites that a resolution must comply with to bring a person to trial. There are three requisites: a declaration by the accused (investigatory declaration), accreditation of the action with criminal characteristics and suspicions based on the participation of the accused.

19 The associate specialists were the doctors Sergio Ferrer and Eugenio Fornazari, both neurologists, designated by the defence and plaintiffs respectively.

closed the case against the former dictator on the grounds of dementia or insanity, with a ruling that was, to say the least, confused.

The ruling was interesting and controversial because, firstly, it referred to and applied international human rights regulations regarding the due process of the accused, but said nothing with regard to the right of the victims' families to justice. Secondly, it was based on the rules of a new Criminal Procedure Code not then yet in force in Santiago.[20] It was contested by the plaintiffs by way of an appeal for annulment, aiming to revoke the ruling. This appeal was finally refused by the Penal Chamber of the Supreme Court in July 2002, effectively bringing the proceedings against Pinochet to a close.

The indictment still stands

Pinochet's defence counsel, as stated previously, appealed against the resolution that had refused to revoke his indictment. However the Santiago Court of Appeals did not deal with this appeal due to the fact that, as the case had been temporarily closed beforehand, all proceedings with regard to Pinochet had come to a standstill.

In consequence, the suspension of the case against Pinochet did not overturn the indictment. In legal terms, Pinochet is still being tried as an abettor in the aforementioned crimes although the trial however has effectively come to a standstill.

The special judges

On 20 June 2001 the Supreme Court resolved that eight judges in courts of first instance (*jueces de primera instancia*) who were conducting preliminary enquiries into human rights violations were to work 'exclusively' on the handling of these cases. It also ordered fifty-one other judges to give 'preferential' treatment to similar cases being dealt with in their courts. The Supreme Court's decision derived from a request from the government to accelerate the investigations, and was based on the need to 'make significant advances' in the investigations in order to end the 'ongoing suffering of the victims' families', with particular reference to the detained and disappeared.

20   There has been a radical change in national criminal proceedings in Chile from 2000 onwards, which has gradually been introduced in the different regions of the country in accordance with a schedule laid down in the Political Constitution and in legislation. The new system brings together the procedural principles and guarantees consecrated in international human rights treaties and lays down a public oral hearing for the accusation, with separation of the functions of investigation and adjudication in different bodies. This is radically different to the previous system, which was inquisitive, in writing and semi-confidential, and where the functions of investigation and adjudication were in the hands of one sole judge.

The procedural consequences of this resolution have been extremely important and notable advances have been made in the investigations. This can be seen in the number of former uniformed personnel and members of the security forces being tried by these judges (around 60 former agents).

All this has precipitated a reaction from the Commanders in Chief of the different branches of the armed forces, who have called for a 'turning of the page' on the investigations into human rights violations – in effect, the closing of the cases. This reaction was prompted by the recognition that, if these cases follow their institutional course, they must end in penal convictions, especially in cases relating to detained and disappeared individuals, in conformity with the jurisprudence of the Supreme Court as referred to above.[21]

Conclusion

Augusto Pinochet remains a political figure in Chile. Most important business people, many in the political right and the armed forces admire and revere the former dictator. However, the figure of Pinochet in Chilean politics is undoubtedly becoming increasingly marginalised. On the other hand, the judicial proceedings initiated in Chile have prompted questions of a political nature from some who have claimed that the aim was to put the 'military government' on trial, and that this trial was a political one motivated by the left's urge to seek vengeance.

Pinochet's arrest in London was a milestone in the advance of judicial investigations into human rights violations. It put the issue of human rights on the political agenda of all parties and social organisations in Chile. In order to justify the arguments advanced for Pinochet's release, the more right-wing sectors were forced to admit that Pinochet could and should be judged in Chile. The Chilean government (under pressure from the armed forces) initially relied on arguments concerning the extraterritorial character (*extraterritorialidad*) of criminal law to request Pinochet's release and to disclaim the jurisdiction of Judge Baltazar Garzón and the British courts, and this meant accepting that Pinochet could be judged in Chile. Later, humanitarian reasons were invoked.

While Pinochet's detention in London was of crucial importance, it should be restated that the Penal Chamber of the Supreme Court had already issued certain rulings establishing that human rights cases should be investigated, *prior* to the detention of the former dictator. One of these rulings, unfortunately the

---

21 In October 2002, for the first time in the history of trials relating to the disappeared, Judge Jaime Salas, of the southern town San José de la Mariquina, handed down prison sentences to two officers of the Chilean army.

only one, even upheld that the Geneva Conventions be applied over and above the Decree Law 2191 on amnesty.

This combination of factors made it feasible for Pinochet to be tried, and this is more or less what happened. Pinochet was stripped of his congressional immunity and put on trial. His 'temporary' release was due to a formality and not his innocence. The Pinochet case, even without the former dictator himself, still continues, however. Judge Juan Guzmán is still investigating numerous episodes of repression in which large numbers of agents of the security forces are being tried. Barring exceptional circumstances, these proceedings will continue for at least three more years. The Supreme Court decision in June 2001 to order a number of circuit judges dealing with cases of human rights violations to work 'exclusively' on and to give 'preferential' treatment to the handling of these cases, has already enabled important advances to be made in the investigations. One question that remains concerns what would happen, with regard to the competence of Judge Juan Guzmán, if Pinochet were to die in the near future. Since the original designation of a Court of Appeals judge was justified on the basis of the congressional immunity of the main individual accused, it might be argued that Judge Guzmán would lose his competence, and the cases would then be dealt with under the natural jurisdiction of the lower courts. Death as grounds for the dismissal of criminal responsibility could also give way to the definitive closing of the case (equivalent to an absolution) in relation to the deceased.

As a final comment, it must be said that while advances have been made in Chilean jurisprudence concerning the investigation of human rights violations, there is still a long way to go as regards the assimilation of the doctrine of international human rights and humanitarian law, still insufficiently considered by the Chilean courts.

PART 3
Politics

CHAPTER 7

The politics of the Pinochet case in the United Kingdom

Madeleine Davis

Augusto Pinochet's detention in the UK lasted seventeen months. His case was without precedent in UK legal, political and diplomatic history and its tortuous and gripping progress through the courts reflected this. The UK's highest court, the Appellate Committee of the House of Lords, heard the case three times as a result of its unprecedented decision to set aside its own judgement in *Pinochet 1*. The two rulings made by the lords (in *Pinochet 1* and *3*) on the issues of immunity and extradition law differed substantially in their interpretation of the law, nevertheless both found that Pinochet could be extradited to Spain. However, the eventual decision to free him on the grounds that he was not fit to stand trial was taken by the then Home Secretary, Jack Straw, not by the courts.

Throughout the UK chapter of the case, Straw and other government ministers insisted that the judicial proceedings would be allowed to take their course. Nevertheless, the political aspects of the case cannot be easily separated from the legal ones. UK extradition law itself demonstrates the complexity of the interplay between legal and political considerations and between the respective responsibilities of the executive and the judicial branches, granting the Home Secretary in his 'quasi-judicial role' a wide measure of discretion. But this is only one illustration of the fact that politics was intrinsically involved in the handling and perception of the case by actors on all sides. In a case of such symbolic and substantive importance, it could scarcely be otherwise. Recognising that 'the case cannot be fully understood solely from a legal perspective', Michael Byers has argued that 'the existence of legal rules and institutions shaped the options available to judges and politicians involved in this case, and ultimately constrained their behaviour'[1] But the point could equally be made the other way around. While the case certainly demonstrates – as other chapters in

---

1 M. Byers, 'The law and politics of the Pinochet case,' *Duke Journal of Comparative and International Law*, Spring/Summer, 2000, p. 416.

this book show – the activism of magistrates and judges acting to a substantial degree independently of their national governments, it nevertheless unfolded within a political context of tremendous sensitivity and importance, and this played a part in shaping its course and its outcome.

Other chapters in this book address the political factors at play in Spain and Chile, this chapter seeks to illuminate the politics of the case in the UK. It focuses on two linked issues. The first is the role of the then-Home Secretary, Jack Straw. At either end of the extradition process it falls to the Home Secretary to take a decision, at the beginning whether or not to authorise the extradition proceedings, and at the end to take the final decision whether to extradite. These are the points, chronologically speaking, at which political factors might most obviously come into play. In relation to both, there has been no shortage of speculation on the precise political motivations and machinations at work. At the start of the case, the nature and extent of communication between the various embassies, officials, and politicians over the arrest was a subject of intense interest to the media and backbench politicians alike. As the UK chapter of the case drew to a close, rumours abounded in the press of 'secret deals' between the Spanish, Chilean and British governments to secure Pinochet's release. Clearly, Straw was under very great political pressure from a number of quarters, domestic and international. The nature and relative weight of these (sometimes competing) political pressures subtly changed over time, and it is against this evolving political context that his role in the case is best understood.

A second issue is the impact of political and contingent factors on the legal proceedings themselves. While most analyses of the UK chapter of the case have focussed on the legal significance and implications of the various rulings, the hearings and decisions did not take place in a political vacuum. The Hoffmann episode in particular brought into sharp focus the lack of adequate protection against the appearance (and possible existence) of bias in the way that Lords' panels are constituted. The subsequent rehearing of the case and its delivery of a judgement substantially different from that given in *Pinochet 1* further exposed the procedures and practices of the UK's highest court to criticism, leaving the court uncomfortably open to charges that its judgements may be determined by the composition of panels. These are issues of some political significance in themselves, and there is no doubt that the Lords in *Pinochet 3* were sensitive to them. Such sensitivity could only be heightened by the parallel awareness that Pinochet was a case of enormous political and legal importance, and by the intense media and public interest that accompanied it. Additionally, the level of media interest may have exerted a pressure of its own on judicial actors – there can be few cases in which the backgrounds, interests and reputations of judges have received such extensive press coverage, or in which the gaze of the world's media was so conspicuously obvious and intense. Lawyers and judges are not impervious to such factors, indeed the lords' vacation of its ruling in the Hoffmann episode demonstrates its own (implicit) recognition of this. There is little to be gained from speculating about why individual law lords reasoned and ruled as they did in this case. Nevertheless, as I shall show, it is not unreasonable to suppose that political considerations may have played a part, in particular in inclining the lords involved in Pinochet 3 toward what was, as legal analysts have pointed out, a peculiarly technical, narrow and disputable ruling.[2]

The Pinochet case was not the first to bring into question issues relating to the structure and practices of the Appellate Committee, and analyses of the interplay between law and politics in its functioning had earlier been offered.[3] However certain unique features of this case, in particular the opportunity it provides to see how the same issues were treated differently at different times and by different panels, raise these matters anew. In its insistence that the Pinochet affair was a matter for the courts, and the repeated emphasis on the restrictions imposed upon Jack Straw by his 'quasi-judicial role', the British government implied a view of the legal process as autonomous, technical and mechanical, impervious to political considerations. The reality is somewhat different. The Pinochet case provides powerful evidence to support the contention that the English court system and the Lords in particular, is far from operating 'mechanical jurisprudence'.[4] The political and the legal are inextricably linked.

The arrest

During the course of the Pinochet affair in the UK the government was often asked by Pinochet's supporters in the Conservative Party why it had not intervened to prevent the arrest of in London of a man whom Margaret Thatcher described as a 'good friend' of Britain who had saved British lives during the Falklands War.[5] The Conservative former Home Secretary Michael Howard made it clear that had he been in Straw's position, he would have sought to

2 See essays in D. Woodhouse (ed.), *The Pinochet Case: A Legal and Constitutional Analysis* (Oxford, 2000); M. Birnbaum, 'Pinochet and Double Criminality,' *Criminal Law Review*, March, 2000, pp. 127–39.

3 D. Robertson, *Judicial Discretion in the House of Lords* (Oxford, 1998), J. Bell, *Policy Arguments in Judicial Decisions* (Clarendon, 1993).

4 D. Robertson, 'The House of Lords as a Political and Constitutional Court: Lessons from the Pinochet Case,' in D. Woodhouse (ed.), *The Pinochet Case*.

5 In a letter to *The Times*, 22 October 1998.

bring a speedy end to the extradition proceedings.[6] We can only speculate on what might actually have occurred if the Conservatives, rather than Labour, had been in power in October 1998, but what is clear is that the arrest itself was the product of a remarkable series of events, some planned, some contingent, which caught politicians by surprise. The Spanish investigations into human rights abuses under the Pinochet regime had been well-publicised since their inception in 1996 (although they had not attracted much press coverage in the UK), and there had been previous attempts by Amnesty International to initiate criminal proceedings against Pinochet in the UK courts during his previous visits (permission to proceed with these was refused by the Attorney General on the basis that there was insufficient admissible evidence).

The British Embassy in Madrid was aware of the investigation by Judge Garzón, and had sent a number of reports on the matter to the Foreign Office in 1997–1998.[7] Nobody, however, seems really to have considered the arrest of Pinochet as a serious, let alone an imminent, possibility until hours before it actually occurred. Only the last two of the British Embassy reports, on 15 and 16 October 1998, raised the possibility of the issuance of an international arrest warrant, and even these apparently made no mention of the timing of such a move. This was partly because the Spanish moves to secure the arrest were themselves made in haste, and with an imperfect understanding of the exact requirements of UK law. The first request to the British authorities by the Spanish investigating judge, made on 14 October, was for a rogatory commission, and it appears to have been only when it became clear that Pinochet might leave London before such a request could be processed, that Garzón changed tack and on 15 October sought, via Interpol, a warrant for Pinochet's arrest. At this stage, the contacts between the Metropolitan Police, the Extradition Section of the Home Office, and the Foreign Office were at official, rather than ministerial level, though Ministers were kept informed of events. In response to a request from the Metropolitan Police, officials of the Foreign Office confirmed on 16 October that Pinochet's passport did not afford him diplomatic immunity from arrest, and a provisional warrant was sought from, and issued by, Metropolitan Stipendiary Magistrate Nicholas Evans. As later became clear, this warrant was legally defective, since none of the crimes alleged were actually extradition crimes under UK law, and a second warrant was

6 In a Commons debate on the case on 27 October 1988, Howard asked the Foreign Secretary, Robin Cook, 'Is the right hon. Gentleman not aware that the Home Secretary had a discretion not to authorise the grant of a warrant and could at that point have taken into account many factors, including the implications of the arrest for the future of democracy in Chile?'

7 House of Commons Hansard written answers for 2 Feb 1999 (pt 17). The reports were: 12 November 1997, 23 January 1998, 15 October 1998, and 16 October 1998.

subsequently issued on 22 October.[8]

By the time Straw himself learned of the issuance of the first arrest warrant on the evening of 16 October the scope for political intervention was limited.[9] Under UK extradition law a person may either be arrested on a provisional or emergency warrant (as Pinochet was), in which case the request goes through police channels and does not require the Secretary of State to authorise it by issuing an Authority to Proceed (ATP) at this stage, or on a full warrant, where the request is made through diplomatic channels with supporting documentation and an ATP is issued before the arrest. Whatever contacts took place in the immediate run-up to the arrest between officials, lawyers and ministers, well-established procedures were being followed and any political interference by the Home Secretary would have been both legally improper and politically risky. By the time Straw had the opportunity to have any hand in the proceedings it was already clear that no political 'quick-fix' would be possible.

At this stage the full import of the case and its potential legal and political significance had not yet been absorbed by ministers. This was shown during the weekend following the arrest, when Peter Mandelson remarked on breakfast television 'the idea that such a brutal dictator as Pinochet should claim immunity, I think for most people in this country would be pretty gut-wrenching stuff.'[10] Alastair Campbell, Blair's press secretary, is said to have immediately paged Mandelson with the rebuke 'I agree with everything you say, but that is not the line',[11] and government sources were reported in the press two days later as describing Mandelson's intervention as 'unhelpful and emotional'.[12] The realisation was dawning that the Pinochet affair placed Blair's New Labour government, and the Home Secretary in particular, in an extraordinarily tricky political situation, in which it had to tread a difficult line between a number of competing pressures.

---

8 Pinochet's counsel applied for judicial review on the basis that the first warrant was defective, but by the time these arguments were heard, CPS lawyers had visited Garzón in Spain and assisted him in the compilation of charges that did specify crimes extraditable under UK law, and which were detailed in a second warrant issued on 22 October by Magistrate Ronald Bartle. Evans was said by some to have been deeply embarrassed by his failure to spot the deficiencies of the initial warrant. The fact that these events occurred late on a Friday evening is privately admitted by some of those involved to have contributed to some confusion in their handling.

9 See House of Commons *Hansard* written answers for 2 Nov 1998 (pt 6)

10 On *Breakfast with Frost*, BBC 1, 18 October 1998.

11 See Andrew Rawnsley's interpretation of the handling of the affair by New Labour in his *Servants of the People: The Inside Story of New Labour* (London, 2000)

Political pressures at the start of the case

Domestic

In the immediate domestic context, there were pressures from the press, public opinion, supporters of Pinochet, and the Labour Party itself. Mandelson's remark betrayed the fact that even the arch-pragmatists of New Labour were not immune from a sense of profound satisfaction that justice might finally catch up with a man who had long symbolised the crushing of hopes for a peaceful route to socialism, the testimony of whose victims was well-publicised and personally felt by many on the left. Jack Straw had himself visited Chile in 1966, and though attempts by Pinochet's supporters to use this to imply that a fiery radicalism motivated his treatment of the ex-dictator struck an unlikely note given his reputation as a sound political administrator and one of the cabinet's safest pairs of hands, such details are nonetheless illustrative of a tension at the centre of the Labour Party's domestic handling of the case.[13] While the bulk of party members and backbench MPs were free to voice their wholehearted support for the Spanish action, the government had little option but to adopt a public position of strict application of the law. The political costs of any other course of action would have been too great.

Labour Party backbenchers made abundantly clear their intention to keep a watchful eye on the government's handling of the affair. Among Labour Party MPs are a number of individuals long associated with Chile and human rights causes, many of them members of the Chile group at Westminster led by Jeremy Corbyn MP. Throughout the UK proceedings, Corbyn and others repeatedly requested debates on the case, and put numerous and detailed questions in the Commons on its handling. Their interventions ensured that the concerns of the vocal crowd of anti-Pinochet protestors who gathered daily were heard inside as well as outside the Commons, and helped keep the case headline news. On the other side, Pinochet's supporters mounted an aggressive and lavishly funded PR campaign defending his record in power and arguing for his release. As well as right-wing Chileans, the pro-Pinochet camp included a number of prominent British Conservatives. Margaret Thatcher visited Pinochet a number of times, spoke passionately in his defence at a fringe meeting of the Conservative Party conference in 1999, and even wrote to the Home Office requesting that he be allowed to take a summer holiday in Scotland.[14] Former chancellor Norman (by then Lord) Lamont was the most publicly active of Pinochet's Conservative supporters, making regular interventions on his behalf both in the

12   *Guardian*, 20 October 1998
13   See House of Commons *Hansard*, 3 November 1998.
14   See UK press reports, 9 August 1999

House of Lords and in the media. His efforts were appreciated by the Pinochet Foundation in Chile, which later awarded him a 'Star of Merit' when he visited in 2000.

The readiness of some Conservative public figures to associate themselves with the Pinochet regime, apparently without regard to the effect this might have upon the public image of their party, was a fascinating aspect of the case. A sense of gratitude for Chile's assistance during the Falklands war may have been one reason, another was the more or less open admiration of Thatcherite ideologues for the neoliberal 'shock-treatment' visited by the Pinochet regime upon the Chilean economy.[15] Thus pro-Pinochet Conservatives did not confine themselves to arguments about Chilean sovereignty and the necessity for heads of state to enjoy sovereign immunity, but also mounted a more aggressive defence of his regime. Along with praise for the Chilean 'economic miracle' came a downplaying of its costs in human terms, and Cold War rhetoric was reheated to damn the record of the Allende regime and justify military takeover as necessary to avert Communist catastrophe. A pamphlet written by a former Thatcher aide supporting Pinochet's record and accusing Allende of atrocities was distributed to British, US, Spanish and Chilean 'opinion-formers' in January 1999.[16] Well organised and funded, the pro-Pinochet camp missed no opportunity to air its views, stepping up the campaign to coincide with critical points in the UK proceedings.

A further source of domestic pressure was the media. Press scrutiny of the government's stance was intense, though editorial opinion was, unsurprisingly, divided. In the early stages of the case, the left or liberal leaning press devoted many column inches to the testimony of victims of the Pinochet regime, publishing and endorsing the opinions of prominent Chileans such as Isabel Allende and Ariel Dorfman, who argued eloquently that justice should be allowed to take its course. Much admiring attention was focused on the 'crusading judge' Baltasar Garzón, and (less admiring) on the backgrounds and supposed political inclinations of the British lawyers and judges involved. The conduct of the Home Secretary and the nature of his discretionary power was minutely analysed – rarely can the precise details of extradition law have been of such intense interest – for any sign that he intended to short-circuit or interfere in the legal proceedings. The liberal news media left the government in no doubt that any attempt to subvert the Spanish action would be a public relations disaster.

The Conservative press, on the other hand, supported the Thatcher/Lamont line, though to varying degrees. *The Times*, for example, tended to emphasise

15 For a lively account of contacts and parallels between the British new right and the Chilean dictatorship, see A. Beckett, *Pinochet in Piccadilly* (London, 2002).
16 Robin Harris, *A Tale of Two Chileans: Pinochet and Allende* (London, 1999).

the supposed threat posed by Pinochet's detention to the stability of Chilean democracy, and the potential damage to Anglo–Chilean diplomatic and trade relations.[17] The *Daily Telegraph* took a more robust line, lauding the economic successes of the Pinochet regime and carrying sympathetic accounts of the captive senator's daily existence at Wentworth. The *Sunday Telegraph* was the only British newspaper to carry a first-hand interview with Pinochet, in which he described himself as 'the only political prisoner in England'.[18] That the Pinochet affair had caught the public imagination was illustrated by its omni-presence in newspaper letters pages. A sample from late 1998, around the time Straw gave his first ATP, includes contributions ranging from the facetious ('am I the only person who would be pleased if Argentina requested the extradition of Margaret Thatcher?')[19] through the heartfelt ('the time has come for us, the victims of persecution, to shout with joy and for dictators to fear'),[20] to the almost hysterical ('if a brave Soviet general had managed to overthrow Stalin, even if this had involved killing a few thousand KGB, would we treat him as those who govern us are treating Pinochet?').[21] Jack Straw received some 70,000 letters and emails concerning the case, and Pinochet became a household name.

As well as these active pressures, there were also other domestic political reasons for the government to be sensitive about the case. Pinochet had been a frequent visitor to London during the Thatcher era, and the Chilean military was a valued customer of UK arms firms. This did not end with the accession of New Labour to office in 1997, indeed he had visited London in September of that year, being granted as usual the use of VIP facilities at Heathrow airport. His arrival on 22 September 1998 was once again facilitated in this way by the Foreign Office, though no British government official greeted him and the visit was viewed as a private one, despite one of its objectives being, as it later emerged, to visit UK arms manufacturers.[22] The Labour government's contin-ued willingness to play host to Pinochet and the questions raised about the latter's role in arms procurement deals, coming on top of an earlier embarrass-ment over the continuation of British arms sales to Indonesia, could only serve to further expose the emptiness of the claim made by Robin Cook in May 1997 to 'an ethical dimension' in foreign policy. Jack Straw could certainly not afford,

---

17 See *The Times* leader, 1 December 1998, and other articles around that time.

18 *The Sunday Telegraph*, 18 July 1999.

19 Letter from Peter Skellern to *The Independent*, 11 December 1998.

20 Letter from Ged Levy to *The Independent*, 11 December 1998.

21 W.G.G. Woodhouse, letter to *The Daily Telegraph*, 30 November 1998.

22 Asked in the Commons for details of Pinochet's previous visits to the UK, the government at first failed to mention the 1997 visit, but later admitted its error. House of Commons *Hansard*, 22 October 1998, 27 October 1998, 5 November 1998.

in the interests of his own political career as well as of the party and government, to be seen to be intervening politically in the Pinochet affair.

International

In addition to these domestic political sensitivities were the pressures exerted in the international political arena. Here too the British government was caught in a contradictory situation. Earlier in 1998 the UK had been among the 120 countries to sign up to the Rome statute proposing the institution of an International Criminal Court. In so doing it had made a clear and public commitment to the view that more effective international legal mechanisms should be developed to bring to justice those guilty of egregious human rights abuses (including Heads of State). The political, legal and diplomatic difficulties of putting such a commitment into practice, however, were dramatically illustrated by the Pinochet affair. Relations between the UK and Chile were a primary political concern. The Concertación government of Eduardo Frei immediately protested against the arrest and demanded that Pinochet be returned to Chile. Behind this inevitable defence of Chilean sovereignty lay a complex reality. Several members of the Chilean government, including Mario Artaza, the then ambassador to the UK, had been exiled or persecuted by the Pinochet regime, and were privately delighted to see the ex-dictator humiliated. Criminal charges had already been initiated against Pinochet in Chile by Judge Juan Guzmán (though at this point they were very far from having any prospect of success had he been returned to Chile), and thus the process of investigating the past, begun under Aylwin, was progressing in Chile, albeit painfully. As Alan Angell has argued in his contribution to this volume, the marginalisation of Pinochet and his legacy had already begun in Chilean politics in this and other ways, and whatever sense of satisfaction was enjoyed by Chilean politicians of the centre-left, there was also room for a justifiable sense of indignation at Spain's interference in its affairs.

Britain's situation in the middle of this diplomatic conundrum was an unenviable one. Relations with Spain, whose centre-right government was firmly opposed to Garzón's action, and whose Prime Minister Aznar enjoyed a good personal relationship with Tony Blair, were a further consideration. The UK government was also acutely aware of the sensitivity of the issue for its 'special relation' the USA. The Spanish investigations into the activities of the dictatorships of the Southern Cone were instrumental in turning up a mass of evidence of the USA's own complicity in the human rights abuses that had occurred, and in forcing the CIA to open its files on such matters.[23] The questions thus raised about US sponsorship of Pinochet and other right-wing dictators

23   M. Davis, *The Pinochet Case* (London, 2000), pp. 8–9.

held out more than simply the prospect of political embarrassment over the past, given the potential dangers posed to Henry Kissinger and others were Pinochet to be extradited. Informally, the USA through Madeleine Albright placed considerable pressure on the UK government to allow Pinochet to return home.[24] Even the Vatican joined in to argue for Pinochet's release on compassionate grounds, transmitting its concern through a diplomatic letter in November 1998.[25]

There were also pressures in the other direction. Switzerland, France and later Belgium all lodged their own extradition requests, while the UN Committee on Torture called (in November 1998) on the UK government to prosecute Pinochet in its own courts should the extradition process fail. The European Parliament called on the Spanish government to back Garzón's action,[26] Lionel Jospin in France and Joschka Fischer in Germany hailed the arrest as good news, while Kofi Annan, UN secretary general, said that the arrest proved the gathering momentum of international human rights law.[27] The weight of international public opinion, transmitted through human rights groups (themselves of course a not inconsiderable source of pressure), was firmly in favour of extradition. Nobody, it seemed, was without a view.

In the politically charged atmosphere surrounding the arrest and the early months of Pinochet's detention, Straw and New Labour had little room for manoeuvre. Whatever the private views of ministers, in political terms the affair could be nothing but a headache, and Downing Street was reputed to be keen to find a quick way out.[28] Straw, however, at whose door the responsibility lay, determined to play the matter by the book, and whatever Downing Street's first inclinations, this was also in the circumstances the politically expedient course. On 21 October, in an attempt to calm an atmosphere of feverish speculation, Tony Blair gave a series of press interviews insisting that the matter was a judicial, not political one, in which Jack Straw would act 'as a magistrate, not a politician,'[29] and a similar view was conveyed to the Chilean deputy foreign minister when he met with Robin Cook a few days later.

A matter for the courts

Before the matter moved to Straw for a decision, it was for the Divisional Court to hear Pinochet's petition for habeas corpus and judicial review of the decision

24 See newspaper reports through October and November 1998.
25 House of Commons *Hansard* 2 March 1999.
26 In a vote taken on 23 October 1998.
27 See press reports 21 October 1998.
28 Rawnsley, *Servants of the People*, pp. 186–7.
29 *The Daily Telegraph*, 22 October 1998.

to arrest him. At this stage, it was widely expected that the arguments of Pinochet's counsel that he was immune from the jurisdiction of the English courts by virtue of his status as a former sovereign, would convince the panel of judges led by Lord Chief Justice Bingham, and this did indeed happen. Bingham's judgement, in asserting that nothing could invalidate the principle that 'one sovereign state will not impugn another in relation to its sovereign acts' demonstrated a reliance by the Divisional Court on a traditional view of international law.[30] The much more surprising judgement was that given almost a month later by the House of Lords, where a 3:2 majority of the panel found that international law did not recognise immunity for crimes such as torture and genocide.[31] This reversal of the Divisional Court's ruling was highly unexpected, and a number of factors may have contributed to bringing it about. One was the reassignment to the case of a panel that had originally been convened to hear an immigration case[32] and which included law lords with a 'progressive' reputation, as well as some of those most knowledgeable in the area of international law.[33] Another was the greater use in the proceedings of specialised counsel and in turn of arguments grounded in public international law. Thus issues such as whether immunity could be claimed for the specific crime of torture given the UK's incorporation of the 1984 Convention on Torture into its domestic law, which had not been fully explored at the earlier stage, were now considered in detail. Two additional and unusual factors of the hearing were the decision to grant human rights groups (headed by Amnesty International) the opportunity to intervene, and the unprecedented manner in which the judgements were delivered live on television in the form of oral summaries from the lords. The latter clearly indicated that the judges were all too aware of the level of media and public interest in the case, while the former was to prove highly significant in the ensuing proceedings concerning Lord Hoffmann, who gave the final judgement tipping the balance in favour of allowing the appeal.

The dramatic reversal of the earlier court decision made Jack Straw's task even more difficult – far from settling the matter for him, as he might have hoped, the courts had complicated it further.[34] He responded to the pressure by

30 Marc Weller, 'On the Hazards of Foreign Travel for Dictators and Other International Criminals,' *International Affairs*, vol. 75, no. 3, 1999.

31 Hazel Fox, 'The First Pinochet Case: Immunity of a former Head of State,' *International and Comparative Law Quarterly*, vol. 48, part 1, Jan. 1999.

32 Byers, 'The Law and Politics of the Pinochet Case'.

33 *Ibid*. Not all, though, ruled as their reputations might have suggested that they would – Slynn, most notably, rejected the appeal.

34 In the meantime also, the Spanish courts had upheld Garzon's claim to jurisdiction in the case, disposing of the possibility that this would bring an end to the process.

proceeding with extreme care, requesting an extension to the normal extradition timetable in order to consider representations, and taking legal advice on the measure of discretion allowed him by the Extradition Act. He also took the unusual step of issuing reasons for his decision, made on 9 December 1998, and received with cheers from the Labour benches, to allow the extradition process to proceed. Having been advised that his discretionary power was a very wide one, he was careful both to demonstrate that his decision had been arrived at in a way which satisfied the requirements of the Extradition Act, and to make clear that he had considered all the representations made to him.[35] These had included pleas to consider the effects of extradition upon Chilean democracy, and to free Pinochet on compassionate grounds because of his age and state of health. These he rejected, though noting also that it was open to him to reconsider such matters in making his final decision at the end of the extradition process. The Home Secretary's statement made it clear that he had chosen to play the issue according to the rules. The external pressures upon him, however, very much narrowed the scope for the exercise of discretion, and had his decision gone the other way, it would almost certainly have been challenged by way of judicial review.

The Hoffmann affair

In a case not short of remarkable moments, the Hoffmann episode was one of the most remarkable, and proved to be a turning point. Before Straw issued his ATP, it had emerged, in slightly murky circumstances, that Lord Hoffmann was an unpaid director of Amnesty International Charity Ltd, and Pinochet's lawyers had already made representations to Straw, which were rejected, that this should have disqualified him from sitting on the panel in Pinochet 1.[36] Pinochet's lawyers then made an application to the House of Lords for judicial review of their decision on the basis that Hoffmann's Amnesty links gave an appearance of bias (no actual bias was alleged, as all concerned were at pains to point out) since Amnesty had intervened in the appeal hearing. This brought about an unprecedented situation, with a panel of five lords being hastily convened to hear the petition, and judging unanimously that Hoffmann's links with AICL were an automatic disqualification to his sitting on the panel. Thus the decision of the Lords in *Pinochet 1* was void, and the case would have to be heard again. David Robertson has argued that the reasoning used here – that Hoffmann was disqualified because he could not be a judge in his own cause –

---

35 See the editor's introduction in Woodhouse (ed.), *The Pinochet Case*.

36 The information was apparently transmitted to Michael Caplan, Pinochet's solicitor, in an anonymous phonecall (source: interview with the author). However Hoffmann's Amnesty links were well known in London legal circles.

was flawed, since 'it really makes no sense to equate the 'interest' Amnesty International had in the case ... to the sort of interest the civil law rule of *nemo in sua causa* involves. The structure of the decision is tainted by this throughout.'[37] It was an unusual decision, and one which has also had unintended effects, as Diana Woodhouse points out in chapter 5.

After the Hoffmann episode a rash of challenges were made on the grounds of the interests of particular judges. The senior law lord, Browne-Wilkinson, did his best to avoid this by presenting the Hoffmann case as exceptional, but the debacle exposed to public scrutiny, in a way that was very uncomfortable for the law lords, questions about the extent to which the ideological, political or moral leanings of a judge may be said to affect the decisions he makes. By using the reasoning they did in *Pinochet 2*, the lords avoided addressing this issue head on, indeed, as Robertson has argued 'the automaticity of the supposed bar on Lord Hoffmann's participation was almost certainly partly to avoid actually investigating a charge of bias'.[38] To do so would have involved constructing an argument around Hoffmann's political views, and this in turn would have involved investigating rather more explicitly than they would have wished the extent to which judicial decisions are affected by non-judicial considerations – something which obviously has broad resonance and implications quite apart from the Hoffmann affair. The notion that judges, like anyone else, are ideological beings who inevitably exercise discretion and apply value judgements 'choosing to be convinced by one, rather than another, legal argument in order to craft an opinion which gets them where their ideological leanings prompt',[39] is hardly new, and the Hoffmann episode does show, in a roundabout way, an implicit recognition of this amongst legal actors themselves. However, in arguing as they did in *Pinochet 2* the lords showed themselves reluctant to abandon a conception of their role as 'legal technicians', (Robertson's phrase) a conception which is surely going to become increasingly anachronistic as the reach of international law continues to extend into the ambit of domestic courts.[40]

The questions raised by the Hoffmann affair about the structures, practices and culture of England's highest court are important in themselves. They also show the emptiness of the claim that by treating the Pinochet affair as a 'matter for the courts', political considerations could be effectively removed from the equation. Justice is and should be a deliberative rather than a mechanical process. The fact that in *Pinochet 3* we see a Lords panel, convened to address the

37 Robertson, 'The House of Lords as a Political and Constitutional Court,' p. 27.
38 *Ibid.*, p. 25.
39 *Ibid.*, p. 29.
40 Such issues were raised and linked to the Hoffmann affair in debates around the Access to Justice Bill then being considered. See House of Commons *Hansard*, 14 April 1999.

same issues as the earlier hearing, deliver a judgement substantially different from that in *Pinochet 1* in itself demonstrates this unequivocally. And yet we also see in *Pinochet 3* the Lords choosing to step back from the application of general principles of contemporary international law (such a striking feature of *Pinochet 1*) into a much more restrictive and narrowly technical treatment of the issues. The 6:1 decision to allow Pinochet's extradition, but only in relation to crimes of torture and conspiracy to torture committed after 8 December 1988, hinged on the Lords' interpretation of the precise requirements of 'double criminality'. They chose to accept the argument that for a crime to be extraditable it must have been a crime under UK law at the time it was committed rather than at the time of the extradition request. Thus the extraditable charges against Pinochet were reduced from 32 to three. This decision has been subjected to a number of critical analyses from a legal perspective.[41] However it also raises the question of the extent to which, in making their decision, the Lords were sensitive to the legal and political pressures upon them.

First and foremost, the Hoffmann episode had caused profound embarrassment and led the structure and practices of the UK's highest court to be subject to a great deal of critical media and public scrutiny. To have overturned *Pinochet 1* in this context could only have prompted further criticism, and would have added to the questions already raised about bias and the inadequacy of the court's ability to deal with it further questions about the effect of the composition of panels upon its rulings. Of the seven law lords assembled to hear *Pinochet 3*, none had been involved in *Pinochet 1*, but four had heard *Pinochet 2*. Lord Browne-Wilkinson chaired the panel and gave the leading judgement. Although a majority assented to his reasoning, there were a variety of positions. Lord Goff at one extreme would have dismissed the appeal, while Lord Millett at the other took a line rather more similar to the majority in *Pinochet 1*. Indeed he went so far as to say that in the absence of an extradition request from Chile, the UK had an obligation to extradite to another requesting state or to prosecute Pinochet itself. Ultimately, the decision of the majority to accept a narrow interpretation of double criminality requirements had the effect of allowing the panel to uphold the decision in *Pinochet 1* while also drastically reducing the number of extraditable charges. Though technically defensible, the ruling sidestepped the broader and more significant questions about the nature and intention of developing international law. The panel's reluctance to articulate a robust view on these critical issues was further shown by the strong hint it gave to Jack Straw that in view of the reduction of the charges he should reconsider

---

41 Woodhouse (ed.), *The Pinochet Case*; C. Warbrick, 'Extradition Law Aspects of Pinochet 3,' *International and Comparative Law Quarterly*, Oct. 1999; Birnbaum, 'Pinochet and Double Criminality'.

his decision to allow extradition to proceed. In sum, the impression given was that the lords were inclined (though in a way that avoided damaging the reputation of the court further) to find a way out of a case that had become both a legal embarrassment and a political liability.[42]

A changed context

Straw's immediate response was to seek legal advice on whether he had the power to reconsider his earlier ATP. Advised that he could not revoke it, but could issue a new one, he did so on 15 April, again allowing the extradition to proceed, but insisting that he had considered the matter 'entirely afresh'. He did not, however, change his approach. The lords' suggestion that he reconsider his earlier decision could not alter the fact that, having publicly committed himself to abide by the letter of the law, it would have been difficult for him now to take a different line, since the crimes alleged, though fewer in number, were still extraditable. Again, Straw had considered representations, and on this occasion the Ministry of Defence voiced its concern about the effects of the case in terms of lost business for British defence manufacturers. None of the arguments put to Straw were considered strong enough at this stage to outweigh what he unequivocally stated as 'the UK's obligation to extradite Senator Pinochet to Spain consistently with the ECE' (European Convention on Extradition).

A long hiatus in the legal proceedings now followed. While the Lords proceedings had been expeditiously organised (though the panel in Pinochet III took two months to release their ruling), the lower courts moved more slowly. Over the summer of 1999 a preliminary hearing set 27 September as the date for the start of extradition committal proceedings, and thus there was a period of five months relative quiet in the case. During that time the political context against which Jack Straw had to act changed. Media and public interest in the case receded somewhat. The court proceedings inevitably became less interesting as they were repeated, and *Pinochet 3*, in focusing on narrower and more technical issues, detracted from the newsworthiness of the story. In contrast to the time of the arrest, which had been a rather slow period for international news, there were in mid 1999 other dramatic foreign policy stories – in particular the NATO bombing of Kosovo that had begun in March. Coverage of the case in the press thus dwindled, although it by no means disappeared. Without

---

42 Some lawyers involved in the case (on both sides) to whom I spoke in the course of this research were privately willing to vouchsafe their conviction that the aggregate decision was the result of behind-the-scenes horsetrading amongst the lords in a bid to find an acceptable way out of the case, both because of its huge political and legal implications, and because of acute sensitivity to criticism about their own role in the wake of the Hoffmann episode.

high-profile court proceedings, attention focused more on Pinochet himself and his experience as 'the only political prisoner in England'. The arguments made on his behalf by his British and Chilean supporters shifted in their focus. Earlier in the proceedings, the wilder pronouncements of the Pinochet lobby – though serving to ensure publicity for the pro-Pinochet cause – had had the unintended effect of making New Labour's handling of the case appear positively principled by comparison. Now the case for his release was developed more subtly, to emphasise humanitarian considerations. Rumours about a decline in Pinochet's health began to circulate more frequently, and the Conservative press accompanied each new stage in the legal proceedings with renewed reports of minor strokes, falls, and depression.

While the tactical shift of the pro-Pinochet lobby helped prepare the ground in the UK for Straw's eventual decision, a corresponding change of diplomatic tack by the Chilean government ultimately proved critical. On 28 June 1999 Juan Gabriel Valdés met Robin Cook and their Spanish counterpart Abel Matutes during a summit in Brazil. With Cook he reportedly raised the possibility of freeing Pinochet on health grounds, and was apparently told that this could only be considered once the legal process was exhausted. With Matutes he discussed the possibility of some form of international arbitration between Spain and Chile to secure the end of the process. Chile was pursuing a dual strategy. In relation to Spain, a letter was dispatched requesting that Spain consider the arbitration route. This, in the event, was formally rejected by Spain in September as unviable, since the Spanish government was unable to intervene in the judicial process. In relation to the UK, Chile now concentrated its diplomatic efforts on persuading the British government of the humanitarian case for Pinochet's release. New medical reports were sent to the UK in August, and a few days later it emerged that Jack Straw had taken legal advice on the possibility of freeing Pinochet in the case of a deterioration in his health. The Home Office insisted that the advice was sought on a contingency basis only, and that there was no intention to interrupt the judicial process.

If the UK authorities were keen to play down any suggestion that the humanitarian route was Pinochet's best hope of freedom, the Chilean authorities were much more open about it. After Pinochet insisted that he did not want to be released on compassionate grounds, in an interview given to a Chilean radio station in July, Valdés made it quite clear that this was a decision not for him, but for the British authorities, and the prospects of success for the proposed 'via humanitaria' were openly discussed in the Chilean press.[43] This makes the

43 Carlos Vergara, 'Reacciones del gobierno chileno durante el caso Pinochet,' in FLACSO Chile (ed.), *Chile 1999–2000: Nuevo Gobierno: desafíos de la reconciliación* (Santiago, 2000).

reports of 'secret deals' that circulated in the aftermath of Pinochet's eventual release somewhat far-fetched.[44] Certainly there were contacts, formal and informal, between officials and ministers of the Chilean and British government. Cook and Valdés met again in Auckland in early September, and once more on 21 September in New York, and no doubt there were other, less well-publicised contacts at official level. Pablo Cabrera, the new Chilean ambassador to the UK who arrived in September 1999 was much more active than his predecessor in communicating the Chilean government's preferences directly to Pinochet himself (Cabrera, unlike Artaza, visited the ex-dictator personally) and to the UK authorities. But this hardly amounts to a 'secret deal' to free Pinochet. While the case proceeded through the UK courts, there was, on the face of things, no room for political manoeuvring. However this did not mean that diplomatic contact between the UK and Chile ceased. The outcome of the affair, and Straw's role in it, is better seen as the product of a changed political and legal context than as the result of secret machinations.

While the more focused approach of the Chileans was one factor, there were also others. Prosaically but crucially, the law on Extradition gives the Home Secretary greater latitude at the end of the process than earlier on. Once Pinochet had been committed on 8 October to await the Home Secretary's decision, Straw had a much freer hand.[45] In deciding whether or not to issue an order for return (i.e. whether to send the person concerned to the requesting state), the Home Secretary may consider a number of issues that are not properly to be considered when deciding whether to issue an ATP (Straw did consider these at the earlier stage, probably to discourage applications for judicial review). These include whether the application for extradition is made 'in good faith and in the interests of justice', and whether, having regard to all the circumstances, it would be unjust or oppressive to extradite. The way was open for Straw to take into account representations that a decline in Pinochet's health made it unjust or oppressive to return him to Spain. The manner in which Straw went about this, and the timing of the exercise of his discretion and of his eventual decision to free Pinochet, may, however, be questioned.

There are several issues here. Firstly, the fact that it was he who requested

---

44 See Hugh O'Shaughnessy, 'Secret Deal Freed Pinochet,' *The Observer*, 7 January 2001, and Mónica Pérez and Felipe Gerdtzen, *Augusto Pinochet: 503 días atrapado en Londres* (Santiago, 2001).

45 There was speculation during the committal proceedings that Bartle, whose right-wing sympathies were extensively examined in the press, would decide to halt the process. This entirely missed the point that Bartle in fact had almost no power to do so, since the procedures specified for committal by Section 9 of the Extradition Act made his responsibility to commit Pinochet quite clear. Had he not done so his decision could have been challenged. In the circumstances, there was no real possibility of the proceedings being halted at this stage.

(on 5 November 1999, and in response to a formal request from Chile that Pinochet be released on compassionate grounds) that Pinochet undergo independent medical tests to determine whether or not he was fit to stand trial, and moreover, that he offered a guarantee that the results of the tests would remain confidential, was an unusual step to take.[46] Still, given the scope of his discretion under Section 12, it would be difficult to sustain the argument that this was improper, and indeed since it was the UK who would have to decide on the evidence available whether Pinochet's health would be a bar to further proceedings, it was arguably necessary that the examinations should be by a team appointed by the UK authorities. More open to question is the timing of his intervention, while an application to seek a writ of habeas corpus from Pinochet's lawyers was still pending. A date of 20 March 2000 had been set by the Divisional Court to hear the appeal, and thus the judicial process could not be said to have been exhausted. For the Home Secretary to intervene at this point, as acknowledged by lawyers involved in the case, is extremely unusual, and the result was effectively to short-circuit the final legal stages of the case. Rather than waiting for the legal proceedings to run their course, Straw declared on 11 January 2000, six days after the tests had been carried out, in his now famous formulation, that he was 'minded' to release Pinochet after seeing the medical reports. He gave seven days for representations.

Representations from human rights groups and the countries seeking extradition centred on Straw's refusal to disclose the medical findings in full, and Belgium lodged an application for judicial review on this basis. However even before the High Court forced Straw to disclose the report to the governments seeking extradition, further criticism of his handling of the case in its final stages centred on the composition of the team who examined Pinochet, and on the findings of the medical report itself (which had been leaked to the Spanish press and were thus a matter of public knowledge before official disclosure). Questions were also raised about the way in which Straw chose to interpret his responsibilities — could it not, for example, have been open to him to have allowed the courts to decide on the issue of Pinochet's fitness to stand trial? Moreover, was it in fact necessary for Straw to take a position on this issue at all — could the issue not have been whether Pinochet was fit to travel to Spain (which, since he travelled to Chile shortly afterward without mishap, he clearly was)?

Straw's presentation of his eventual decision to free Pinochet as effectively the only option available to him was debatable, and indeed in one sense it

---

46 This correspondence is published along with much other useful primary material in Reed Brody and Michael Ratner (eds.), *The Pinochet Papers: The Case of Augusto Pinochet in Spain and Britain* (The Hague/London/Boston, 2000).

contradicted simultaneous claims about the broad scope of his discretionary power. Despite this, no legal challenge was made to Straw's final decision, announced at 8 a.m. on 2 March 2000, to free Pinochet on the grounds that he was unfit to face trial, and thus Pinochet left Britain from RAF Waddington at lunchtime the same day. Whether any such challenge might have succeeded can only be guessed at. Garzón's attempt was frustrated by the Spanish government. No other party attempted it. The consensus seems to have been that while certain aspects of Straw's conduct and the precise manner in which he chose to exercise his discretion could be questioned, this was unlikely to provide sufficient grounds for legal challenge, since in the end, the decision lay with the Home Secretary.

In a sense, the outcome of the UK chapter of the case was predictable, since it was always clear that compassionate circumstances could be considered as a reason for refusing extradition. In setting aside such considerations until after the committal stage, Straw had acted quite properly in his 'quasi-judicial' role, and indeed the matter was handled throughout in typical New Labour fashion – cautious, technocratic, yet simultaneously with an acute awareness of political sensitivities and of the requirements of pragmatism. However the political circumstances pertaining after seventeen months were somewhat different from those at the start, and this undoubtedly made it easier for Straw to exercise the discretion given him under the law. Whereas the early phase of the UK chapter of the case was to a significant extent media and public opinion driven, with political and emotive issues very much to the fore, the later stages of the case unfolded against a more complex and politically nuanced background. By this point the issues had been tested in court several times, and notwithstanding the rather ambivalent judgement in *Pinochet 3*, an important legal precedent had already been set – nine of the twelve law lords who heard the case concluded that Pinochet could be extradited to Spain for acts committed when he was head of state. In one sense, then, the key principle was already established, and the freeing of Pinochet on humanitarian grounds could not alter this. That in itself went a long way toward defusing the political tension surrounding the case, and created a context in which Pinochet's release, though a symbolic defeat for many, was not in truth a disastrous outcome.

It was also clear by this point that things had changed in Chile. In October 1998 it was unthinkable, despite diplomatically motivated claims to the contrary, that Pinochet could ever face trial in Chile. By the time of his return, investigations by Judge Guzmán were well advanced, and an application was almost immediately made for the lifting of his senatorial immunity from prosecution. What Alan Angell has called the 'Pinochet factor' in Chilean politics was now being constructed in a different way, in part as a result of his long absence and the circumstances of it. Additionally, while the lengthy UK proceedings continued, the genuine complexity of the political and diplomatic issues it raised became clearer. Several commentators have pointed to the irony of the fact that it was Spain, of all nations, whose own transition to democracy in the 1970s was predicated on an unspoken agreement to absolve the crimes of the Franco regime, that sought to try Pinochet. However this might be interpreted, there was something to be said for the view that Chile should be allowed to deal with its own past in its own way. Once the important legal precedent had been set, there was more room for these kinds of considerations to affect the decisions and motivations of the actors in this drama.

Conclusion

The Pinochet affair, by further entrenching the principle that there should be no immunity for the most egregious crimes against human rights by whoever committed, has advanced the cause of international justice significantly. It has also demonstrated the very real problems and paradoxes that may be encountered in putting this principle into practice, in a context where political and legal imperatives may conflict. In cases of this nature the political and the legal are inextricably intertwined. The only decision that the UK had to make in this case was whether or not Pinochet could, under UK law, be extradited to Spain. Notwithstanding the government's stated position of strict application of the law, political considerations were of necessity involved, not only in the way that the executive branch of government perceived and acted in the case, but also in the way that the matter was treated by the courts. In an obvious sense, the politically expedient decision for the UK authorities was always to free Pinochet – neither Cabinet nor judiciary had wanted to be caught in the middle of the affair, which had enormous potential costs in all sorts of ways. In the UK, as in the international arena, what the case demonstrated is the paradoxes that exist where political sensitivities and practicalities constrain the options available to legal and political actors in a way that made it unlikely that Pinochet would ever actually be brought to trial. This is not to imply that events were pre-determined or solely determined by political considerations. The dramatic twists and turns the affair took in the UK show that this was not the case. Nor should it be forgotten that the UK proceedings resulted in a landmark legal decision, the status of which was not altered by Pinochet's eventual release. Nevertheless, it remains the case that whether and how the Pinochet precedent may be applied in the future will depend as much on the exercise of political will as on the application of law.

CHAPTER 8

Spanish Public Opinion
and the Pinochet Case

Carlos Malamud

The Pinochet case was headline news worldwide in October 1998. International public opinion was suddenly confronted with demands for justice for the horrors committed by the Chilean military dictatorship. In Spain, where this international shockwave began, the actions of Baltasar Garzón polarised public opinion, with a majority in favour of his attempt to indict the dictator. The case had numerous facets – legal, political and international – and its repercussions were felt in various countries, initially Spain, Chile and Great Britain, and subsequently Argentina, the United States and several other European and Latin American countries. Using mainly press sources, this chapter analyses the current of public opinion in Spain and the behaviour of the different political and social forces during the first few weeks following the general's arrest. No in-depth study of the subsequent reactions is attempted here since, in broad terms, all the protagonists discussed maintained their initial positions with little variation throughout the proceedings in London and even after Pinochet's return to Chile.

Spanish justice

The conduct of justice was a central issue conditioning the reactions of all the other protagonists. The responses of public opinion, the government and political parties depended upon decisions made by the Spanish judicial system and also by the British courts, most notably the House of Lords. The legal rulings always preceded the political and media response, and they influenced the tenor and volume of the subsequent attitudes adopted. This may be seen with respect to Garzón's initial decision to arrest Pinochet and also subsequently with respect to the decision of the Pleno de la Sala de lo Penal de la Audiencia Nacional (Plenary Session of the Criminal Chamber of the Spanish National Court) establishing the competence of the Spanish judicial system to try the lifetime senator. The same can be said for the various rulings by British judges and the House of Lords concerning the extradition proceedings.

On 13 October Judge Manuel García Castellón, responsible for the investigation of the disappeared in Chile, requested authorisation from the British authorities through Interpol to interrogate Pinochet, who was convalescing following an operation. England was one of the few risk-free places the general could visit and he had been received with the same privileges as on previous occasions. All this was to change, however, in October 1998. García Castellón rejected the request by plaintiffs for cautionary measures to prevent Pinochet from leaving England without being questioned.[1] At this point, nobody dreamt that he would be imprisoned and the most vehement plaintiffs would have been satisfied simply with his being questioned. Expectations were to soar, however, to the point that any scenario that stopped short of extradition and conviction by the Spanish courts came to be seen as defeat.

Since 4 July 1996 García Castellón had been conducting an investigation into crimes of genocide, terrorism and torture during the Pinochet dictatorship, a case that was originally begun by Miguel Miravet, a public prosecutor at the Tribunal Superior de Justicia (High Court) in Valencia and president of the Unión Progresista de Fiscales (UPF – Union of Progressive Prosecutors), an association which played a leading role in the case. Initial uncertainty about how Great Britain would respond was reinforced by indications that it would not be possible to detain and subsequently interrogate Pinochet following his discharge from hospital. Two days later, however, events accelerated and took a different course. Judge Garzón, who was investigating a similar case relating to crimes committed by the Argentine military, begun by Carlos Castresana of the UPF on 28 March 1996 in parallel to the García Castellón case, requested authorisation from the British authorities to interrogate Pinochet on the basis of his being an accused person in the investigations underway. The answer was affirmative, however in order to interrogate the general an international warrant for his arrest would be required.

On Friday 16 October two complaints for private prosecution relating to Pinochet's involvement in Operación Cóndor were filed in Garzón's court of first instance, one by Juan Garcés and the Comisión de Desaparecidos en Chile and the other by the political party Izquierda Unida (IU – United Left), who held him responsible for the disappearance of over 70 people. At 4 p.m. that day Garzón accepted the complaints and filed an urgent warrant for Pinochet's

---

1 According to *El Mundo* (EM), 18 October 1998, García Castellón did not want to request Pinochet's detention because he had insufficient evidence and because he considered the proceedings to be too speculative.

arrest in London.[2] There has been some speculation that the order was signed in the afternoon to forestall any reaction from the Chilean embassies in Madrid and London. For months, Garzón had been in doubt as to whether to include Operación Cóndor in his indictment, believing that it would not be a fruitful avenue, despite the contrary opinion of the civil action plaintiffs, who were motivated by propaganda considerations and had few hopes of the trial actually prospering. Garzón abruptly changed his opinion. On 14 October[3] the press was still reporting 'Garzón is thinking about it', although his decision must have been influenced by the wider media response. In circles close to the plaintiffs there was overwhelming joy at the prospect of Pinochet's capture and Operación Cóndor began to be used as a decisive line of argument.[4]

After submitting a request to question him, Garzón called for Pinochet's extradition on charges of genocide,[5] terrorism and torture. For procedural purposes, he also joined his request to that made by García Castellón. Why was Garzón in such a hurry to include Operación Cóndor in the proceedings and to try Pinochet in a case in which he was not named? The haste with which this all occurred points to some kind of co-ordination between the various plaintiffs and the examining magistrate. Some news items pointed to the fact that some of the plaintiffs' lawyers, especially those of the IU, worked together with the judge in his office to draw up and immediately file the arrest warrant. In the spring of 1998, the plaintiffs, aware of the pressure from the Attorney General's Office (*fiscalía*) of the Audiencia Nacional upon García Castellón to end his proceedings, had filed a complaint with Garzón relating to Operación Cóndor in order to guarantee the continuation of the proceedings against the Chilean dictatorship in the event of García Castellón's lawsuit being prematurely dismissed. While Garzón did create a separate line of investigation, he did not come to a final decision.

2 *Diario 16* (D16), 18 October 1998.
3 D16, 14 October 1998.
4 From D16 on 14 October 1998: 'The counsel for prosecution (in this case Enrique Santiago for IU in the Argentine process and Juan Garcés, president of the Allende Foundation and lawyer for various victims in the Chilean case) considers Pinochet to be one of the main people responsible, through the DINA, for the so-called 'Operación Cóndor', a plan in which the intelligence agencies of various South American dictatorships were involved to eliminate people who were opposed to their interests by means of terrorist acts. The development and consequences of this operation [Condor] make up a separate section within Garzón's investigations due to the direct command of the DINA, which suggests the direct implication of Pinochet in the disappearance of Spanish nationals during the Argentine dictatorship'.
5 'The persecution of opponents of the regime brought about the "elimination" of the members of a Nation with the aim of "purifying" it.' *ABC*, 18 October 1998.

Garzón went much further than García Castellón in that he requested an international warrant for Pinochet's arrest for the disappearance and torture of various Chilean nationals,[6] and also asked the authorities in London to guarantee that Pinochet would remain on British soil pending his statement. García Castellón had not done this, as there was no formal accusation against Pinochet in his summary proceeding. Despite the specific nature of the accusation, the days following Pinochet's arrest saw a continual insistence that in both cases against members of the Chilean and Argentine military, the disappearance of Spanish citizens was a fundamental issue in order for the Spanish judicial system to intervene, a strategy clearly aimed at gaining the support of domestic public opinion. *ABC* stated that Garzón was seeking to 'interrogate Pinochet about the disappearance of Spanish citizens during the military regime' and a five-column headline appeared in *El Mundo* that read, 'Pinochet detained in a London clinic for the murder of Spanish citizens.'[7]

Once Pinochet had been detained, it was for the Audiencia Nacional to decide on Spanish competence in both summary proceedings. In the Argentine case, the *fiscal* (attorney general) deemed that Spain had no jurisdiction because the crimes being investigated were neither committed by Spanish nationals nor had they occurred in Spanish territory. Moreover, the accusations of genocide and terrorism were ruled out on the grounds that the prevailing law dated from 1985 whereas the crimes had been committed prior to this. Garzón maintained that there was Spanish legislation prior to 1973 that provided jurisdiction over crimes of genocide and terrorism outside the national territory and that the *punto final* laws (which put an end to domestic prosecutions of military personnel in Argentina), beyond any democratic legitimacy that they may have had, did not affect Spain as such.[8] On 19 October, the Attorney General's Office of the Spanish National High Court appealed against Garzón's arrest warrant. One argument made was that since Pinochet was a senator for life (with sovereign immunity) the petition for arrest and extradition had to be processed by the Supreme Court and not by a judge from the Audiencia Nacional. It was further considered to be contradictory for the indictment proceedings to be based on the Rettig Report (quoted various times as having evidential validity in the arrest warrant of 16 October) since this had also been used to try the same events in Chile.[9]

6 'Auto de Prision' in EM, 20 October 1998.
7 *ABC*, 18 October 1998 and EM, 18 October 1998.
8 *ABC*, 19 October 1998. Whereas the Amnesty Law in Chile was passed under the dictatorship, the Argentine Laws of Due Obedience and *punto final* were passed by a democratic parliament although some senior Argentine judges now question their constitutionality.
9 EM, 20 October 1998.

A particularly controversial element of the case against Pinochet was the charge of genocide, made by Garzón on the grounds of various 'illegal detentions followed in certain cases by the murder or disappearance of 91 ... victims'.[10] The crimes committed by Pinochet and the Argentine dictatorship were abhorrent, indeed words can hardly do them justice, but this should not be allowed to lead to serious errors of categorisation, which in legal terms must be precise. In attempting to convert the cases against the Argentine and Chilean military, due to the nature of the crimes they are supposed to have committed, into more wide-scale accusations against dictatorships as a whole, the crime of genocide and what it signifies was devalued. Furthermore, what is valid for Argentina or Chile is out of place in Spain. Political trials involving the Argentine and Chilean military dictatorships should not be held in Spain but in Argentina and Chile. Further, if a political trial was wanted in Spain, this should have been directed against the Franco regime. Such criticism however is for the Spanish people to make and not for the Argentine or Chilean authorities, whose use of this argument only muddied the waters further.

In his indictment of 98 Argentine military, Garzón insisted on the issue of genocide (racial, ethnic and religious persecution), making reference to Jews, and also, on 10 December 1998, to the Mapuche Indians. While it is true that a sector of the Argentine military is anti-Semitic, as is also the case with the federal and provincial police forces, the Jews had not actually been repressed. Neither did this argument fit with what was possibly the most emblematic case, that of Jacobo Timmerman, author of *Preso sin nombre, celda sin número* ('Prisoner with no name, cell with no number'), a chronicle of his arrest and torture. Timmerman was arrested for being a contentious journalist, although the fact that he was Jewish aggravated the conditions of his arrest. The Jewish community, or the Argentine Jews as such, was not systematically persecuted, nor was this considered. The Chamber of Criminal Proceedings (Sala de lo Penal) persevered in this line of argument, however, and, twisting its interpretation of genocide to the limit, it pointed out that the 1948 Treaty specified that 'the term 'national group' does not signify 'group made up of people who belong to the same nation', but simply national human group, distinctive human group, with a particular characteristic, integrated into a larger collective group as a whole ... The prevention and punishment of genocide as such ... cannot exclude particular distinctive national groups, due to the very nature of the system, by discriminating against them with respect to others'. It concluded by pointing out that 'all the victims, real or potential, and Chileans or foreigners in the country, formed a distinctive group that they [the dictatorship] tried to exterminate'.[11]

10 'Auto de prision,' EM, 20 October 1998.
11 Antonio Remiro Brotóns, *El caso Pinochet. Los límites de la impunidad* (Madrid, 1999), p. 80.

This interpretation of genocide is highly debatable. What group did the dictatorship want to destroy? What was the common denominator of the victims? Were they opposition, or possibly 'guerrillas'? If the group was some kind of 'opposition', were all those who were opposed grouped together or were there some who were exempted from repression? While some members of the Chilean Christian Democrat party, such as leading trade unionists, underwent repression, why not the majority? In an archive on the victims of the repression found in police premises in the province of Buenos Aires, all the files, carefully bound in wood, bore the inscription DS (*delincuentes subversivos*) – criminal subversives. Though itself a broad and diffuse definition lending itself to the wildest aberrations, this does convey the real target (in terms of both 'passive' and 'active' subversive activity) of repression in Argentina and Chile. There was indeed severe repression against the opposition, but this does not mean that there was genocide in either of these countries.

On Sunday 18 October Pedro Rubira, public prosecutor at the Audiencia Nacional, requested the revocation of Garzón's warrant, contending that the judge was exceeding his area of competence and that there had been a failure to notify the Attorney General's Office of the measures adopted in the issuing of the mandatory report. Senator Pinochet's status of sovereign immunity was also alluded to.[12] The Director of Public Prosecutions at the Audiencia Nacional, Eduardo Fungairiño, justified the opposition of the Attorney General's Office to extradition by arguing that Garzón's order to imprison Pinochet contravened the Constitution. He considered the international arrest warrant to be 'null and void in the full legal sense'. A key event for the future of the case then occurred on 20 October. García Castellón ceded the Chilean case that he had been dealing with to Garzón, on the basis that the genocide of which Pinochet was accused was a single crime, and that Garzón had begun to investigate it before him. Now the sole examining magistrate in both cases, Garzón gave them new momentum and applied his own personal style – an important element of which was his love of the limelight and media attention.

On 30 October the Audiencia Nacional's Chamber of Criminal Proceedings confirmed Spanish jurisdiction over the crimes of the dictatorships in Argentina and Chile, delivering a blow to the position of the government defended by the prosecutors Cardenal and Fungairiño. After four hours deliberation, the eleven judges of the Audiencia Nacional unanimously approved an unappealable resolution allowing Pinochet to be tried. While not alluding directly to genocide, the senior judge Carlos Cezón indicated that jurisdictional confirmation entailed the indirect acknowledgement of other crimes of genocide and

12 *El País* (EP), 20 October 1998 and ABC, 20 October 1998.

terrorism that should be investigated.[13] Other senior judges on the committee made similar comments. That same day the High Court of England and Wales released Pinochet on bail, dividing Spanish public opinion. *El País*'s account of the delivery of the decision eloquently conveyed the feelings of those present; 'The decision was read out to a public audience by the member of the bench ... in what was an extremely emotional ceremony. The judge had read just ten lines of the clauses in the resolution when relatives of the "disappeared" from both countries, who were present in the courtroom along with fifty or so reporters and around twenty lawyers, broke out in a combination of applause, hugs, shouts of "viva la justicia", or burst into tears of relief and joy.'[14]

The Spanish government and the extradition proceedings

The 6 November decision by the Council of Ministers (*Consejo de Ministros*) to file the petition for extradition marked another important moment in the proceedings. Chilean President Frei's government responded by recalling its ambassador in Madrid, Sergio Pizarro, a measure which did not signify the breaking off of relations with Spain but rather a strong expression of the Chilean government's dissatisfaction with the political handling of the case. From the first, the position of the Spanish government was controversial for the Chilean authorities, over and above the personal position of Aznar and his cabinet. The Chilean government's anger was focused in particular upon the Spanish Minister for Foreign Affairs, Abel Matutes, and this distrustful attitude was maintained throughout the proceedings, until the Spanish government finally rejected the possibility of international arbitration proposed by the Chilean Minister for Foreign Affairs, Juan Gabriel Valdés.

Aznar was in an uncomfortable situation. He wanted to avoid a conflict that would be detrimental to Spanish financial interests in Chile, and to avoid provoking the enmity of Christian Democrat President Frei, with whom he had a special relationship. His difficulty was exacerbated by the fact that the majority of public and press opinion, including many of his most loyal supporters, was in favour of extradition. The government believed that any support on its part for Pinochet to be tried in Chile, and the rejection of Garzón's aspirations to try him in Spain, would undermine Aznar's attempt to occupy the political centre ground. Its main objective was to distance itself from the right-wing associations that had long accompanied both the governing People's Party (Partido Popular – PP) and Aznar. For this reason, from the start of the Pinochet case, Aznar refused to hold a political debate on the matter.

13 EP, 18 October 1998.
14 EP, 31 October 1998.

The government's reaction must be examined in the context not only of developments in bilateral relations with Chile but also of an internal political conflict conditioning the behaviour of the main protagonists, all of whom had their own particular interpretation of the conflict from the Spanish point of view. With opinion poll data showing a majority in favour of extradition, and in the midst of his 'journey to the centre' (the PP's modernising enterprise to be seen as a moderate centre-right party rather than a hard-line party with authoritarian tendencies harking back to the Franco dictatorship), Aznar could hardly take Pinochet's side, for this would have associated him with the hardline position of the traditional right wing. While Margaret Thatcher was defending her Chilean 'friend', for the Spanish government to take a similar attitude would have given a political advantage to the Socialist Party (PSOE). Thus, the parliamentary spokesman for the PP, Luis de Grandes, declared that the PSOE 'had yet again reacted cynically and irresponsibly to a matter that affected the international relations of Spain'.[15] The ideal solution for the Spanish government would have been for a Chilean or British judge to have requested Pinochet's trial, effectively blocking the request for extradition (although, in the case of Chile, the Santiago Court of Appeals would first have had to accuse him). Aznar demonstrated his unwillingness to make a decision in a statement on 20 October, 'Depending on the result of the appeals, it is possible that it won't involve the government, the government probably won't even have to make a pronouncement.' The governmental position was also influenced by the ongoing debate over extraterritorial justice, an issue bound up with Spanish opposition to the application of the Helms–Burton Law, which threatened to have a negative impact on significant Spanish investments in Cuba, especially in the hotel sector.[16]

The Spanish authorities, in particular Foreign Minister Matutes, insisted on the government's respect for the judicial decisions[17] and refused to make any political gesture to bring their position closer to the Chilean government's, especially concerning the issue of the executive's role in making the extradition request. News of Pinochet's arrest coincided with the Eighth Latin American Summit in Oporto, attended by presidents Frei and Aznar, and Pinochet's extradition became a central issue in the discussion. An *El Mundo* editorial concluded that 'Garzón can request the extradition of the former dictator directly through

15 EM, 20 October 1998.

16 See Bert Hoffmannn, 'The Helms–Burton law and its consequences for Cuba, the United States and Europe,' paper delivered at the 1998 meeting of the Latin American Studies Association, http://136.142.158.105/LASA98/Hoffmannn.pdf.

17 The official position could be summed up as 'The Executive does not support the judges' actions in these cases [against the Chilean and Argentine military], but... there is very little that it can do to prevent it' EP, 18/x/98.

Interpol without Spanish diplomacy having to get involved at all'.[18] The Spanish government had 40 days from the time of Pinochet's arrest to request the British government to extradite him.

Aznar, in Oporto, called for 'responsibility and sound judgement' in a message directed at Garzón, at the same time asserting 'relations between Chile and Spain are splendid and I trust that nothing in the world will alter this'. According to Aznar, his government would respect the judicial decisions, co-operate with justice and assume international legality, though it would also demand 'real (… and sound) grounds' before requesting Pinochet's extradition through the Ministry of Justice. However, Aznar warned that 'there may be attorneys in Spain, in the Office of the Attorney General, for example, who believe that the investigation of certain events in other countries does not fall within the competency of the judges'.[19] Government sources signalled that the government's scope for action was very limited,[20] although the Chilean authorities urged them to be more explicit. The matter was concluded when the ruling that confirmed Spain's jurisdiction to judge Pinochet became known and the government spokesman, Josep Piqué, declared that the extradition request would be authorised.

So intense was the political and media pressure on the government that, according to the government-supporting *El Mundo*, a statement was issued from La Moncloa (the prime minister's official residence in Madrid) saying that 'the Government will respect the decisions of the competent courts'. According to the same source, 'the Government is of the belief that public opinion will not understand why the Council of Ministers opposed the Audiencia Nacional's decision to request the handing over of the former dictator … It will understand even less after having seen how the PSOE yesterday began to make political capital from a matter that came out of the blue and created one of the most uncomfortable situations for the Aznar government since 1996'. The vice-president Francisco Alvarez Cascos made a statement along the same lines; 'this is a judicial matter. The role of the Executive is to await their decisions with reiterated and insistent respect for the rulings.'[21] In the midst of the ambiguity of both the government and PP, one of the few dissonant voices on the right belonged to Manuel Fraga, former Francoist minister and president of the Autonomous Government of Galicia, who claimed that nobody had the right to

18 EM, 18 October 1998.
19 *La Vanguardia* (LV), 19 October 1998. The attorney general is appointed by the president of the government and there is a close interdependency between this position and the executive. The current head of the Attorney-General's Office, Jesús Cardenal, who occupied the post at the time, often conforms excessively with the wishes of the executive.
20 EM, 19 October 1998.
21 EM, 20 October 1998.

get involved in the affairs of another country.[22] Economic relations with Chile were another concern for the government, given the investments in Chile of some of the largest Spanish companies (Endesa, Telefónica, Banco Central Hispano, Banco Santander, BBV, Caja de Madrid, Dragados, Bazán) and a contract (worth 480 million euros) with the Chilean navy to supply Franco–Spanish 'Scorpene' submarines, the cancellation of which would have had negative effects for certain sectors of the Spanish economy.

The extradition procedure

After the government confirmed that it would authorise the extradition request a debate commenced over the precise nature of its role in the extradition proceedings. According to Enrique Gimbernat, professor of Criminal Law and a member of the editorial board of *El Mundo*, the extradition petition would have to be transmitted through the Ministry of Justice, which would act solely and exclusively as a 'mere courier, without entering into the underlying issues and without the power of veto'. His forthrightness was again shown when he emphatically affirmed that it would be difficult for the United Kingdom not to grant [Pinochet's] extradition given that genocide was one of the crimes that he was being charged with.[23] (Subsequently, in fact, the House of Lords consented to extradition but this was not on the basis of genocide.) Lawyers for the plaintiffs declared that it was a case of active extradition and that no adverse political decision was admissible; 'The government is a mere means of transmission and if it were to be rejected, this would be the first time in Spanish judicial history'.[24] The fact that it would have been the first time that something like this had occurred did not necessarily imply that it was illegal, but this was not mentioned.

Other jurists claimed that, as it was the government's responsibility to formulate the petition, it could evaluate the grounds for doing so. In line with this interpretation and, given that the petition for extradition is made by the Council of Ministers, it is quite logically a political decision. The state would thus be legally entitled not to file the petition for extradition if it considered that it was defending the national interest.[25] A central issue is whether the Spanish government relinquished its control over foreign policy by putting the matter into the hands of the judiciary. The handling of Pinochet's extradition was a serious matter not only because it created a dangerous precedent but also because it had a negative impact upon diplomatic relations with two South American countries and with Latin America in general. It should also be

22 D16, 20 October 1998.
23 EM, 19 October 1998.
24 EP, 19 October 1998.
25 EP, 19 October 1998.

recognised that, according to the Spanish Constitution, responsibility for the conduct of foreign policy corresponds to the government and not the judiciary.

Another line of argument was offered by Diego López Garrido, professor of Constitutional Law and secretary general of Nueva Izquierda, a minority splinter group of IU that inclined towards the PSOE. He opined that the government could in fact block the extradition by simply letting the legal period of 40 days expire. Accepting this interpretation, the PSOE parliamentary deputy María Teresa Fernández de la Vega, declared 'that would be scandalous'.[26] The various opinions expressed not only reflected different points of view, but also sought to influence the government's decision. Lawyers for the plaintiffs claimed that a negative decision by the Executive 'would leave the Government seriously marred' and that both Fungairiño and Cardenal had 'acted as defence lawyers for Pinochet by placing all possible obstacles in the path of the investigation'.[27] Another topic of discussion was the grounds for extradition. A British jurist described Garzón's indictment as a 'botch job' (*chapuza*) and doubted that British justice would concede it on the basis of accusations of genocide and terrorism, a position that contradicted that of Gimbernat. According to this British jurist, the position would have been much clearer had the accusations been classified as murder – although Garzón would have had serious problems applying Spanish jurisdiction to this.[28]

Both the judicial system and public opinion were concerned as to whether or not Spain had jurisdiction to judge Pinochet. Carlos Castresana pointed out

the public prosecutors of the Audiencia Nacional maintain that Spanish jurisdiction is not competent to try Pinochet, but this is not true. The competence of the Spanish Courts has been recognised in this case by the Plenary Session of the European Parliament, by the Office of the Director for Public prosecutions of the Swiss Confederation, by the Courts of Justice of France, Italy, Sweden, Germany and Uruguay, by the United States Department of Justice, and also now by the United Kingdom. It has also been upheld by Amnesty International and numerous institutions, bodies and associations and by the most highly prestigious academic authorities. It is surprising to see the stubbornness of Spain's denial, in an institutional position supported by president Aznar in statements made last year to the Chilean newspaper *El Mercurio*, of what has been recognised in Spain itself by the entire international community.[29]

The issue of Spanish competence initially became one of the few ways open to the government to extricate itself. A decision concerning the dispute would

---

26 EP, 19 October 1998.
27 EP, 19 October 1998.
28 EM, 20 October 1998.
29 Carlos Castresana, 'Crimen y castigo,' EM, 20 October 1998

eventually devolve upon the Plenary Session of the Audiencia Nacional, all except the judges of Section Three, as they would theoretically be responsible for Pinochet's trial, if events ever came to that.[30]

Social forces

The government's position became increasingly difficult with the alignment of the opposition and majority public opinion behind the request for extradition. As an *El Mundo* editorial put it after the ruling on Spanish jurisdiction, 'The social majority in favour of the despised general paying for his sins is so significant that even the judges themselves must have taken it into account. Conceptually speaking, the bad guys lose this time and the good guys win … The decision of the Audiencia Nacional can be described as 'historic' because it will enable Garzón to pursue those responsible for thousands of disappearances and murders in Chile and Argentina wherever they may be'.[31]

The day after Pinochet's arrest, both the PSOE and the IU, together with the Asociación Progresista de Fiscales (APF), asked the government to uphold the extradition proceedings. For Rafael Estrella, PSOE spokesman in the Commission on Foreign Affairs in Congress, Pinochet's arrest was 'good news for all democrats and for those of us who maintain that crimes against humanity have no frontiers', as it entailed Pinochet's 'humiliation'. The IU Secretary for Foreign Policy, Pedro Marset, expressed satisfaction at the 'arrest of one of the biggest criminals in humanity' and asked the government to 'rise to the occasion'. The APF considered the arrest to be a 'historic event'.[32] Various associations, including the moderate senior judges' association Francisco de Vitoria, the progressive group Judges for Democracy (Jueces para la Democracia) and the Association of Attorneys (Asociación de Fiscales), expressed satisfaction at the arrest, while the conservative Asociación Profesional de la Magistratura (Association of Magistrates) 'expects actions to be based on solid judicial criteria'.[33] On 22 October the Consejo General de la Abogacía (Law Society) hoped for 'not one case of the crimes that Mr Pinochet is charged with to remain unpunished'.

The UPF adopted a belligerent position and on 19 October asked for Cardenal, Fungairiño and the attorneys representing the Argentine and Chilean causes to stand down, arguing that their systematic opposition to the investigations amounted to a failure to comply with the function of the Ministerio Público (Public Prosecutor) to defend the law.[34] Carlos Castresana appeared outside the

30 EP, 20 October 1998.
31 EM, 31 October 1998.
32 EP, 18 October 1998 and LV, 19 October 1998.
33 LV, 19 October 1998.
34 ABC, 20 October 1998.

Audiencia Nacional as people celebrated the ruling confirming Spanish jurisdiction to say, 'This is the first decisive step made in fulfilment of the moral obligation that Spain owes to its citizens who were among the disappeared, along with the entire international community'.[35] Here, the figure of Franco may be seen as linked to that of Pinochet and a psychoanalytical interpretation might point to a transference effect – the impulse to do to Pinochet what was not done to Franco. Francisco Umbral plays with this idea in an article entitled '*El caudillo*'; 'for the Spanish people, Pinochet's arrest is the vicarious dream of a historical impossibility, that of Franco being arrested in bed ... *Qué fuego de justicia se despierta en nosotros, qué tardía revancha, qué cuchillo* (How the fire of justice burns within us, what belated revenge, how the knife [cuts]).'[36] PSOE official spokesman Alfredo Pérez Rubalcaba declared, 'If only we could have done the same with Franco'.[37] The message sent out to public opinion was clear; as it was not possible to punish those who repressed us, given the exigencies of the transition process in Spain, now that it is possible, let's do it to others, in this case Pinochet and the Chilean people, irrespective of their own process of transition.

The political debates were reproduced in judicial circles, in associations of lawyers and attorneys and also as far as individual opinions were concerned. It is important here to emphasise the polarised and politicised nature of Spanish justice, which may be observed every time parliament has to elect the members of the Council for the Judiciary (Consejo General del Poder Judicial) or the Constitutional Court (Tribunal Constitucional), and also in the pattern of promotions of judges and investigating magistrates. When Spanish jurisdiction was upheld, Juan José Martínez Zato, head of the Board of Public Prosecutions (Inspección Fiscal) and politically speaking a progressive, called for the team of public prosecutors to be dismissed and expressed satisfaction at the pronouncement of the Audiencia Nacional; 'Today is a great day for Spanish justice, and [... what has occurred] has reinforced its international prestige.'[38]

Similar claims were made by human rights associations and by relatives of the disappeared Argentines and Chileans in Spain. Carlos Slepoy, a lawyer for the plaintiffs against the Argentine military, became another media star,[39] expressing 'satisfaction' at Pinochet's detention and 'its enormous symbolic

35   EM, 31 October 1998.
36   Francisco Umbral, 'El caudillo,' EM, 20 October 1998.
37   EP, 19 October 1998.
38   EP, 31 October 1998.
39   An article in EP on 31 October 1998 commenting on the ruling by the Audiencia Nacional that recognised Spanish jurisdiction, reports: 'Carlos Slepoy, one of the lawyers who has fought hardest in the proceedings relating to disappearances and murders in Argentina, burst into tears on hearing the court's decision and could not stop until over an hour later.'

value, for it is a clear message to those who commit genocide anywhere in the world'.[40] Another constant element in the proceedings began to take shape in the form of references to recourse to law as a panacea against impunity, encapsulated in the slogan '*viva la justicia*'.[41] The same people who, before the fall of the Berlin Wall, advocated armed revolution and loathed bourgeois institutions, starting with justice and corrupt judges, now placed their confidence in the unlimited possibilities of the selfsame justice. Ana María Flores of the Chilean Human Rights Association (Asociación Pro Derechos Humanos Chilena) claimed Pinochet's arrest as a tremendous advance for justice in the struggle against dictatorial impunity.[42] After the 30 October ruling by the Audiencia Nacional, Slepoy waxed lyrical,

> This example needs to be repeated everywhere, in all the countries of America, Africa, Asia and Europe … where tribunals need to be set up to pursue persons guilty of genocide so that they know that they will be ceaselessly persecuted. If justice in Spain or in other countries had acted when the military coups began to occur, thousands of people would be alive today.[43]

No thought was given to the fact that it was a Chilean who was being persecuted and not a citizen of the United States or Great Britain, France or Germany. In the field of global justice, the figure of Garzón was soon to stand out like that of a visionary, followed by a cohort of flatterers and supporters, a latter-day Robin Hood and a courageous and righteous judge. 'Garzón is a judge who is hunting down widespread international fascism, a man who is globalising justice, a kind of Montesquieu in a helicopter.'[44] After the Audiencia Nacional confirmed Spanish jurisdiction, 'the most enthusiastic applause and cheering could be heard when Baltasar Garzón left the Audiencia Nacional.'[45]

Victims' relatives and Chilean and Argentine human rights associations also became omnipresent protagonists in Spanish public life and a further factor exerting pressure on justice and the authorities. When the Audiencia Nacional met to decide on Spanish jurisdiction, around 200 relatives of the disappeared and sympathisers from human rights associations assembled at the doors of the Court from 9 a.m. with placards demanding Pinochet's punishment, justice for the victims and declaring support for Garzón. They remained chanting slogans and singing songs until 2.30 p.m. when the ruling was made known, breaking

40 LV, 18 October 1998.
41 This cry erupted when the Audiencia Nacional ruling on Spanish jurisdiction was made known, EP, 31 October 1998.
42 LV, 18 October 1998.
43 EM, 31 October 1998.
44 Francisco Umbral, 'El caudillo,' EM, 20 October 1998.
45 EP, 31 October 1998.

out with cries of joy in the midst of hugs and sobbing.[46] One senior judge from the Audiencia, who was in the courtroom when the ruling was read out, was next to one of the *madres de Plaza de Mayo* who told him 'Thank you'. The judge replied 'No, thank you.'[47]

The Opposition

From the time of Pinochet's arrest, the Opposition feared that the government would not process the extradition request or would stymie it. The Socialist deputy Joaquín Leguina expressed his suspicion that it would all 'come to nothing' in the face of biased action by the Attorney General's Office. IU, itself a plaintiff in the proceedings, announced its intention to present the extradition request before the end of the stipulated time limit.[48] Víctor Ríos, a leading figure within IU, accused Aznar of protecting Pinochet,[49] which was undoubtedly untrue. In truth, the Spanish government was concerned more about relations with the Chilean government and with Frei than with protecting Pinochet. There was intense pressure in its ranks in favour of trial and extradition, while voices defending the senator were isolated or practically non-existent.

The PSOE, the main opposition party, responded to the Pinochet case in the same way as to other political challenges; internally divided and with serious leadership problems as a result of an ongoing struggle between the Secretary General, Joaquín Almunia, and the party's hierarchy's preferred leadership 'candidate' José Borrell. The PSOE had held primary elections for a candidate who would stand up to Aznar, in which Borrell had defeated Almunia. From then on the PSOE was characterised by a strange bicephalism which obstructed its internal functioning. Faced with these serious internal problems, the Pinochet case provided the PSOE and its leaders with a golden opportunity to reinforce their role as the opposition and to humiliate the government by harping on its right-wing character. The Socialist spokesman in the Senate, Juan José Laborda, exaggeratedly accused the government and the PP of adopting a 'pro-Franco ideological attitude' by subordinating the law and democratic values to 'supposed national interests'.[50]

The PP struck back by accusing the PSOE of incoherence and once more stirred up the GAL issue (*Grupos Antiterroristas de Liberación* – an organisation

46 EP, 31 October 1998.
47 EM, 31 October 1998.
48 D16, 19 October 1998.
49 EM, 20 October 1998.
50 Accusations of something or somebody being 'pro-Franco' are frequently used in political language and in the press when trying to discredit them. Such accusations are not just the preserve of the left.

responsible for a 'dirty war' against ETA in the 1980s and in whose activities the PSOE was implicated) to accuse both the PSOE and the former heads of the Ministry of the Interior of state terrorism. On 22 October Luis de Grandes, the PP parliamentary spokesman, said 'the scant sensitivity shown [by the PSOE] for the transgression of human rights undermines the opposition party's demands to the government in relation to the request for the extradition of Augusto Pinochet'. Three days later, responding to Socialist criticisms of his position, Aznar expressed his concern that 'we all show ourselves capable of respecting the judicial decisions and of not making foolish remarks and so turn this matter into a political issue.'

PSOE spokesman Pérez Rubalcaba initially welcomed Pinochet's detention as good news, although he made no announcement concerning the party's position, which would be decided at the Federal Executive Meeting on 19 October;[51] several days later he recalled that, in articles written twenty years previously, Aznar had professed support for Pinochet. The secretary general of the PSOE, Joaquín Almunia, called on the government not to obstruct the extradition proceedings, and to confine itself to requesting extradition, arguing that any attempt to hinder the proceedings would be 'interfering' in the jurisdiction of the courts.[52] The PSOE wanted to bring the Pinochet case into Parliament and prepared a series of motions against the government. Borrell would put forward a question for Aznar and the Socialist group would request the attendance of the Minister of Justice, Margarita Mariscal de Gante and the Chief Prosecutor, Jesús Cardenal.[53]

As part of its policy in support of extradition proceedings and against the PP, the PSOE wanted to take the matter to the European Parliament, in order to maximise pressure on the government. It was supported in this by the European Socialists and other parliamentary groups (Greens, Liberals, Radicals and the IU) and a proposal was adopted urging the government to process the request for extradition. Consequently, the PP and the PSOE confronted each other in the Eurochamber, with the PP arguing that the chamber should not interfere in a judicial matter pending resolution. On 22 October a plenary meeting of the European Parliament adopted a ruling urging the Spanish government, 'in case the judicial authorities so require it', to request Pinochet's extradition 'as soon as possible'.

From the start, former PSOE president Felipe González deviated from the party line, adopting a studiedly respectful stance towards Chile and the Concertación government. During the week of Pinochet's arrest, he cancelled a

51 EP, 19 October 1998.
52 EM, 20 October 1998.
53 D16, 20 October 1998.

visit to Chile at Ricardo Lagos' invitation because the Spanish government had not yet made a pronouncement concerning the extradition proceedings, and because he did not want to interfere in the debate between the Chilean Socialists and Christian Democrats.[54] His forthright words and the clear contradiction between his stance and that of the PSOE led Almunia to declare on 26 October that 'Felipe González has every right to express his opinions but the position of the (Socialist) Executive has been, is and will continue to be that the government cannot restrain, boycott or engage in governmental filibustering to delay [the extradition]'. González's position was inconvenient for Borrell, who tried to distance himself from the former secretary general's statements. This was interpreted by some in the media as part of the internal struggle between the Socialists for the control of the party.[55] When the Audiencia Nacional upheld Spanish jurisdiction, González expressed satisfaction and asked the government to 'process the decision of the courts'.[56] Aware that he was going 'against the current', he clarified his opinions, saying that he would not like the case to 'be a precedent to be used by other countries as an abuse of power' and that 'it is very difficult for extraterritoriality to be applied in criminal justice without consequent abuses occurring and [I'm] not [talking about] small and medium-sized countries like us'. Finally, he hoped that 'we won't regret this decision in the future'.[57] González's attitude was heavily criticised, especially by *El Mundo*, which had carried out a veritable crusade against him during the last years of his government. 'Politicians and judges congratulated themselves on the ruling by the Audiencia Nacional [on Spanish jurisdiction]. There was only one exception, Felipe González, who took the precaution of warning of the danger that this decision might set a precedent 'in other countries'. Was he thinking about the GAL case by any chance?'[58]

Rosa Aguilar, a parliamentary spokeswoman for IU, called on the government to respect the judicial proceedings and not to interfere in the extradition process.[59] López Garrido (Nueva Izquierda) announced that his party would back declarations of support for Pinochet's extradition in town halls, the autonomous regional communities and in Congress and called for absolute respect from the government for the autonomy of the judicial authorities; he also considered the possibility of co-ordinating with other parties to call for street demonstrations.[60]

54 EP, 20 October 1998.
55 EM, 4 November 1998.
56 EP, 31 October 1998.
57 EM, 31 October 1998.
58 EM, 31 October 1998.
59 EP, 19 October 1998.
60 EP, 19 October 1998.

The autonomous government authorities and nationalist parties also participated in the debate. Both the Partido Nacionalista Vasco (PNV) and Convergència i Unió (CiU), the parties in power in the Basque Country and Catalonia, were allies of the central Spanish government and supported it in Parliament. Iñaki Anasagasti, spokesman for the PNV in Congress, applauded the bold judicial action and called for the government to request extradition, saying that not to do so would be to 'give precedence to commercial interests over human and democratic ones'.[61] Jordi Pujol, president of Catalonia, said that 'Pinochet's arrest is morally positive for everybody's conscience and for each of us individually', because the acts of the dictatorship 'have not been forgotten and are not covered by a statute of limitations' and for this reason 'it is right and positive that someone like Pinochet knows that he can't go around doing things with total impunity'. He also called for the legal and political dimensions of the case to be clarified by the governments of Madrid, London and Santiago.[62]

A further issue debated was the process of transition in Chile and the ability of Frei's government to withstand what Spain and Europe generally seemed to view as constant and overwhelming pressure from the army. Announcements of meetings of the Chilean National Security Council (Consejo de Seguridad Nacional) were met with concern, with the intentions of the military chiefs, rather than the response of the government, seen as the main issue. Fear was also expressed about a deep division in Chilean society between supporters and opponents of Pinochet. This picture of a country irreconcilably divided in two was exaggerated and bore little or no relation to the reality within Chilean society – the majority of whose members experienced the Pinochet case as a matter of minor importance. The economic situation and the presidential elections were much greater preoccupations than the Pinochet case. Moreover, with considerations about bilateral relations and the future of Spanish investments in Chile at stake, Spanish public opinion was sensitive to the show of anti-Spanish sentiment by Pinochet's supporters in Chile. This however was merely one more piece of information feeding existing feelings in favour of extradition; the reasoning behind which could be summed up as 'if they are protesting against us and burning the Spanish flag, then it is because Garzón is right.'

One of the few dissenting voices was that of Chilean writer Jorge Edwards, who wrote regularly for *El País*. His bold points of view conflicted with those expressed by most of his compatriots both in that newspaper and others such as *El Mundo* and *Diario16*. His leading articles were often flanked by comments from Chileans including Ariel Dorfman, Isabel Allende and Luis Sepúlveda

---

61   EM, 20 October 1998 and D16 20 October 1998.
62   EM, 20 October 1998, EP, 20 October 1998 and D16 20 October 1998.

who opposed his arguments and advocated Pinochet's trial in Spain. Only a few people supported the idea of a trial in Chile on the basis of democratic arguments. This was the case of Oscar Alzaga, Emilio Lamo de Espinosa and the present author.[63] In his first article, Edwards wondered about the real reaction of Chile and commented optimistically, 'I believe that the country will declare itself in favour of becoming a modern democracy that is free of tutelage and ghosts, and in favour of being part of the contemporary world.'[64] The problem was the scant impact of Edwards' good sense and the lack of interest in really getting to the bottom of the problems that Chile was facing. Very little attention was given to the lawsuits against Pinochet and others in Chile despite the fact that at the time of his arrest eleven cases had already been initiated in Chile. *El País* was the first to print this news, which appeared as a small inset.[65]

One of the first arguments against extradition to Spain was made by the associate director of *La Vanguardia*, Lluis Foix, who declared,

> Garzón and García Castellón are entitled to hold a dictator responsible for the many deaths of Chileans and several Spanish citizens that he caused. The thing that troubles me, however, is what historical and moral authority does Spanish justice have to hold a dictator in a foreign country to account? The lure of the limelight for some judges knows no bounds.[66]

This stance combined the question of Spain's right to judge Pinochet in light of its own process of transition while aiming a poisoned dart at Garzón who, throughout the proceedings, received a great deal of criticism for his lust for being at centre stage.

The press

In the days following Pinochet's arrest, press coverage (as well as that of radio and TV) was intense. Numerous pages and leading articles were devoted to the story, though most showed a lack of awareness of the real situation in Chile.

---

63 Carlos Malamud: 'Garzón y la dictadura argentina,' *El Correo* (Bilbao) (EC), 29 September 1996; 'Un antidemócrata vitalicio,' EC, 19 February 1998; 'Las desdichas de un senador (vitalicio),' EC, 22 October 1998; 'Con golpe, Pinochet no vuelve,' EC, 1 December 1998; 'Preguntas y reflexiones en torno a Pinochet,' *Escenarios Alternativos*, No. 6 (Buenos Aires, 1999); 'El factor Pinochet,' D16, 14 December 1999; 'La solution está en Chile,' EC, 13 January 2000; 'Chile, su futuro y sus fantasmas,' D16, 18 January 2000; 'Las perplejidades de Chile,' *Expansion* (E), 21 January 2000; 'La hora de los Chilean está más cerca,' D16, 1 February 2000; 'La rueda de la justice,' D16, 3 March 2000; '¿Quién manda en Chile, Lagos o Pinochet?,' EC, 8 March 2000.
64 Jorge Edwards, 'El susto del dictador,' EP, 20 October 1998.
65 EP, 20 October 1998.
66 LV, 18 October 1998.

The affair continued to be of great interest over the following months, the level of coverage fluctuating along with developments in the proceedings. The press, which mostly supported extradition (especially *El País*, *El Mundo* and *Diario 16*), was an important source of pressure. A more subtle line was taken by both *ABC* and the Barcelona-based *La Vanguardia*. *El Mundo* was the most radical: 'Judicial sources have declared ... that it is improbable that the Ministry of Foreign Affairs will oppose the processing of extradition proceedings ... because it would be a great scandal both nationally and internationally.' We are also of the belief that it will not use the strategy of drawing out the extradition proceedings in order for the 40 mandatory days to expire.' 'We know that both Matutes and Aznar have made comments to the effect that they will not oppose the extradition proceedings', the same sources pointed out. 'The Government has declared its formal opposition, expressed through the prosecutor, although we do not believe that it will go any further than this. We even believe that Eduardo Fungairiño will realise that he has been giving the impression of being a fascist and will finally change his position,' they added.[67] The same newspaper commented in an editorial that 'Aznar's caution is unsettling. He appeals to the "[moral] sensibilities" that are in play. So in the final analysis, he should be pointing to the repudiation of the human rights violations committed during the Pinochet dictatorship. That is what the centrist position that Aznar advocates so much is all about.'[68]

The less strident line followed by *La Vanguardia* was demonstrated in an editorial which recognised that; 'the wish of democratic Europe is that Pinochet's crimes should not remain unpunished', but added three important caveats, pointing out that; (1) Pinochet is not the only cruel dictator in the world's recent history, (2) it would have been better for an international criminal court to act instead of Spanish justice, and (3) it was advisable to work in support of Latin American stability, which could be affected by such an event. On the same day, the newspaper published a leading article aimed at focusing attention upon issues of stability and democracy in Chile and Latin America as a whole.[69]

The first leading articles favourable to the trial in Spain referred repeatedly to two aspects of the matter, one being the idea that 'well, if we can't do it, it's good that another country should' (Isabel Allende) and the other being the obstacles imposed by the Attorney-General's Office (*Fiscalía*) of the Audiencia Nacional, together with the negative work carried out by Chief Prosecutor Fungairiño (who is supposed to have written a report in which he defined the Argentine and Chilean dictatorships as 'temporary interruptions of the

67 EM, 19 October 1998.
68 EM, 19 October 1998.
69 LV, 22 October 1998.

constitutional order' in the name of national peace).[70] In an editorial on 20 October *El Mundo* criticised the attitude of President Frei, who had questioned the legitimacy of Spain to judge Pinochet while doing nothing about the crimes of the civil war and the Franco dictatorship, and raised the question of what would happen if the Chilean judicial system started a lawsuit to do with the GAL case. After refuting Frei's arguments, the newspaper added, 'He says … that crimes committed by Chilean citizens should be judged in Chile. But that's the whole problem, in Chile they don't want to try Pinochet!'[71] Along the same lines is the argument, repeated again and again, that nobody is above the law. People also talked about the globalisation of justice, the International Criminal Court and the idea that the end of the Cold War had put an end to the principle of non-interference in the internal affairs of each country which had benefited dictators up until that time. An editorial in *La Vanguardia* stated, 'Fortunately, the situation has changed, or is changing, and there are more and more voices and facts that proclaim exactly the opposite … the right to intervene in the internal affairs of a country to put an end to situations where there is continual violation of human rights.'[72]

Many journalists with regular columns, such as Gabriel Albiac and Martín Prieto in *El Mundo*, or Ernesto Ekaizer and Manuel Vázquez Montalbán in *El País*, launched a crusade against Pinochet. Martín Prieto said, 'We'll know how much consideration Aznar gives to human rights according to whether the Spanish government supports the judges in the Audiencia Nacional or not' and 'I fear the worst; the triumph of the most despicable diplomacy over justice … The pathway to moral destitution has already been well trodden and the prosecutors Fungairiño and Cardenal have presented an abundance of legal theories endorsing institutional barbarity, deeming it impossible for any armed forces to turn into a band of bloodthirsty criminals. Ultimately it is the purchase of Spanish armaments by Chile or Anglo–Chilean friendship from the days of the Falklands War, as Fidel Castro recalled, that will prevail. Of course, there is still the possibility of bombing Milosevic's Belgrade. Judging the barbarian who broke the hands of Víctor Jara before he was shot in the Santiago stadium is an inappropriate extravagance of State justice.'[73]

Manuel Vázquez Montalbán touched upon a central issue for the supporters of extradition, namely that action was necessary because Chile was a supervised democracy, that the process of transition was incomplete and that Pinochet could never be tried in Chile. 'Democracy in Chile is on probation, just another

70   D16, 14 October 1998.
71   EM, 20 October 1998.
72   'Cerco a Pinochet,' LV, 20 October 1998.
73   EM, 19 October 1998.

in a geopolitical network of open societies that are merely open until the curfew is sounded.'[74] This is why Chilean society 'finds itself dramatically divided'.[75] According to the Spanish press, the growing polarisation of Chilean society was shown in the demonstrations by Pinochet's followers and anti-Pinochet demonstrators in Santiago, yet no reference was made to how minor these demonstrations were. According to *El Mundo*, 'While there is an increasing feeling in Europe that Pinochet will be tried, in Chile the situation is so tense that it could endanger the process of transition itself.'[76] What the Spanish journalists did not understand, or preferred to say nothing about, was that the confrontation between the staunch defenders of Pinochet and the relatives of the victims did not involve all Chileans, but only a minority.

Fear of judging Pinochet and of the reaction of the armed forces was another subject commented on in the Spanish press. The *El País* correspondent in Chile, Francesc Ralea, stated that 'the fear that has prevailed in Chile during seventeen years of dictatorship and eight years of democracy hamstrung by the omnipresent figure of Pinochet is still choking people's consciences' and reinforced his view with the words of the jurist Andrés Dominguez, 'People are frightened, paralysed with fear.'[77] He saw the Concertación as at risk of breakdown at any moment; 'The Christian Democrat and Socialist coalition government is going through its worst time since the beginning of the transition nine years ago … The PS (Socialist Party) is increasingly uncomfortable with the Government's steps to secure the former dictator's release at any price, in which it has hardly been consulted.'[78] This account reveals how highly sensitised public opinion had become in Spain. Qualifying adjectives easily crept in concerning the Pinochet case or human rights violations and it was difficult to hold any calm discussion in the news media. I experienced this in two TV discussions with Carlos Slepoy where the mere fact of upholding the view that Pinochet should be tried in Chile, or that Chile could try Pinochet, was considered to be an act of complicity with the dictator. Sentences like 'It would be tremendous if the Chilean butcher's last lawyer turned out to be Spain'[79] featured frequently in the discussion.

There were those who were against putting Pinochet on trial, though their opinions tended to be indirectly expressed. José María Carrascal, in *ABC*, pointed out that it would be right if Fidel Castro was simultaneously tried for

74   EP, 19 October 1998.
75   Baltasar Porcel, 'El fiel Augusto,' LV, 20 October 1998.
76   EM, 19 October 1998.
77   EP, 21 October 1998.
78   EP, 31 October 1998.
79   C. Sánchez-Vicente, 'Sensibilidad,' LV, 20 October 1998.

his crimes or that a similar measure might allow for the imprisonment of Felipe González in France in the GAL affair, and concluded by arguing that initiatives of this type would make dictators reluctant to stand down, as Pinochet had done in his time.[80] Federico Jiménez Lozanitos was more forceful, saying; 'It is decidedly sinister to try to apprehend a retired dictator while an acting dictator like Fidel Castro, who is much more of a criminal and has been around a lot longer than Pinochet, is treated with such consideration.'[81] Francisco Umbral also invoked the figure of Castro but from an opposing perspective, in accusing Aznar of neo-fascism – 'turning his nose up at Fidel whereas for him Pinochet was untouchable'.[82] Coinciding in some aspects of the previous argument were those, such as Antonio Burgos, who argued that human rights are not the preserve of the left and that Aznar should head the campaign for Pinochet's extradition instead of being opposed to it, since such opposition was tantamount to tarring oneself as the 'same old bad old right'.[83]

The figure of Castro was invoked almost throughout the media, beginning with his astonished reaction (when at the Oporto summit) to Pinochet's arrest, and continuing with many columnists calling for Castro and all dictators to undergo the same fate. The media was also concerned by the anti-Spanish sentiment detected in certain Chilean circles, especially those closest to the right, and the potential for this to jeopardise the future of Spanish investments in Chile. A headline in *Diario 16* said, 'There is an increasing anti-Spanish sentiment amongst the Chilean people who support the general', and cited the words of Joaquín Lavín 'we are fed up with being humiliated'.[84]

Conclusion

I have argued here that throughout the case, and not simply in the initial stages, all the protagonists, including those more strictly involved in the legal aspects, were involved in political intrigue, and thus emphasis must be placed on how the matter was interpreted from the domestic political point of view. Political parties tried to obtain political advantage that, if possible, could be translated into electoral support. The Pinochet case was a matter of international politics and also of national law and order at the same time, and thus the particular political situation in Spain influenced the reactions of the various leading characters. Particularly important was the fact that, for the PSOE, the Pinochet

80   ABC, 19 October 1998.
81   Federico Jiménez Losantos, 'X-2,' EM, 20 October 1998.
82   Francisco Umbral, 'El caudillo,' EM, 20 October 1998.
83   Antonio Burgos, 'Aznar y la capa de Pinochet,' EM, 20 October 1998.
84   D16, 25 October 1998.

case came at a time of profound division in the party following its experience in the primary elections, while for the PP, it came as it was in the midst of its 'journey to the centre'.

These circumstances gave rise to a curious unanimity within the parties regarding people's judgements and attitudes toward the Pinochet case. There were two notable exceptions, one in the PP and the other in the PSOE, and both were cases of top-rank members in their respective parties. Both Manuel Fraga, the president of the Autonomous Community of Galicia, and Felipe González, the former prime minister, are above and beyond their party leaderships with a political substance of their own, independent of their party, that enabled them to express their private views in public when others would have preferred them to keep their thoughts to themselves. This explains why they were among the few to criticise the prospect of Pinochet's trial in Madrid and why they maintained their independence of mind over and above any tactical considerations connected with the party struggle in Spain.

In general, very few voices were to be heard defending Pinochet in the discussion in Spain, because public opinion had overwhelmingly demonised the figure of Pinochet, condemning him prior to his trial to the extent that any support for the general's position was viewed as equivalent to defending fascism. There were also a very few people who, while not defending Pinochet, nevertheless opposed his being tried in Spain or any other European country on the grounds that it was a matter that directly concerned Chile and the Chilean people and their own process of democratic transition.

Notwithstanding its erratic policy during the conflict, it is important to place on record the concern of the Spanish government for the state of diplomatic and economic relations with Chile. In this respect, Aznar's government showed itself to be in a difficult position, hostage to events, and so always dragged along by them rather than being in charge of the situation. Nevertheless, the Chilean government was particularly outraged by the way that Aznar's government handled the crisis because it felt that, rather than fully assuming its responsibilities, it had reacted to events, not from the perspective of State policy, but rather from short-term political considerations. It thereby relinquished the role of leadership in foreign policy which, according to the Spanish Constitution, corresponds to the executive and not the judiciary.

CHAPTER 9

The consequences of the Pinochet case for Chilean politics

Carlos Huneeus

The arrest of Pinochet in October 1998 had serious consequences not only for the Chilean political system but also for the man who had been Chile's powerful dictator for seventeen years,[1] now detained as a common criminal.[2] The government of the Concertación de Partidos por la Democracia (Group of Pro-Democracy Parties) under President Eduardo Frei Ruiz-Tagle found itself in the uncomfortable situation of having to reject Spanish jurisdiction and take measures to ensure the old general's return to Chile, seen by many as 'defending' Pinochet. Changes from one political regime to another are far more complex than they appear on our television screens. The Chilean government's stance can only be understood in the context of Chile's particular transition to democracy, guided by the strategy of reform rather than rupture,[3] which passed through the institutions set up by the dictatorship. It had been respect for the rule of law that had induced the military to return to their barracks following Pinochet's defeat in the plebiscite of 5 October 1988, and which had permitted the consolidation of democracy during the 1990s.

Faced with the fact of the arrest, the Chilean Government's position could hardly have been more uncomfortable. Three important members of President Eduardo Frei Ruiz-Tagle's cabinet (1994–2000) had themselves been victims of the Pinochet regime. Chancellor José Miguel Insulza had been exiled in Italy and Mexico. The Minister of Public Works, Jaime Tohá, had been held in a

I am grateful to Alejandra López of CERC, Chile, for her help.

1 See C. Huneeus, *El régimen de Pinochet* (Santiago, 2001)
2 For an excellent account of Pinochet´s detention see Mónica Pérez and Felipe Gerdtzen, *Augusto Pinochet: 503 días atrapado en Londres* (Santiago, 2000). The authors are journalists from Chile's *Televisión Nacional* who covered the case in Madrid and London, using previously unknown material. Gerdtzen is President Frei's son-in-law.
3 For further information see Juan J. Linz and Alfred Stepan, *Problems of Democratic Transition and Consolidation* (Baltimore, 1996).

concentration camp for several months and had undergone torture; his brother José, Allende's ex-Interior minister, had died as a consequence of the physical and psychological abuse he had suffered while detained on Dawson Island in the extreme South of Chile, where ministers and leaders of Allende's Unidad Popular (Popular Unity) were held after the military coup. Jorge Arrate had been president of the Partido Socialista (Socialist Party) at the beginning of the 1990s and was now General Secretary of the Government. After serving as minister for mines for a few weeks in 1972, he was later to suffer exile in Holland. President Frei's own father, Eduardo Frei Montalva, had himself been president between 1964 and 1970. He died at the end of January 1982, in a Santiago clinic, whilst undergoing routine surgery. His death has been blamed by some on the involvement of the dictatorship's Secret Services.[4]

This chapter is divided into five parts. The first briefly describes General Pinochet's role in Chilean politics since 1973, as a background for analysis of the far-reaching consequences of his arrest in London. A second examines the policies followed in relation to the Pinochet case by President Frei Ruiz-Tagle's government and the differences evident in the governing coalition, the Concertación por la Democracia, made up of the Partido Demócrata Cristiano (PDC, Christian Democratic Party) the Partido Socialista (PS, Socialist Party), the Partido por la Democracia (PPD, Pro-Democracy Party) and the Partido Radical Social Demócrata (PRSD, Radical Social Democratic Party). In the third part, the role of the army is analysed, while the fourth deals with the policies of the right and of business leaders during the affair. The fifth and final part discusses the internal factors which ensured that Pinochet's detention in London led to his trial by the Chilean courts, resulting in the stripping of his senatorial immunity by the Supreme Court on 8 August 2000.

Augusto Pinochet, a strong dictator with popular support

The great impact that Pinochet's detention had in Chile and the high-profile coverage it attracted in the international press can be attributed to the unique character of the detainee. He was a 'strong' dictator, to use the language historians employ when debating the extent of Hitler's power,[5] another emblematic twentieth century dictator. Pinochet established the DINA (Directorate of National

---

4 See the important biography of Frei Montalva written by Cristián Gazmuri, Patricia Aran-
    cibia and Alvaro Góngora, *Eduardo Frei Montalva y su época* (Santiago, 1996), especially
    vol. II, pp. 933–6, in which they describe the circumstances of his death in the clinic, not
    discounting the possibility that non-medical factors were involved.

5 Manfred Funke, *Starker oder schwacher Diktator? Hitlers Herrschaft und die Deutschen*
    (Dusseldorf, 1989).

Intelligence) and waged war against communism and terrorism without ever distancing himself from the extreme violence used in this war, even when his participation in the attack which cost Orlando Letelier his life in Washington, DC in 1976 became well known. The first director of the DINA, Manuel Contreras, was still being invited to military ceremonies in Chile after he had been forced to quit his post under strong pressure from the United States. During the economic crisis of 1982–3, Pinochet backed the technocrats, and brutal coercion was used to stem opposition protests. Among the 'new authoritarian' regimes, he was the only leader to remain as head of state for as long as seventeen years, becoming thus the longest serving governor in Chile's history, surpassing even the governors of the colonial period. Unlike his peers in other Latin American countries his economic policies were successful and his regime was, like Franco's in Spain, a modernising dictatorship – according to the concept of Von Beyme[6]– which pushed forward radical economic policies that led to a sustained annual growth rate of 7 per cent during the period 1985 to 1997. During his mandate, he enjoyed the support not only of right-wing groups but also of business and trade union leaders, as well as a large part of the population as a whole. This was a result of the systematic use of propaganda to demonise Chile's pre-1973 democracy and the Unidad Popular (Popular Unity) government of 1970–1973, of the practice of political cronyism which sought popular support, as well as of mass-mobilisation initiatives such as acclamatory events[7] and non-competitive elections – the *consulta* (consultation) of 1978 and the plebiscite of 1980 – which gave his leadership all the elements of a personality cult.

Nor, unlike his counterparts in the region, was he ejected from power, but rather was able to hand over leadership according to the rules established by the 1980 constitution, having been defeated in the plebiscite of 5 October 1988 despite receiving an impressive 43 per cent of the votes. Pinochet did not lose control of events after his defeat and implemented a policy of '*amarres*', leaving things well and truly secured, to make life difficult for the first democratic government. He did have to resign himself, however, to reforming the Constitution by negotiating with the opposition to remove its most undemocratic elements.[8] He did this from a sense of pragmatism: it was preferable that he

6 Klaus von Beyme, *Vom Faschismus zur Entwicklungsdiktatur – Machtelite und Opposition in Spanien*, (Munich, 1971).

7 The main events were on 11 September to commemorate the military coup, 1 May to celebrate 'Labour Day' and 9 July, which was declared 'Youth Day'.

8 The negotiations pushed forward by the Concertación after the plebiscite have now been recognised as an inevitable necessity even by the strongest critics of the transition. 'The Concertación, now close to their goal of governing, faced up to an inevitable round of negotiations. Under the circumstances, the cost of not negotiating was higher than the cost of the worst possible deal. Given the number of designated senators foreseen under the old

should eliminate some elements of the Foundational Charter rather than let the Concertación do it, since he knew that they would call for the complete dismantling of the protected and authoritarian democracy.

In a manner previously unseen in the new democracies, he availed himself of a clause that he himself had established in the 1980 constitution, by which he could remain as commander-in-chief of the armed forces for eight years after handing over power to Patricio Aylwin on 11 March 1990. This was intended to maintain his influence in political life and also to make sure that no military man, beginning naturally with himself, would be tried in the courts for human rights violations.[9] He made it quite clear that he would be forced to act in the event that anyone in uniform was threatened. One of the principal *amarres* was his retention of the power to appoint new members – those whom he knew he could rely on – to the Supreme Court. He was convinced that the left wing parties would not allow Aylwin to govern, that the latter would end up like President Allende, and therefore that it was necessary to maintain his own position as head of the army so that he could act once more in the event of any new and deep crisis. After handing over control of the military on 10 March 1998 to General Ricardo Izurieta, he became a life senator, with the intention of continuing to exert influence on national politics.

In the end, the fact that he had retained command of the military in 1990 boomeranged against him because it kept fresh the memory both inside and outside Chile of his responsibility in severe human rights abuses, a factor leading to his humiliating detention in London. Once arrested, he was openly defended by his admirers, who were to be found not only in elite circles but also in large sections of the general population. Even after being stripped of his privileges by the Supreme Court, Pinochet continued to enjoy support from a large proportion of the citizenry; in a poll taken in September 2001, one in every five Chileans maintained a favourable opinion about him, one in every three considered that he would go down as one of the best governors in the history of Chile and 23 per cent rejected the idea that he would go down in history as a dictator.[10] For him personally, the main consequence of his arrest in London

---

constitution, it would have been very difficult for the Concertación to achieve a double majority, even with a favourable electoral system.' Tomás Moulián, *Chile actual. Anatomía de un mito* (Santiago, 1997), p. 335.

9 He made use of a direct method: he offered compensation equivalent to 28 times actual salary to those who retired within a prudent timespan. This was taken up by six of the sixteen ministers, thus allowing him to designate their successors and thereby avoiding their retirement during the term of the first democratic government.

10 National urban poll of 1200 subjects carried out by the CERC corporation under the author's guidance.

was the loss of the protective mantle that had defended him from the course of justice. Not only was he forced to remain in detention for 503 days and answer to the justice of a foreign country, an intolerable situation for a military man, he was also subsequently prosecuted in Chile for his responsibility in the crimes committed by the so-called 'Caravan of Death' in October 1973. On 5 June 2000 he was stripped of his immunity as a senator by the Santiago Court of Appeal, a sentence confirmed by a 14 to 6 majority of the judges, and he was then officially made a prisoner. In order eventually to stop the proceedings against him, his lawyers were forced to use the legal sophism that he suffered from 'insanity and dementia', a measure resisted by his family who refused to accept that he was insane. In this way he was able to escape justice, but he was not able to prove his innocence.

From the time of the arrest onward, Chile was deeply shaken, although this did not manifest itself in massive street demonstrations either in support of or against Pinochet. Although his supporters defended him and rejected the measures taken by the British police and the Spanish judicial system, they also preserved a certain distance from the regime of which he been leader and from his personal character. Pinochet's arrest coincided with the start of the campaign for the presidential elections of 1999. Opinion polls had predicted a good result for the candidate of the Pinochetist UDI (Unión Demócrata Independiente, Independent Democratic Union) Joaquín Lavín. He had managed to capture some support among the Concertación's natural voters, especially from the Christian Democrats, which entailed that he distance himself somewhat from Pinochet. Behind the Pinochetist rhetoric of the leaders of the UDI and the RN (Renovación Nacional, National Renovation) lay the pragmatic decision not to weaken their electoral support.

The position of the government and the concertación parties

After initial irritation about the way that President Frei had been informed of Pinochet's detention had subsided – he had been attending a summit meeting of Latin American countries in Oporto, Portugal – his government took a position based mainly on the possible effects that the case might have at home and particularly within the armed forces. Its policy was couched in legal terms based on the same principle of respect for the rule of law that had been the basis for the change from dictatorship to democracy. At first, the government argued that Pinochet possessed diplomatic immunity, as he had gone to the UK under a diplomatic passport and on state business. It soon had to abandon this position when, after a few days, it turned out that Pinochet's visit to London had not been officially sanctioned. It then decided to reject the right of Spanish law, which had instigated the arrest, to act outside of its own borders. Later, when these legal avenues had failed and the law lords in London had confirmed that proceedings to extradite Pinochet to Spain should begin, the government used political arguments, emphasising that the general's delicate state of health would justify his return to Chile on humanitarian grounds. There was a legal basis to this argument, too, since Jack Straw, the British Home Secretary, had it in his power to stop extradition proceedings whenever reasons of ill health could be used to justify it.

The Concertación found itself in a difficult position. As the coalition which had formed the government it could not now adopt a stance which differed from that of the government. The government position of denying Spanish jurisdiction in the case and rejecting Pinochet's extradition to Spain thus had the firm support of its ministers and of the coalition parties and their deputies, with the exception of a sector of the Socialist Party.[11] These socialists, along with human rights groups and the non-parliamentary left rejected the government position as an unacceptable defence of the dictator who, moreover, would never be tried in his own country. They favoured extradition to Spain. A group of PS deputies, among whom were a daughter of President Allende and the distinguished lawyer Juan Bustos, who had acted for the family of Orlando Letelier in the trial that resulted in prison sentences for General Manuel Contreras and Brigadier Pedro Espinoza, travelled to London to express their support for the measures taken against Pinochet. They carried a letter to Jack Straw supporting extradition to Spain and emphasising the fact that trying Pinochet in Chile was unfeasible, which was delivered while Chancellor Insulza was visiting London at the end of November 1999.[12] The delegation then publicly criticised the government's argument of diplomatic immunity for the ex-head of state and its rejection of the concept of international law.[13] Their anger was focused on Insulza, who was made to appear in front of his party's central committee to defend the government's position.[14]

---

11 The then General Secretary of the PS remembered it thus: 'The defence of Pinochet by those who should defend the common good of the nation has affected me greatly. I've felt shame and pain for those who fell and I feel the country has been disgraced…These events have given an inevitable feeling that we are going backwards and fear, which I can't hide, of the danger that this habit of not knowing what to do, except give in to the anti-democratic pressures and problems posed by the military, with and without uniform, will become the norm,' Camilo Escalona, *Una transición de dos caras* (Santiago, 1999), pp. 7–8.

12 'Insulza Accuses in Pinochet Case: Socialists' Letter Affected Government Policy,' *El Mercurio*, 3 December 1999.

13 'PS responds sharply to Insulza's deception,' *El Mercurio*, 25 January 1999; 'Escalona calls on Government to right 'historical wrong' *El Mercurio*, 31 January 1999.

14 His statement was recorded in *La Segunda*, 10 November 1998; Camilo Escalona answered him in the same journal two days later 'Justice must prevail; Reply to Chancellor Insulza'.

The stance taken by this Socialist sector in favour of trying Pinochet in Spain pleased the right, whose aim was to polarise the presidential election campaign against the left by reviving the old image of an extreme left, in order to capture centrist votes which had previously gone to the Concertación. It also raised sensitive issues for the Concertación, whose own pre-candidate, Ricardo Lagos, was himself a left-winger. The affair showed up a sensitive issue of difference between Lagos and the pre-candidate of the PDC, Andrés Zaldívar, the senate president and a long-serving politician.[15] Zaldívar had been president of the PDC in the seventies and had been exiled by Pinochet due to his strong opposition to the 'yes' vote in the 1980 plebiscite. His position was complicated. His party had lost a lot of votes in the parliamentary elections of 1997, and in 1999 he found himself lagging behind Lagos in the opinion polls. As president of the senate, he could not remain indifferent whilst one of its members was under arrest and he was forced to take steps to secure the return of the life senator. However, he had to measure each step carefully because Pinochet was as unpopular in the PDC as he was in the PS and the PPD, although not as explicitly rejected. Zaldívar had always maintained a respectful attitude towards Pinochet since he had become a life senator in March 1998 and later (in spite of opposition from right wing deputies) he negotiated the repeal of the public holiday declared by the dictatorship on 11 September to celebrate the military coup. He went to Madrid and Brussels to lobby for Pinochet's return to Chile, which was not popular with other leaders. Some of his public declarations also damaged him in the eyes of his voters, who saw him as being too close to Pinochet.[16] Later, his position became even more complicated when an ex-senator of the PDC, Arturo Frei Bolívar, the president's cousin, travelled to London in November 1998 to support Pinochet. Relations between Pinochet and the PDC deputies were more conflictive. In January 1998, two months before Pinochet relinquished control of the armed forces, some deputies had tabled a motion against him on constitutional grounds for 'gross dereliction of duty'. Although lack of back-bench support meant that this was not passed in

---

The text does not reveal political differences, rather ethical and juridical ones. The emotionally charged atmosphere of that time did not allow Insulza's critics to see quite how strongly he had attacked Pinochet. The newspaper headlines read; 'I haven't the slightest interest in creating martyrs for the right' declared minister Insulza, *La Hora*, 23 October 1998; 'Minister Tohá: "I was tortured, but I still wish to see this gentleman (Pinochet) released",' *La Segunda*, 23 October 1998.

15 He had been Finance Minister in the government of Eduardo Frei Montalva (1964–1970), was elected Senator in 1973, again in 1989 and re-elected in 1997.

16 His declarations were used against him in the press, which was clearly pro-Lavín. Take, for example, the headline 'Pinochet is important for the transition,' *La Tercera*, 23 October 1998.

the lower house, the outcome in fact owed more to political considerations, since the measure would not have made it through the senate where the right held a majority.

Added to these internal domestic political issues was the fact that relations between the Chilean and Spanish governments were not easy, for reasons that had nothing to do with the Pinochet case. José María Aznar's government was never particularly popular with President Frei's PDC party. The crisis of Spanish conservatism that followed the disappearance of the Unión de Centro Democrático (Union of the Democratic Centre – UCD), the coalition founded by Adolfo Suárez which had guided Spain through the first years of its own political transition before imploding dramatically, saw the Spanish right lurch from hard-line to populist positions in the search for electoral success. The PDC, like much of the Spanish electorate hitherto, saw the Partido Popular – with Aznar as leader from the beginning of the 1990s – as a right-wing conservative party in the mould of its predecessor, the Alianza Popular (People's Alliance), whose leader during the transition, former Francoist minister Manuel Fraga Iribarne, had not supported the Chilean democratic opposition. The PDC leadership was not convinced by the move towards the political centre ground that the PP carried out under the leadership of Aznar. This was a process of modernisation and pragmatic change, which also included the recruitment of important figures from the UCD,[17] and would eventually lead to electoral success. In spite of the fact that both the PDC and the PP were members of the Christian Democrat International, Aznar was never much liked by the main leaders of the Chilean party as he was seen, erroneously as it turned out, as a lacklustre politician who would never be able to defeat Felipe González (1982–1996), the dominant figure in Spanish politics since his victory in the election of 28 October 1982. The visits previously made by Aznar to Chile as both president of the PP and as leader of the opposition had done nothing to change this opinion. Neither was there the same kind of personal warmth between President Frei and Aznar that had existed between President Patricio Aylwin (1990–1994) and the German chancellor, Helmut Kohl (1982–1998).[18]

17 See Carlos Huneeus, *La Unión de Centro Democrático y la transición a la democracia en España* (Madrid, 1985).
18 This relationship had begun when Aylwin, as president of the PDC, had been invited to participate in the Hamburg Congress of the CDU a few weeks after the 1973 coup and a few months after Kohl had himself been elected as president of his party. The new leader of the CDU was able to offer constant and effective help to the PDC, which was very important for the party's survival attempts during the difficult years of the military dictatorship. It was a friendship and political understanding that was to prove very useful in December 1991 when the last dictator of East Germany, Erich Hönecker, took refuge in the Chilean Embassy in Moscow, whilst being sought by the German judiciary to answer to charges of human

The response of the army

Pinochet's arrest was a hard blow for the army to take. He was worshipped by officers and NCOs alike and admired for having exercised command for a quarter of a century and for having been a successful president of the republic. His detention came as a shock to the new commander-in-chief, General Ricardo Izurieta, who had been making efforts to find a new professional role for his organisation, efforts which involved cutting links with the old authoritarian regime and with the image of Pinochet. Izurieta was convinced of the need to start a new era in the army rather than simply continuing the policies of his predecessor. He had been appointed by President Frei after a long process which had also involved Pinochet. Pinochet had prepared for his retirement by holding military parades and trade union rallies during 1997, at which he was praised for services rendered to the nation. His aim was to maintain his political profile as he became due to enter the Senate as life senator.[19] The new head of the army was a distinguished officer and a member of a well-known military family: his father, Pelayo Izurieta Molina was an army general and his uncle, General Oscar Izurieta had been commander-in-chief of the army during the six years of the Jorge Alessandri government (1958–1964). During the dictatorship he had held only institutional posts and was therefore free from the suspicion of responsibility for human rights abuses which hung over many other high-ranking officers. From the beginning Izurieta made it known that the army would now fulfil only strictly professional duties. In a measure that clearly distanced him from his predecessor, he indicated that he would not obstruct the course of justice in the event that trials for human rights abuses affected any member of his organisation.[20] One of his first decisions was to hand over the lists of employees of the CNI (successor of the DINA) that the courts had been

---

rights abuses. I served as ambassador in Germany during Aylwin's Government and was able to observe the warm personal relationship between the two, which helped greatly to solve the conflict. Honecker had entered with the approval of the Chilean ambassador, Clodomiro Almeyda, who had been Foreign Office minister in the Allende Government.

19 Pinochet was decorated in public ceremonies by the Cámara Nacional de Comercio (National Chamber of Commerce) and the Sociedad Nacional de Minería (National Mining Society). The criticism that these acts received in right wing circles led to other institutions, the Sociedad de Fomento Fabril (Society to Aid Manufacture) and the Confederación de la Producción y el Comercio (Confederation of Production and Commerce) refusing to organise this kind of event.

20 There were at least four important cases in the courts, including the Operation Albania of 1987, the murder of the Trade Union leader Tucapel Jiménez, of the MIR leader Jecar Neghme and the journalist José Carrasco. One minister, Juan Guzmán, was answering questions about the 'caravan of death'.

unsuccessfully demanding for years. Officers called to appear in court now also began to turn up, something that had not previously been the case before he took charge of the army.

The army made efforts to secure Pinochet's return to Chile, working through official channels jointly with the government. The military proved able to leave sentimentality to one side and adopted a pragmatic position in order to achieve their goal. Still, Izurieta had publicly to challenge the initiatives of some retired officers, and particularly of some retired generals who had worked for many years with Pinochet, who called for drastic measures incompatible with democratic government.[21] He was also under pressure from members of the Pinochet family and from some right-wing politicians, who had grown accustomed to the army taking action against Concertación governments in defence of their interests or those of their subordinates. This kind of pressure was aimed at forcing him to take action against the government outside the democratic legal framework, just as Pinochet had rattled his sabre at the Aylwin government with acts of military defiance such as the *ejercicio de enlace* of December 1990 and the *boinazo* of May 1993. The Pinochet family and the circle of retired officers felt that Izurieta displayed weakness when dealing with the government and were annoyed that he did not go immediately to London to support the general, leaving it until April 1999.[22]

During the long months of Pinochet's detention in London Izurieta refused to bow to pressure and continued to work through official channels, demonstrating an authoritative strength as commander-in-chief that was highly valued by the government and by the parties of the Concertación.[23] In order to soothe dissident voices he reduced the rank of the army's representative in Madrid from general to colonel, something the navy had already done in their London office. However, he did not take more drastic measures such as reviewing his policy of arms acquisitions, which would have had economic repercussions for Great Britain and Spain. In order to support General Izurieta's efforts, President Frei called for several meetings of the Consejo de Seguridad Nacional (National Security Council), the body most emblematic of Chile's protected and authoritarian democracy, set up under the 1980 constitution to give military institutions tutelage over political power. This body, which had previously only been

21 Some ex-soldiers, such as Cristián Labbé, the last Government General Secretary, occupied public office. As mayor of the Providencia district he made known his protest by stopping refuse collection from the Spanish embassy.

22 To make a clear distinction, Izurieta took care not to wear uniform, wearing civilian dress when visiting him in Virginia Water.

23 This image had to be altered slightly on Pinochet's return to Santiago due to the ceremony which had been prepared for him, which Izurieta changed according to the wishes of the head of state. In any case, it was an event of minor importance.

summoned four times,[24] was convoked by Frei at each decisive moment during Pinochet´s detention in London so as to give the military an institutional forum to air their opinions rather than taking direct action. Frei also used it as a way of keeping the military informed of the steps that the Government was taking and to listen to the concerns of the armed forces. This became very important when Spain confirmed the legitimacy of Garzón's request for Pinochet's extradition on 6 November 1999.

The navy also played an important role. Its new commander-in-chief, Admiral Jorge Arancibia, appointed at the end of 1997 by President Frei, had been Pinochet's aide-de-camp at the beginning of the 1980s and had come to enjoy a close relationship with him. He succeeded Admiral Jorge Martínez Busch, who had himself been appointed by Admiral José Toribio Merino, a member of the *Junta del Gobierno* under the military regime. Toribio named Martínez as his successor before 11 March 1990, so that he could stay in office for eight years and not four, as would have been the case had he been nominated under the new regime. He could thereby accompany Pinochet who would also remain in command of the army after the accession to power of the civilian regime. Martínez Busch performed his duties with such diligence that it was only after his retirement in 1997 that the navy began once more to act in a purely professional capacity.[25]

The navy bore little responsibility for human rights abuses. It had participated in coercive action only in the first few months after the coup and had initially been a member of the DINA until Merino ordered the withdrawal of navy personnel due to the highly personalised leadership of General Manuel Contreras and the army's dominant position in the executive. It also had a low profile in government – only a few naval officers were ministers or under-secretaries in the seventies. From 11 March 1981, when Merino became president of the Junta (which held legislative power), the navy concentrated its power in the legislature. He also endeared himself to many Concertación supporters when, on the night of the plebiscite of 5 October 1988, he called for Pinochet, who had remained silent for several hours,[26] to accept that the 'yes' vote had been defeated.

---

24 The first time was in April 1991, at the request of General Pinochet and the navy after President Aylwin released the Rettig report; the second was in 1992 and concerned constitutional accusations against three Supreme Court ministers; the third was in 1994 under President Frei as a result of the Laguna del Desierto sentence that went against Chile; and the fourth, when five terrorists of the Frente Patriótico Manuel Rodríguez escaped from prison.

25 He put the navy at the disposal of General Contreras' attempts to escape the Supreme Court's sentence by taking refuge in a naval hospital in 1995. It played an important part, strongly supporting the army's position.

26 Merino always considered that he had a historic right to leadership as it had been he who precipitated the coup in 1973, whereas the army had been indecisive.

The navy could exert leverage through the acquisition of submarines. Under Martínez Busch, the navy had taken the controversial decision to sign a contract with a Franco–Spanish consortium for the construction of two submarines to replace those supplied by Germany in the 1970s. During Pinochet's detention no action was taken against the consortium, although the navy made sure that delivery was made in France rather than in Spain, where the submarines were built, in order to avoid any possible action on the part of the Spanish judiciary against either the submarines or the officers entrusted to receive them.

Finally, Pinochet's detention forced the military to make concessions on the issue of human rights abuses. As part of their efforts to secure Pinochet's return, the military agreed to take part in a 'Mesa de Diálogo' or Forum for Dialogue, with church leaders, academics and human rights lawyers. After a year's work, a declaration was signed in June 2000 recognising both that state terrorism had existed and the military's involvement in it. This recognition would have been impossible without the actions of Judge Garzón and the British police in London.

The right wing and business leaders

Pinochet's arrest took the Chilean right by surprise just as they were preparing for the 1999 presidential elections. They had a good candidate in Joaquín Lavín,[27] whom the polls showed as enjoying widespread popular support. After the election debacles of 1989 and 1993 the right were at last in a position to defeat the Concertación. They counted on the fact that the Concertación candidate would be the socialist Ricardo Lagos and not a candidate from the Christian Democrats, hoping thereby to capture the support of conservative Christian Democrat voters unhappy with a left-winger. In order to sway those voters Lavín was obliged to adopt a critical position towards the abuse of human rights committed under the dictatorship. This implied confronting the issue of the arrested and missing persons and required that he distance himself somewhat from Pinochet. He took steps towards both in July 1998 when he met the families of people still missing or arrested.[28] This irritated Pinochet, who took no trouble to hide his rejection of the young 'gremialista' politician,[29] whom he considered immature. He came out in favour of the Senate president, Andrés

27 He had briefly been General Secretary of the UDI and a sucessful mayor in the wealthy district of Las Condes, after being elected in 1992. His attempt to be elected as deputy in 1989 failed, and he was beaten by the Renovación Nacional candidate.

28 He also publicly announced that one of his cousins ha d been a victim of the 'caravan of death'.

29 For a fuller discussion of the background to and activities of 'gremialists' see Carlos Huneeus, 'Technocrats and Politicians in an Authoritarian Regime; the "ODEPLAN Boys" and the "Gremialists" in Pinochet's Chile,' *Journal of Latin American Studies*, vol. 32, issue 2, May 2000, pp. 461–501, and also Huneeus, *El régimen de Pinochet*.

Table 1: The Military Regime's Image, 1989–2001.

Q. *In your opinion concerning General Augusto Pinochet's regime, do you think that … ?*

	It was a very good thing	It was only bad	It was only good	Don't Know/ No Response
October 1989	54	22	24	0
March 1991	58	29	11	2
March 1992	54	26	17	3
October 1993	51	28	18	4
July 1995	53	29	14	4
June 1996	50	29	17	4
September 1997	53	27	14	6
September 1998	56	25	14	6
Sepember 1999	58	26	13	4
September 2000	56	24	16	4
September 2001	54	24	16	6
Average	54	24	15	4

Source: National Pollsters CERC, 1200 interviews in each sample.

Zaldívar, believing, not without reason, that he would enjoy more political influence in a third Concertación government than in a new right-wing one.

The arrest of Pinochet had a great impact on the right, especially due to the unexpected fact that nobody in Europe, with the exception of Margaret Thatcher,[30] raised their voice to criticise Spanish justice or to defend the ex-dictator. For the right it was a bitter irony that Spain was the country to call for his arrest, since the Pinochet regime had shaped its discourse and its institutions by drawing inspiration from the authoritarian ideas underpinning Franco's long dictatorship in Spain from 1939 until 1975. Moreover, they saw that Spanish justice was backed up by a centre-right government with which they had previously identified. The widespread support that Pinochet still enjoyed among the elite and the masses during the military regime resurfaced after his arrest. His regime was remembered, for good and ill, by a large sector of the population and Pinochet himself was seen by many as a great man who would occupy an important place in Chilean history (see Tables 1 and 2).

30 The 'Iron Lady' asked Pinochet about the missing and arrested persons during their interview in Virginia Waters, which was a terrible shock for Pinochet. See Pérez and Gerdtzen, *Augusto Pinochet,* p. 185.

Table 2: How will General Pinochet go down in history, according to age and voting intentions? (Open question)

	UDI	RN	PDC	PPD	PS	Total	2001	2000	1999	1998	1995
Positive opinions	39	39	18	3	4	20	20	24	15	19	22
– Good President	15	8	2	1	2	6	10	11	5	9	6
– Saved Country from chaos*	–	–	–	–	–	–	–	6	3	4	6
– Hero	13	16	7	0	1	6	9	7	2	5	4
– Others	11	15	9	2	0	8	1	0	5	1	6
Negative opinions	24	26	53	77	74	44	43	45	49	53	38
– Dictator, tyrant	11	9	22	32	33	17	22	22	28	30	19
– Murderer, genocidal	1	3	8	22	21	10	11	11	8	10	9
– Bad president	4	0	4	7	8	5	6	8	5	12	7
– Others	24	25	16	11	10	18	7	3	9	4	9
Neutral opinions	24	25	16	11	10	18	7	3	9	4	9
– Just one more President	8	3	2	2	0	5	5	--	5	2	4
– Military Man	0	5	1	1	0	1	1	–	3	0	3
– Coup leader	1	0	2	0	0	1	1	1	1	1	2
– Others	16	17	11	8	10	11	0	2	–	1	0
Others	–	–	–	–	–	–	10	11	12	11	6
Don't know/ No response	11	9	13	9	12	18	18	16	12	10	15
Total number of respondents	212	102	148	94	87	1200	1174	1200	1200	1188	1240
						70%	70%	70%	67%	67%	67%

(*) In this case we have used this indicator as part of the option 'good president'.
Source: National pollsters CERC, September 2002.

In right-wing circles Pinochet was seen as a statesman who deserved support during a difficult time. Hundreds of people went to London to show their support for him and to repudiate those who had been instrumental in his humiliation. They ranged from the presidents of the RN and the UDI, deputies of these parties, and leaders of the Confederación de la Producción y el Comercio (CPC, Confederation of Production and Commerce) to humble people who were given a free ticket to London as representatives of the poor who had supported Pinochet while he was head of state. The CPC president, Walter Riesco, who had been a member of one of the Junta's legislative commissions, came out strongly in favour of Pinochet, even suggesting that Chile break off relations with Spain and Great Britain after the British government stated that humanitarian grounds would only be considered after extradition proceedings against Pinochet were over.[31] He visited Pinochet twice in London and even went to Madrid in an unsuccessful attempt to garner support among Spanish business leaders.

The main political formation that supported Pinochet at this time was the 'gremialista' movement, founded in the mid-sixties by a young law student, Jaime Guzmán. The *gremialistas* had always been enthusiastic Pinochet supporters, and Guzmán took care to place young *gremialistas* in various state bodies, especially in the Secretaría Nacional de la Juventud (National Youth Secretariat) an entity in charge of youth mobilisation, the Oficina de Planificación Nacional (ODEPLAN – National Planning Office) a body set up to support the president and form a bridge with the 'Chicago Boys' movement, and at local government level where they obtained the office of mayor in all the major cities.[32] In 1983 he founded the UDI as a way of gaining representation for Pinochet's supporters and in the parliamentary elections of 1989 he gained a seat in the Senate, assisted by the electoral law which secured this outcome even though he had obtained fewer votes than the Concertación's second candidate, Ricardo Lagos. In spite of the reappearance of the traditional two-party politics of the right – the other party being the RN which gained more votes than the UDI in the 1989 parliamentary elections – it was the UDI which continued to grow both in organisation and in electoral support until it became the main conservative party. This was ratified in the 1997 parliamentary elections when Carlos Bombal secured a seat in the Senate for a Santiago district at the expense of the RN president, Andrés Allamand.[33]

---

31 'Riesco calls for the breaking off of relations with Great Britain,' *El Mercurio*, 1 July 1999.
32 This is dealt with more fully in Huneeus, *El régimen de Pinochet*, chapter seven.
33 For more information, see Huneeus, 'La derecha en el Chile después de Pinochet: el caso de la Unión Demócrata Independiente,' *Working Paper* No. 285, July 2001, Kellogg Institute, University of Notre Dame.

The UDI strongly condemned Great Britain and Spain with fiercely worded declarations in defence of national sovereignty. Defending national sovereignty and attacking the actions of European governments were arguments that struck a chord with popular nationalist sentiments and were also pleasing to the military. This position, in fact, covered up a coolly calculated political gambit, because by giving voice to the large pro-Pinochet section of Chilean society, it enabled the UDI to depersonalise the controversy surrounding the ex-dictator, so as not to be seen defending him on personal terms. The strategy also created tensions between the government and its supporters, as well as with foreign governments. Behind the nationalist rhetoric, the UDI was far more interested in achieving its election aims than in defending Pinochet's character, and thereby running the risk of losing the presidential elections. When it seemed that the government's emphasis on the humanitarian grounds for Pinochet's release was beginning to pay off, the UDI did all in its power to avoid it succeeding, to make sure that the old general did not return during the election campaign. They had good reason to fear that his return might see the loss of enough votes to stop them gaining a majority.

Internal factors favouring Pinochet's trial in chile

The consequences in Chile of Pinochet's detention in London made it possible for Pinochet to be tried and condemned by the Chilean courts. Human rights groups and a sector of the Socialist Party had argued that it would be impossible to try him in Chile and that the stripping of his immunity as a senator by the Supreme Court had only been made possible by the action of Spanish justice. This approach underestimates the importance of national factors in permitting Pinochet's trial in Chile. External factors can only have internal consequences when there are favourable conditions that allow the effects to spread through the political system.

It is worth remembering what those internal factors are. Firstly, the remarkable and brave activities of human rights groups over many years. Judge Garzón would never have been able to issue an extradition warrant had he not had access to the case histories compiled over years by the Comité pro Paz (Peace Committee) the Vicaría de la Solidaridad (Vicariate for Solidarity) the Comisión Chilena de Derechos Humanos (Chilean Commission for Human Rights) and other organisations. Their labours facilitated the compiling of the Rettig report after just one year's work. Secondly, the work of the various judges who had had the courage to act independently both during the dictatorship and after the transition to democracy, such as José Cánovas in the case of the *degollados* (a 1985 massacre in which the victims' throats were cut) and of Adolfo Bañados in the Letelier case.

Thirdly, the very important contribution made by investigative journalists, amongst whom Mónica González and Patricia Verdugo, in particular, stand out.[34] This made it possible to compile case histories and documents proving the involvement of state agents in attacks that cost the lives of important opposition figures.

Nobody in Chile thought that Pinochet would ever be brought to justice. He was protected by strong legal and political provisions that made prosecution unfeasible. These provisions were to be found not only in the Amnesty Law of 1978 and in the Constitution which permitted him to remain as head of the armed forces for eight years, but also in the *amarres* established after the plebiscite of 5 October 1988 which forced him out of office. These included prohibiting Congress from investigating any irregularities committed before the changeover and appointing one third of the sixteen Supreme Court judges, who would uphold the decisions made during the years of the dictatorship to safeguard against trials being held for human rights abuses. Also, Pinochet felt confident of staying out of the courtroom because the army, along with the other branches of the armed forces, would be ready to take the necessary measures if those previously mentioned failed. It never crossed his mind that he could possibly face an attack from the legal system. Judge Garzón's decision and its prompt enactment by the British police broke through the armour that had previously protected Pinochet.

A further important internal factor is the change that had taken place in the judicial system as a result of the Concertación government's policies during the 1990s.[35] The authoritarian stranglehold which had kept the judiciary above the law when it came to human rights, especially in the Supreme Court, was already very much weakened by the time the Spanish judge gave the order to arrest Pinochet. Firstly, 'las leyes cumplido' (fulfilled laws) meant that proceedings for human rights violations could now be transferred from the military to the civil courts. In the military courts it was deemed impossible to get justice because of military control. Secondly, at the beginning of 1992, a group of deputies of various Concertación parties, all linked to the human rights movement, moved a constitutional accusation against three Supreme Court ministers for 'gross dereliction of duty'. The accusation was finally upheld against one of the

34 Mónica González carried out detailed investigations about the murders of General Carlos Prats and his wife in Buenos Aires, 30 September 1974, the results of which were published in Edwin Harrington and Mónica González, *Bomba en una calle de Palermo* (Santiago, 1987), and about the 'Combined Commandos' of the Air Force which she published along with Héctor Contreras, *Los secretos del comando conjunto* (Santiago, 1991). Patricia Verdugo published her results in a book which had a huge impact, *Los zarpazos del puma*, (Santiago: Ediciones ChileAmérica CESOC, 1989).

35 Jorge Correa, 'Cinderella stays at the party. Judicial power in Chile in the nineties,' in Paul Drake and Iván Jaksić (eds.), *El modelo chileno. Democracia y desarrollo en los noventa* (Santiago, 1999), p. 281.

ministers, Hernán Cereceda, although only on the charge of corruption, with the support of senators of the RN. For the first time in 120 years, a Supreme Court minister was dismissed from his post. To the Supreme Court this came as a severe blow. Thirdly, President Frei's government managed to pass a constitutional reform through Congress that changed the composition of the Supreme Court. In effect, this abolished the rule which allowed members to stay in office after they had reached 75 years of age, which meant that the older ministers appointed by Pinochet soon began to retire in the ensuing years. The number of ministers was also increased from sixteen to twent-one and of these, at least five had to come from a non-legal background. Thus, the wind of change began to blow through the highest tribunal in the Republic.[36] Fourthly, the cloak of immunity covering the Supreme Court was broken by a constitutional accusation against its president, Servando Jordán, at the beginning of 1997, made by Carlos Bombal, a UDI deputy. Bombal faced a tough election bout with the RN president Andrés Allamand for an important seat in Santiago. Both were on the same right wing electoral list. Bombal's action enabled him to take centre stage and wage a campaign that led to the defeat of his fellow right-winger. This made it clear that the UDI was at liberty to act against one of the 'bastions of authority' most representative of the dictatorship.

It is a fallacy of hindsight to criticise the various Concertación governments for accepting Pinochet's continuation as head of the army. The change from dictatorship to democracy had been made, as we have seen, in a constitutional way and it was not easy to change this in Pinochet's case. He had constitutional legitimacy that was enshrined in the Foundational Charter on his side. He had the backing of the army and of the other branches of the armed forces. He was also supported by the parties of the right and the business community, who saw him as a guarantee against the dangerous centre-left coalition whom they feared would apply 'centralising' policies and plunge the country back into the chaos of 1973. Now that democracy is well established, it is easy to suggest that President Aylwin, or Frei after him, could have forced Pinochet to resign as commander-in-chief. Those who hold such opinions forget the context of the fledgling democracy, especially in the first few years. In that climate of insecurity, nobody could have discarded the possibility that the army might once again intervene in politics, least of all the analysts and politicians of the non-parliamentary left.

It must also be remembered that the transition in Chile took place whilst democracy in Argentina, established at the end of 1983, had suffered blows from several army rebellions led by middle-ranking officers who were protesting

36 This reform was made possible with the support of the right. It established that the appointment of ministers needed the ratification of two-thirds of the Senate. This was the President's proposal and it differed from an earlier one made by the Supreme Court.

about President Raúl Alfonsin's military policies.[37] Alfonsin was forced to hand over power to the new president, Carlos Menem, before his term was over because of a deep economic crisis that threatened the new democratic order. If the first democratic government in Argentina was able to take drastic action against the military by cutting the budget of the armed forces and putting high-ranking officers on trial, it was because those institutions had become severely weakened in public opinion after their defeat in the Falklands war started by the 'Proceso' dictatorship (1976–1983), and they lacked support both among the elite and the masses. None of these circumstances obtained in Chile.

Maintaining discipline among the military institutions was a priority for President Aylwin's new administration in order to consolidate democracy, even if this meant counting on the help of the ex-dictator who had stayed on as commander in chief.[38] At the same time, Aylwin let it be known from the beginning of his government that he was not going to be intimidated by Pinochet, and he stood up to him on various occasions. When, in April 1990, Pinochet criticised the make-up of the Truth and Reconciliation Committee, Aylwin demanded an apology. He did the same in September 1990 during a lunch at which Pinochet, who had probably had too much to drink, criticised the German army. The third occasion was when Aylwin refused to accept the promotion of General Parera due to his behaviour during the military parade of 19 September 1990, when Parera blatantly ordered the parade to begin without first asking for permission.

Not all the Concertación's political gestures struck the same tone as Aylwin's. The Senate, whose president, Gabriel Valdés of the PDC, had been elected after a deal between the Concertación and the UDI, invited the commanders in chief of the armed forces to a lunch a few weeks after the beginning of democracy. Photographs of smiling parliamentarians alongside General Pinochet were used to reinforce the 'nice guy' image that the general was so anxious to project, and gave ammunition to critical sectors of the Concertación concerned at the good relations maintained with Pinochet. Relations between ministers and the supreme commander of the army were also far from uniform. While the defence minister, Patricio Rojas Saavedra, clearly kept his distance, the government Secretary General, Enrique Correa, a Socialist Party militant, had a more moderate attitude, a situation which Pinochet was able to use against Rojas.[39] Such examples show that the change from dictatorship to democracy is a complex process with an aesthetic that may be irritating to those who, when looking back, do not take into account the circumstances in which it happened.

37 For army mutinies, see Deborah L. Norden, *Military Rebellion in Argentina* (Lincoln, NE, 1996).
38 This was what Pinochet said to him during their first meeting after Aylwin was elected President on 14 December 1989, when Aylwin made clear his disagreement with Pinochet's remaining in control of the army. Interview with the ex-president, 2 April 2002.

Conclusion

General Pinochet's arrest in London had far-reaching consequences for Chilean politics. It put to the test the principle of respect for the rule of law that had motivated the change from dictatorship to democracy, as the government was forced to make efforts to ensure the former dictator's return. This was an unpopular policy with wide sections of the Concertación and meant a loss of support for Ricardo Lagos in the presidential elections of 1999. For the first time since the 1989 elections, a second round of voting was necessary to choose the president, which Lagos won thanks to the votes of the Communist Party. A second important consequence was the creation of favourable conditions for the development of an autonomous judiciary, now much more inclined to accept cases put by human rights lawyers. It also led to Pinochet's isolation and the eventual stripping of his senatorial immunity. In addition, Pinochet's detention caused the right to distance itself from him, as may be illustrated by the declarations of Pablo Longueira, the UDI president, who described Pinochet as 'a man of the past'.[40] This has created a favourable situation for the consolidation of democracy in Chile, because it breaks the relationship that all right wing parties had with Pinochet up until the beginning of the presidential election campaign in the winter of 1999.

Judge Garzón's action provoked political tensions which almost led to a Pinochetist triumph in the elections, but in the end served to isolate him in Chile, which will in turn weaken any nostalgic appeal associated with him. His arrest in London, aside from the myriad juridical and procedural implications, was a political event which humiliated the once-powerful dictator, the man who had once boasted that 'not a leaf could move' without his permission. Pinochet's long-term reputation will surely now be dominated by this event, and by the accompanying image of human rights violations.

39 In declarations referring to a visit made by Pinochet to London in 1991, which had sparked a fierce rejection in that country, the Conservative junior defence minister, Alan Clark (though rather a supporter of Pinochet in private), said that they would never invite Pinochet and a Labour MP described him as 'the butcher of Santiago'. Correa defended the commander in chief's visit and added that 'it's always disappointing when anyone from another country, no matter how friendly that country is, uses language that does not correspond with their official status,' *La Nación*, 5 May 1991, quoted by Felipe Portales, *Chile: una democracia tutelada* (Santiago, 2000), pp. 113–14.

40 He was able to do this because he needed the votes of the centre and because he himself had never occupied high office under the dictatorship. He had served as an advisor in the Ministry of Housing.

PART 4
Implications and Effects

CHAPTER 10

Of catalysts and cases: transnational prosecutions and impunity in Latin America

Naomi Roht-Arriaza

In tracing the ripple effects of the Pinochet case throughout the world, at first glance the depth and breadth of effects seems puzzling. The Pinochet case was not the first to use a theory of universal jurisdiction.[1] Nor was it the first case brought outside Argentina or Chile for the crimes of the military dictatorships in those countries – the Italian cases on Argentina began long before, in 1982.[2] But the case touched a global nerve, in large part because of Pinochet's status as the poster child of Latin American implacable dictators. It touched off or inspired a series of investigations in a number of countries, both European countries connected to the victims, and countries throughout the Americas, including the United States.

This chapter discusses some of the cases that either followed from or were inspired by the Pinochet case. In doing so, I am aware that tracing cause and effect in social phenomena is a risky business: more than one factor contributes to every change. These cases all arose out of a specific domestic political context, affected by actors who wanted investigations and prosecutions for reasons of their own, and by pressures from organised human rights groups and family members of victims. Nonetheless, it is obvious that a burgeoning field of transnational prosecutions followed Pinochet. It is also obvious that the pace and scope of investigations and prosecutions within Argentina and Chile has changed considerably since 1996, when the Spanish cases were filed, or even

The research for this chapter, and for a forthcoming book on the same subject, was supported by a grant for Research and Writing from the John D. and Catherine T. MacArthur Foundation, and by a grant from the United States Institute for Peace. For these author is profoundly grateful.

1 See *Attorney General of Israel v. Eichmann*, 36 Int'l L. Rep. 18 (Israel Dist. Ct. Jerusalem 1961), *aff'd* 36 Int'l L. Rep. 277 (Israel Sup. Ct. 1962).

2 Criminal Tribunal of Rome, Sentence of 6 December 2000 against Riveros, Gerardi, Suarez-Mason and others, available at http://www.derechos.org/nizkor/italia.

since 1998. The effect of the cases within Chile is examined elsewhere in this volume; the present chapter considers firstly, the effects in Argentina. Secondly, it briefly outlines some of the other cases arising out of, or in connection with the Spanish investigation. Thirdly, it considers a subsequent investigation by the Spanish courts into atrocities committed by military forces in Latin America: that initiated by Nobel Peace Prize winner Rigoberta Menchú into genocide, terrorism, torture and related crimes in Guatemala. The Guatemala case in Spain illustrates some of the paradoxes in the increasing use of transnational litigation to overcome impunity. Indeed, the very success of transnational prosecutions like the Pinochet case in stimulating judicial and legislative action against continued impunity within the territorial states (Argentina and Chile) has created its own set of difficulties. As formal amnesties and pardons for those who commit crimes against humanity lose currency, the question of when other national courts should step in, and whether they should require it to be demonstrated (as does the newly-created International Criminal Court) that the domestic courts are unwilling or unable to do so, is becoming more urgent.

Amnesty, domestic investigations and the role of the judiciary

The Spanish investigation into the crimes of the Chilean and Argentine military regimes was predicated on the idea that domestic jurisdiction was unavailable, even though domestic courts were the preferred forum for hearing these cases. In the Chilean case Pinochet had a limited immunity from prosecution as a senator-for-life. In both Chile and Argentina, as elsewhere in countries emerging from years of dictatorship, amnesty laws protected the bulk of the military's crimes from judicial scrutiny.[3]

An initial spate of legal challenges to amnesty laws in Chile, Argentina, El Salvador, Guatemala, Honduras and Peru was unsuccessful.[4] Over the following years, lower courts began carving out exceptions and interpretations of those laws that allowed some investigations to go forward. In Chile, for instance, one case invoked international humanitarian law to invalidate the 1978 amnesty,[5] while other cases in Honduras and Chile found that application of the amnesty required a thorough investigation into the nature of the charges and the identity

---

3 See Robert J. Quinn, 'Will the Rule of Law End? Challenging Grants of Amnesty for the Human Rights Violations of a Prior Regime: Chile's New Model,' *Fordham Law Review*, vol. 62, no. 4, 1994, pp. 905-960 for a description of the Chilean amnesty law. Re Argentina, see Law No. 23, 492 (Dec. 1986) (*punto final* law); Law No. 23, 521 (4 June 1987) (due obedience law).

4 For descriptions and analysis, see Roht-Arriaza and Gibson, 'The Developing Jurisprudence on Amnesty,' *Human Rights Quarterly* , vol. 20 (1998), p. 843.

5 Caso Poblete Córdova, Sept. 9, 1998, Rol No. 895-6. Corte Suprema de Chile.

of those benefiting from the law. This approach was not new: in the Chilean case, at least, it had been proposed by Judge Carlos Cerda as far back as 1986, but at the time the Supreme Court not only rejected it but sanctioned the magistrate for applying it.[6] In a variant of this approach, courts found that disappearance cases did not fall within the ambit of the amnesty because they are continuing crimes and thus could potentially persist beyond the amnesty period. (This was the strategy used by Judge Guzmán in the Caravan of Death case that led to the indictment of Pinochet in Chile.)[7] In El Salvador, similarly, the Supreme Court by the year 2000 ruled that that country's sweeping amnesty law had to be applied by each judge taking into account whether its application in the particular case would violate the state's international human rights commitments or the fundamental rights of victims.[8] By carving out a sphere of judicial investigation despite such laws, these decisions set the stage for a frontal assault on the laws.

The decisions of the Inter-American Commission criticising amnesty laws throughout the Americas proved especially important. In decisions involving Argentina, Uruguay, El Salvador, Chile and Peru, the Commission found that those laws violated several provisions of the American Convention on Human Rights, including the right to a fair trial, the right to a remedy, and the obligation of the state to protect rights.[9] The Commission was especially critical of the effect on the victims and survivors of the inability to use either civil or criminal proceedings to find out what had happened to loved ones, and who was responsible. In the *Barrios Altos* case the Inter-American Court essentially endorsed the Commission's approach.[10]

Judges outside the region also considered the effect of the amnesties. Judge Garzón, for example, found that these laws had no effect on his investigation, both because Spain does not allow general amnesties and because the laws violated international obligations of the enacting states.[11] Similarly, in the extradition case in Mexico involving Argentine Ricardo Miguel Cavallo, a then-naval lieutenant who served in the infamous torture and detention camp at the Naval Mechanics School (ESMA), trial judge Jesús Guadalupe Luna found that Argentina's

6 Interview with Judge Cerda, Santiago, Chile, June 2001.
7 Corte de Apelaciones de Santiago, Rol. No. 2,182-98'A,' 1 Dec. 2001 (indictment).
8 Sala de lo Constitucional de la Corte Suprema de Justicia, No. 24-97/21-98, 26 Sept. 2000.
9 Las Hojas Massacre Case, No. 10,287 (El Salvador); Leonardo et.al. Case No. 10,029 (Uruguay); Herrera et.al., Case No. 10, 147 (Argentina), all in 1992–93 Ann. Rep. Inter-Am. Comm'n H. Rts. 88, 154, 41 (1993); Garay Hermosilla et al, Case No. 10, 843 (Chile), in 1996 Ann. Rep. Inter-Am. Comm'n H. Rts. 156 (1997).
10 Corte Interamericana de Derechos Humanos, Caso Barrios Altos (Chumbipuma Aguierre y Otros vs. Peru), Sentence of 14 March 2001.
11 See Orden de prison provisional incondicional de Leopoldo Fortunate Galtieri, Juzgado No. 5 de la Audiencia Nacional, 25 March, 1997, at 7-8.

amnesty laws had no legal effect outside Argentina because they violate the international obligation to investigate and prosecute the alleged crimes.[12] The House of Lords also seemed little impressed by the 1978 Chilean amnesty law. By negating the validity of blanket amnesty laws for disappearances, killings and torture, these decisions by third-party national courts have greatly devalued amnesties within their home countries. Moreover, potential defendants have begun to realise that a domestic amnesty may not be worth as much if it does not apply outside the borders of their country. The Pinochet case illustrated the dangers of foreign travel and of possible extradition even when the home country has an amnesty law in place.

Thus, even before the Pinochet case became front-page news, the barrier of amnesty laws was becoming more porous. The case accelerated that trend, with substantial effects throughout the region.

Developments within Argentina

As the 1990s began, the prospects for victims and survivors of the repression seeking justice looked bleak. The 1985 trial of the nine ex-commanders who had led Argentina's three military governments had imposed life-sentences on General Videla and Admiral Massera, and jail terms on most of the other defendants. As the number of complaints in the courts increased, so too did military unrest. Then-President Alfonsín reacted by limiting almost all prosecutions. He promulgated a law which set a cut-off date for trials relating to the crimes of the military governments (the *punto final* law) and soon after, another law directing the courts to presume that most lower-ranking military personnel were following orders and therefore not criminally liable (the 'due obedience' law). Subsequently, then-president Menem's pardons of those few generals and other top officers still either convicted or subject to prosecution made the existing amnesty complete. There was no information forthcoming about the fate of the disappeared, and, while compensation had been paid, the military was unwilling to admit any wrong-doing. The human rights movement was demoralised, and the prevailing view even among many human rights lawyers was that it might be time to move on.

In 1995 this panorama began to change. Former navy captain Adolfo Scilingo admitted to a local journalist that he, along with many others, had participated in 'death flights'.[13] The confessions caused a stir, leading eventually to the commander-in-chief of the army, General Martín Balza's admission that the

---

12 Extradicción de Ricardo Miguel Cavallo, No. 5/2000, Juez Sexto de Distrito de Procesos Penales del Distrito Federal, Mexico, 11 Jan. 2001.

13 His confessions were later published in a book, Horacio Verbitsky, *The Flight: Confessions of an Argentine Dirty Warrior* (New York, 1996).

army had used unacceptable methods in fighting the 'dirty war.'[14] That same year, Judge Garzón opened his investigation in Spain, and human rights groups began finding witnesses and organising existing files to contribute to the Spanish case. Witnesses began travelling to Spain, while others presented testimony before the Spanish embassies in Buenos Aires and elsewhere.

Since then, the Argentine courts have taken a more and more aggressive stance in favour of investigating and prosecuting past crimes. The legal developments include recognition of a 'right to the truth' which permits courts to reopen investigations even where the amnesty law would ultimately apply,[15] the affirmation that crimes against humanity are not subject to a statute of limitations,[16] investigations into criminal conspiracy in the cases of babies taken from mothers who were prisoners and given away to pro-military families, and the landmark decision in March 2001 by Federal Judge Gabriel Cavallo, upheld by the Buenos Aires Court of Appeals, that the *punto final* and due obedience laws are unconstitutional under international and Argentine law.[17] Even more spectacularly, a case brought against the ex-military leaders of Argentina, Chile, Paraguay and others in connection with the disappearances and killings under the auspices of Operation Condor has led to a wave of indictments and arrests.[18] As a result of these developments, several of the leaders of the military during the mid-1970s are either in prison or under house arrest, as are many of the most notorious operatives and torturers of the time. Others are in hiding or subject to extradition requests from one or more governments.

These developments clearly signal a change in the attitude of the judiciary as well as a renewed enthusiasm by lawyers and activists. Again, I do not want to suggest that this change is a simple cause-and-effect result of the filing of the case in Spain, or of the detention of Augusto Pinochet. Many other factors no doubt intervened, including changes in the constitution, reform of the judiciary (much less pronounced in Argentina than in Chile, however), the deteriorating image of the Menem (and later de la Rúa) administrations, and the coming of age of the children of the disappeared as well as the emergence of a new generation of judges and military officers, many with no links to the repression

14 For Balza's speech, see Marguerite Feitlowitz, *A Lexicon of Terror: Argentina and the Legacies of Torture* (New York, 1998), p. 223.

15 Cámera en lo Criminal y Correccional Federal, Sala II, Privaciones Ilegales de Libertad en el Centro Clandestino de Detención Club Atlético, Buenos Aires, 14 October 1997.

16 Corte Suprema de Argentina, Extradicción de Erich Priebke, 1995.

17 The case, which like the Chilean one involved a victim named Poblete, was decided by Judge Cavallo on March 8, 2001, and upheld by the Appeals Court in November. Fallo de la Salla II de la Camara Federal, Cause no. 17,768 Simón, Julio s/procesamiento, Nov. 9, 2001.

18 For a description of all these cases, see Human Rights Watch, *Argentina, Reluctant Partner: The Argentine Government's Failure to Back Trials of Human Rights Violators*, Dec. 2001.

and others with a desire to point public scrutiny away from current corruption or arms sales scandals. However, the Argentine/Chilean cases in Spain acted as significant catalysts for the local judiciary. In part, the 'Garzón effect'[19] was responsible: local judges saw that Garzón's investigation was considered legitimate, that the legal theories espoused had international currency, and that the judge himself received widespread support and renown. Local judges then felt more comfortable using similar theories, and may well have considered themselves in a better position than a far-off Spanish judge to take up these matters while the eyes of the world were watching. In addition, the Argentine government, like the Chilean, denounced the Spanish case as a violation of sovereignty and insisted that only local courts had jurisdiction. It became easier for judges to take the government's invitation to exercise that jurisdiction at face value, and harder for the government to overtly intervene. Furthermore, Argentine courts have historically been among the most open to reasoning and rationales adapted from other national courts or international tribunals. Argentine law incorporates international law, including customary law, and earlier cases involving ex-Nazis had established the vitality of crimes against humanity, and their imprescriptibility, as part of Argentine law. So parts of the judiciary were predisposed to consider Garzón's *autos* as persuasive legal texts, along with other international materials. And finally, the Pinochet arrest disproved the theory that any efforts at justice would lead to chaos and a return to dictatorship. Indeed, the General's arrest caused relatively little instability within Chile. Both the political parties and the military went out of their way to stress their respect for democratic institutions. That lesson – that justice and stability could coexist –was not lost on the judiciary in other countries.

The first cases to breach the wall of impunity were those that declared that, even if the amnesty laws precluded punishment of offenders, those laws could not affect investigation into the fate of the disappeared. The family members of victims had a 'right to the truth' that was independent and that persisted despite the amnesty law. That right, plus the associated 'right to mourn' common to all peoples, gave rise to an obligation to reopen investigations and pursue them until the manner of death and fate of the body of the disappeared was known.

As a result, not only were cases involving notorious torture centres like the ESMA and the Club Atlético reopened, a number of courts began so-called 'Truth Trials'.[20] While slightly different in each city where they operate, these in essence provide a judicial forum for victims and witnesses to appear before a panel of trial judges and describe their experiences, in the context of investigations

---

19 I thank Roberto Garretón for the phrase.
20 For articles on the trials, see http://www.derechos.org/nizkor/arg. For example, Susana Colombo, 'Derechos Humanos: Reanudan las Audiencias en la Plata,' *Clarín*, 12 March 2001.

into specific police or military facilities. While the courts have subpoenaed alleged perpetrators, few have appeared and given testimony. In some cases, officers have refused to appear on grounds that, even though their testimony cannot be used to incriminate them domestically (due to the amnesty laws), it might well be relevant in investigations and extradition requests issued by a foreign court. Those that have done so have shed light not only on the operation of specific detention centres but on the high degree of coordination among different military branches involved in the repression. The 'truth trials' mechanism, then, becomes a type of hybrid trial and truth commission. According to Judge Leopoldo Schiffrin, who with two other judges heads the 'truth trials' in La Plata, the hope is that eventually the information gathered will create momentum for full prosecutions.[21] Meanwhile, a number of military officers have been charged with contempt for failing to appear before the 'truth trials' or giving false information.[22]

Another line of attack has involved the children of the disappeared. Over 400 children were either born in captivity or kidnapped as infants along with a parent. Almost all the women were killed after giving birth, and the children were given new identities and adopted by military or pro-military families. The crime of child kidnapping was excluded from the amnesty provisions, and while the issue was briefly raised in the 1985 trial of junta members, no one was ever convicted. Nonetheless, until the late 1990s the cases lay dormant, some at an early stage of investigations, some never even the subject of complaints. Judge Garzón's examination of the issue coincided with a number of high-profile cases in which, for the first time, DNA profiling was able to identify disappeared children through their grandparents, as well as with evidentiary breakthroughs establishing that the Campo de Mayo and a few other detention centres had contained specialised 'birthing rooms' for detainees. Garzón issued arrest warrants in a number of high-profile kidnapping cases: for example, when Cecilia Viñas testified in Madrid that Jorge Raúl Vildoza, one of the ESMA officials, had stolen her son, Garzón put out an arrest warrant for Vildoza that resulted in the son (now in his twenties) asking the courts to establish his ancestry through DNA testing.[23] In a number of cases, witnesses came forward in the Spanish investigation who had never testified or filed complaints in Argentina out of fear – the distance, and the prestige of the tribunal, convinced

21 Interview, *La Plata*, 21 June, 2001.
22 The Supreme Court eventually held that witnesses could not be forced to testify under oath if they could possibly incriminate themselves, despite the amnesty laws, because of the possibility of foreign prosecutions or prosecutions for crimes not covered by the amnesty. Human Rights Watch, supra. Note 18.
23 Available at http://www.derechos.org/nizkor/arg/juicio

them to talk. For the first time, a number of judges began simultaneously investigating various child-kidnappings, as well as looking into the systematic nature of the practice throughout the military. Thus, again, the Spanish case was not the sole 'cause' of renewed interest in child-snatching charges against many of the major operatives of the 1970s, but it clearly was one major factor in reinvigorating investigation into the practice.

One of the cases involving child kidnapping was that of a disappeared couple, José Liborio Poblete Roa and his wife Gertrudis Marta Hlaczik. Poblete, a Chilean-born disability rights activist who used a wheelchair, and his wife were held in the El Olimpo camp and ultimately killed; their eight-month-old child Claudia was taken away and given to a military family who established a false identity for her. In 1998, as a result of a complaint from the child's grandmother, the prosecutor filed a criminal complaint; Judge Gabriel Cavallo was assigned the case. As a child-kidnapping case, it was not covered by the amnesty laws, although the parents' disappearance was. Cavallo found that it was illogical to be able to investigate and arrest those responsible for the crime against the child, but not the crimes against the child's parents. The obstacle, of course, was the *punto final* and due obedience laws. Judge Cavallo, in a 156-page decision,[24] found those laws to violate both international law and Argentine constitutional law. He held that under principles of customary international law as well as treaty obligations, Argentina could not refuse to prosecute crimes against humanity. The Federal Court of Buenos Aires has since confirmed both this and similar rulings made by other judges, prompting a final appeal to the Supreme Court (which already once upheld the same laws). If it is confirmed, Cavallo's ruling could allow for the reopening of hundreds of other cases.

Related cases in other national courts

Cavallo

One of the more interesting extensions of the Pinochet case involves the detention of alleged ESMA torturer Ricardo (Miguel Angel) Cavallo in Mexico in August 2000. The facts of the Cavallo case seem novelesque: Cavallo, using the ill-gotten proceeds of his work identifying and interrogating prisoners at the ESMA (and confiscating their property), eventually started a company creating 'smart' vehicle registration identification cards for governments. The company won contracts in Bolivia, El Salvador and Mexico. The Mexican contract was controversial because it privatised public records, quadrupled costs to drivers and was awarded by the notoriously corrupt PRI-led government, which

24 Cited at note 17.

justified it as useful to impede car theft and the falsification of documents. In conjunction with the contract, Cavallo went to Mexico and made a televised appeal to Mexicans to obtain their i.d. cards. A Mexican newspaper began investigating the contract, found out about Cavallo's military past, interviewed ESMA survivors who identified him, and published the story. Alarmed, Cavallo booked a flight back to Argentina, but on Friday, August 24, as the plane was refuelling in Cancún, he was served with an arrest warrant issued by a public prosecutor for using a false identity.

The incoming administration of President Fox was happy about the arrest, as the policies of Cavallo's company, Renave, were associated with the worst elements of the discredited PRI. Meanwhile, Judge Garzón had listed Cavallo as a suspect, but through an oversight no international arrest warrant was pending. Garzón, who was then on vacation, got word from his substitute judge that Cavallo had been arrested but that to hold him, an arrest warrant needed to be issued within 48 hours; the Spanish lawyers in the Argentine case convinced the substitute judge to file the warrant for him based on the existing record. Garzón flew back to Madrid and issued an amplified warrant and request for extradition to Spain on charges of genocide, torture and terrorism.

On January 11 2001 Mexican federal circuit court judge Luna agreed that Cavallo could be extradited to Spain for genocide and terrorism.[25] He found that Judge Garzón had probable cause to find that Cavallo was implicated in these crimes, as required by Mexican law and the Spain–Mexico Extradition Treaty. He relied on the Convention Against Torture and other international treaties, as well as Mexican and Spanish law, to ground extraterritorial jurisdiction. He followed the Spanish Audiencia Nacional's 1998 decision on Argentina and Chile,[26] holding that the fact that the 1983 Spanish law establishing extraterritorial jurisdiction was subsequent to the alleged crimes did not violate the prohibition on *ex post facto* laws. That law merely provided a procedural vehicle, while international treaties had long prohibited the substantive offences. The rules regarding non-retroactivity apply only to substantive, not procedural, rules.

Judge Luna refused to allow extradition for torture, holding that the Mexican statute of limitations at the time the crimes were committed was the applicable law, and that statute had expired. Even though the law might be different now, the principle of lenity (most favourable law for the defendant) required that the torture charges not be allowed. The Ministry of Foreign Affairs disagreed. As

25 The decision is cited at note 12.
26 Auto de la Sala de lo Penal de la Audiencia Nacional confirmando la jurisdicción de España para conocer de los crímenes de genocidio y terrorismo cometidos durante la dictadura argentina, Nov. 5, 1998.

in the UK, the final decision to approve extradition lies with the political branch, in this case Foreign Minister Jorge Castañeda. The Foreign Ministry not only approved the extradition on genocide and terrorism charges, but reinstated the torture charges as well.[27] It relied primarily on Mexican law, which allows the accumulation of charges and the application of the longest statute of limitations (in this case, 30 years for genocide) to all the charges. Secondarily, they noted that Mexico's international obligations under the Convention Against Torture and other international instruments require prosecution of the crime, and that domestic rules on prescription should be read consistently with those international obligations.

Cavallo's pursuit of all possible legal challenges finally placed the issue of Mexico's international obligations and their intersection with domestic law before the Mexican Supreme Court. In June 2003 the Supreme Court ruled in favour of Cavallo's extradition on charges of genocide and terrorism (the torture charges were finally ruled out on the basis that they exceeded the statute of limitations).[28] Mexico thus became the first Latin American country to extradite someone to a third country on the basis of universal jurisdiction.

In the course of the Cavallo case, an interesting side issue arose. The defendant's attorney apparently tried to avoid extradition to Spain by obtaining an Argentine arrest warrant arising from a criminal investigation into his client in Argentina for misappropriation of stolen goods.[29] The Argentine courts eventually declined to issue the warrant, but the attempt raises some of the most interesting questions in the developing practice of universal jurisdiction. Could a defendant defeat extradition and/or jurisdiction by the court of another country prosecuting under a universal jurisdiction provision by showing that a complaint had been filed/accepted by the domestic courts, under a theory that the territorial court has 'primacy'? If so, would the complaint have to be for the same crimes, or related crimes, and to what extent should the extraditing court look into the circumstances underlying the second warrant? Or is the question merely one of 'first in time,' so that the first court to ask for extradition of the defendant gains priority over any others? That is the position of the Mexican government, which reflects current extradition practice. I will return to this question of 'subsidiarity' in considering the Guatemalan case.

Other cases arising from the facts of the Chilean and Argentine investigations in Spain

Following Pinochet's arrest in London, requests for his extradition came from a number of other European countries, including Belgium, France and Switzerland.

27 Acuerdo de la Secretaría de Relaciones Exteriores, 2 February 2001.
28 The decision is available at www.scjn.gob.mx/inicial.asp
29 As reported in the Argentine press at the beginning of 2001.

The Belgian case arose out of a complaint by a number of Chilean exiles living in Belgium, and was grounded on the country's 1993 law[30] allowing universal jurisdiction for war crimes (in this case ill-treatment and killing of civilians, a violation of Article 3 of the 1949 Geneva Conventions given that the Chilean military itself had declared a 'state in time of war'). The Belgian investigating magistrate did not find that the situation in Chile was an internal armed conflict, and therefore could only rely on the statute to invoke the general premise of universal jurisdiction. Instead, he held that the crimes alleged constituted crimes against humanity under customary international law, and that therefore they were directly applicable in Belgian law (despite the fact that they had never been codified in the penal code) and provided sufficient grounding for universal jurisdiction.[31] The Belgian law also specifically excluded the application of immunities. To date, the Belgian case remains open, to discourage any further foreign expeditions by the ex-general, although it has clearly been affected by recent developments in Belgian law.[32]

In Switzerland and France, requests for Pinochet's extradition were based on cases involving Swiss and French citizens, respectively. Neither country has universal jurisdiction legislation that would apply to the relevant time period and crimes, and so the cases were brought under the jurisdictional rubric of 'passive personality.'[33] Recent attempts by French judges Roger Le Loire and Sophie Hélène-Chateau[34] to interview Henry Kissinger about his role in crimes against French citizens in Chile, and the subsequent French indictments against Pinochet, Contreras and others demonstrate that the investigations are continuing. Lawyers representing the families of the French victims have also

---

30 For a description of the law and its evolution, see Luc Reydams, 'Universal Criminal Jurisdiction: The Belgian State of Affairs,' XI Criminal Law Forum No. 2 (2000).

31 Tribunal de 1er. Instance de Bruxelles (Vandermeersch, J.), in re Pinochet, 26 Nov. 1998, partially translated at 93 Am. J. Int'l Law 700 (1999).

32 On June 26, 2002, the Brussels Court of Appeals found, in a case involving Israeli Prime Minister Ariel Sharon, that the 1993 (amended 1999) Belgian law providing the courts with universal jurisdiction could only apply when the defendant was present in Belgium. Since then, the rash of cases based upon the law, including some naming George Bush and General Tommy Franks, commander of US forces in the recent war in Iraq, has contributed to mounting political pressure on the Belgian government to change the law. In June 2003 the government agreed to reduce the scope of the law by limiting the reach of Belgian courts to cases involving Belgian citizens.

33 In France, three separate requests for extradition were filed on Nov. 8, 12 and Dec. 10, 1998, all involving French citizens killed or disappeared in Chile. The Swiss request was based on the disappearance of a Swiss-Chilean citizen, Alexei Jaccard. Formal extradition request filed Nov. 11, 1998. http://www.bap.admin.ch/e/archiv/median/1998/11111.htm (Swiss Federal Department of Justice and Police).

34 Rupert Cornwell, 'The Trials of Henry Kissinger,' The Independent, April 23, 2002.

announced their intention to pursue trial *in absentia* of Pinochet, permitted under French (but not Spanish) law.[35]

At the same time, the Pinochet case gave new impetus to long-standing investigations in Italy and Germany, both of them concerning Argentina. The Italian case dates from 1982, when relatives of Italian citizens or descendants of Italian citizens who were killed or disappeared in Argentina filed the first complaint against the military for killings, disappearances and torture. In 1993 some of the investigating judges visited Argentina to take testimony, causing quite a stir within the Menem government. After a bid by the public prosecutor to close the cases in 1995 for lack of cooperation by the Argentine judicial authorities, the court reduced the number of pending cases from over a hundred to eight. These, under the leadership of a new, more enthusiastic public prosecutor, proceeded in 2000 to the trial *in absentia* of Generals Suárez Mason and Riveros, two of the main architects of the detention camps, and six of their subordinates. The private prosecutions in the case eventually involved the Italian presidency, several regional governments, Italian trade union confederations as well as the family members. A dozen witnesses travelled from Argentina and elsewhere to testify. In December 2000 the accused were found guilty by the Rome court, which included both professional judges and lay jurors.[36]

Cases in Germany are still at the investigative stage, although the Nuremberg public prosecutor has agreed to go forward. A Coalition Against Impunity, made up of lawyers and NGOs, has been urging the prosecutor to investigate 85 disappearances of German citizens or persons of German descent in Argentina. An interesting detail of the German cases is that some of the plaintiffs are descendants of German Jews who left Germany in the 1930s and lost their German citizenship during the Nazi period. Their children were disappeared in Argentina, and the parents are now claiming the protection of the German courts, arguing that the denial of citizenship was illegal and therefore should not impede their ability to bring a complaint.[37] Although the prosecutor originally closed the cases on these grounds, the Federal Supreme Court reversed this and remanded the cases for investigation. Like Spain, Germany does not permit trials *in absentia*. The German government asked its Argentine counterpart to try or extradite the suspects. When the Argentine government, predictably enough, refused, Germany appealed the refusal to the Argentine courts, which

35 Thierry Leveque, 'France Demands Arrests of 15 Pinochet-Era Officials,' Reuters, 25 Oct. 2001.

36 The decision is cited at note 2; this account is based on interviews with participants and attendance at the trial in October 2000.

37 Information on the Coalition's work is available at http://www.desaparecidos.org/arg/coalicion/, http://www.menschenrechte.org/NMRZ/humanrights.htm.

are considering the case.[38]

A related line of investigation stemming from the Pinochet case has involved the multi-governmental repressive strategy known as Operation Condor. An 'anti-subversive Interpol', Operation Condor was a coordinated effort, centred in Chile, by the governments of Brazil, Bolivia, Paraguay, Uruguay, Chile and Argentina to track down and eliminate suspected subversives from all those countries. Those picked up by one military secret service were usually returned to their home country and eventually killed or disappeared; Operation Condor operatives also pursued opponents outside the Southern Cone, and were responsible for the assassinations of Carlos Prats in Argentina and Orlando Letelier in Washington, DC, the attempted assassination of Bernardo Leighton in Italy, and others.[39]

Operation Condor became a focus of Judge Garzón's investigation at an early stage. It was the reason he began investigating Pinochet and the rationale for combining the Argentine and Chilean investigations in Spanish courts into a single umbrella investigation under his jurisdiction.[40] Both Judges García Castellón and Garzón asked the US for documentation about Operation Condor operations. In addition to the information obtained through judicial channels, at the request of US members of congress then-president Clinton agreed to review and release some of the government's files on the Operation.[41] Material from FBI and CIA files has been very useful to people in a number of countries pursuing investigations into the long reach of the Condor.

Since 1998, a number of courts have taken up Operation Condor cases. In Italy, a group of Argentine exiles filed a complaint in 1999 against notorious operatives and torturers including Jorge Acosta, Alfredo Astiz and Jorge Raúl Vildoza for the murder of Italian-Argentine citizens as part of the Operation. The Rome court in charge of the investigation requested the extradition of Astiz as part of the case.[42]

In Argentina, a 1999 case involving Operation Condor led to indictments against ex-Junta members Jorge Videla and Emilio Massera of Argentina, ex-

38 For the German pleadings (in Spanish) see http://alsurdelsur.wanadoo.es or http://www.desaparecidos.org/arg/coalicion/. At the time of this writing (June 2003) the issue is before the Argentine Supreme Court.

39 For a description of the evidence in the Paraguayan archives on Operation Condor, see Katie Zoglin, 'Paraguay's Archive of Terror: International Cooperation and Operation Condor,' 32 U. Miami Inter-Am. L. Rev. 57 (2001).

40 Auto del Juez de Instrucción No. 5, 10 Dec. 1998 (Pinochet indictment, details crimes in connection with Operation Condor).

41 The declassified material in the files is available through the Institute for Policy Studies Pinochet Watch and the National Security Archive in Washington, DC.

42 http://www.hrw.org/reports/2001/argentina/argen1201-08.htm.

president Stroessner of Paraguay, the ex-head of the Uruguayan army and a half-dozen other Uruguayan officers, and Augusto Pinochet, Manuel Contreras (ex-head of the Chilean DINA) and his deputy for, among other things, participating in an illegal conspiracy (*asociación ilícita*). The complainants are family members of Argentines who disappeared in another Southern Cone country, or of Uruguayans, Chileans, Paraguayans or Bolivians detained and/ or disappeared in Argentina. Jurisdiction is based on the fact that the offences either began or were continued on Argentine territory or were part of a conspiracy that committed crimes within Argentina. The complaint also asks the court to apply the Inter-American Convention on Forced Disappearances (which would give Argentina jurisdiction over the case) and to follow existing Argentine jurisprudence that statutes of limitations do not apply to crimes against humanity. The case came before the Federal Court in Buenos Aires, and in April 2001 Judge Rodolfo Canicoba issued arrest warrants for the defendants.[43] Since then, the Chilean and Uruguayan governments have denied the extradition requests, as did Brazil. However, Chilean and Uruguayan courts have opened some domestic enquiries prompted by these investigations.

The Argentine Operation Condor case also resulted in arrest warrants being issued for a number of Uruguayan police and military officials implicated in the torture and disappearance of Argentine citizens sent from Uruguay to the Argentine detention centre at Automotores Orletti. In addition, a Paraguayan prosecutor has asked for the extradition of former Paraguayan dictator Alfredo Stroessner from Brazil, and the Brazilian Congress has demanded an investigation into the local military's participation in Operation Condor.[44] The ramifications of the case have even reached Honduras, where Argentine counter-insurgency advisors were implicated in a spate of disappearances there in the early 1980s.[45]

The investigative work of Judge Garzón on Operation Condor also stimulated the reopening of investigations into the assassination of Orlando Letelier, ex-Foreign Minster under the Allende government, and his aide Ronnie Moffit in Washington, DC, carried out by Chilean operatives as part of Operation Condor. The Letelier investigation had led to convictions in the US of the low-level bombers, plea bargains for others, and the eventual conviction of Manuel

43 A Chilean judge in response to the warrant ordered the arrest of Manuel Contreras. Human Rights Watch, supra, at ch. I.
44 Re Brazilian Congressional investigation into Operation Condor, see Alexandra Barahona de Brito, 'The Southern Cone,' in Barahona de Brito et.al., *The Politics of Memory* (Oxford and New York, 2001).
45 See Honduran National Commissioner for the Protection of Human Rights, *The Facts Speak for Themselves* (New York, 1994).

Contreras and his deputy of the crimes by a Chilean court.[46] The case was never closed because extradition requests for Contreras and Espinoza (although refused by the Chilean Supreme Court) remained pending. Pinochet had never been investigated or charged for his part in the affair. After the Justice Department agreed to cooperate with Garzón's investigation, and began sending some classified materials to Spain, lawyers for the Letelier and Moffit families began pressing Justice Department officials to reopen the investigation. The department sent a letter rogatory to Chile requesting information in August 1999, which was quickly answered by the Supreme Court. In March 2000, a team of Justice Department investigators visited Santiago, interviewing Contreras and a number of other military officers and sparking speculation that an indictment against Pinochet might be forthcoming. While the change of US administrations curtailed its momentum, the investigation remained at least formally ongoing. A group of members of Congress asked the US Justice Department in early 2002 to indict Pinochet for his role in the Letelier affair.[47]

The murder of General Carlos Prats, Allende's Defence Minister, who fled to Buenos Aires after the coup, has also been linked to Operation Condor. In 1974 he and his wife were killed by a car bomb. A Chilean secret police operative, Arrancibia Clavel, was convicted in 2000 of planting the bomb, but until recently investigation into who gave the orders was stalled. After Pinochet returned home, Argentine investigating judge Maria Servini asked to question him (as well as Contreras and other DINA and military operatives) about the case. The judge then issued an indictment against Pinochet and several others, and asked for their extradition from Chile on charges of masterminding the Prats murder. The Chilean Supreme Court twice denied Pinochet's extradition: first (on 6 August 2001) because his immunity needed to be removed, and the second time (8 November 2002) definitively on health grounds. On 2 December 2002 the Chilean Supreme Court decided not to grant extradition of the remaining defendants, but ordered that local courts reopen the Prats case in Chile. The Prats daughters filed a criminal complaint against the defendants on 23 January 2003, thus becoming party to the ongoing criminal investigation.[48]

A final aspect of the renewed lines of investigation concerns the ties between US government officials, especially ex-Secretary of State Henry Kissinger and ex-CIA head Richard Helms, and crimes committed in Chile and Argentina. In addition to Judges Le Loire and Hélène-Chateau of France, Argentine and

---

46 See Mark Ensalaco, *Chile Under Pinochet: Recovering the Truth* (Philadelphia, 2000), pp. 233–5.

47 *Poítica Cono Sur*, Resúmen No. 607, April 21 2002. 25 Members made the third request to the U.S. on February 20, 2002.

48 For a chronology of events, see www.memoriayjusticia.cl/english

Chilean judges have both expressed an interest in questioning Kissinger as a potential witness. A civil suit filed in Washington, DC court by the son of Chilean ex-general René Schneider accuses Kissinger and Helms of complicity in Schneider's killing by a right-wing proto-military group in 1970.[49] In these cases, more information about US backing for the military regimes may come to light.

In short, Operation Condor has been the most fruitful of a number of lines of inquiry originating in the Spanish investigation. By mobilising human rights lawyers and activists, by changing perceptions of the possible, by demonstrating the vulnerability of the once sacrosanct General Pinochet, by forcing governments and judges to allow (or encourage) domestic investigations as a way of proving that outside procedures were unwarranted – in all these ways, the cases acted as a catalyst in both Chile and Argentina, and, to some extent, in the rest of the Americas. Success, however, has its price.

The loosening of interpretations of the Southern Cone's amnesty laws and the consequent resurgence of domestic investigations has created its own contradictions. After all, the premise of the Chilean and Argentine cases was that the most appropriate forum, that of the territorial state, was unavailable. The next-best alternative, investigation and trial elsewhere, was licit because there was no other place to go. Indeed, a number of well-known Chilean human rights lawyers submitted affidavits in the Pinochet case to the effect that domestic prosecutions were impossible. As that impossibility diminished, the potential for cases to undermine, rather than support each other grew. In the Chilean case, lawyers in Spain were careful to cite as specific instances of killings, disappearances and the like only cases that were not the subject of pending complaints in the Chilean courts. As the number of such local complaints climbed over 250, however, avoiding stepping on others' toes became more difficult. With respect to Argentina, a number of incidents are now under investigation in several other countries, with multiple detention and/or extradition requests for the same defendants. One result has been increased direct communication and cooperation among investigating judges, but the potential for confusion remains.

The complexities of extraterritorial jurisdiction emerged in the next such case to come before the Spanish Audiencia Nacional. Enthusiasm for a newly-reinvigorated concept of universal jurisdiction, especially combined with the liberal rules of the Spanish courts on standing and victim participation, led to a

49 Schneider v. Kissinger et.al., Dist. Ct. Washington, DC, filed September 10, 2001. There is also a civil suit pending in the USA against Armando Fernandez-Larios, one of the admitted killers of Orlando Letelier, for his role in the killing of Winston Cabello as part of the Caravan of Death. Cabello v. Fernandez-Larios, C.D.Fla., filed February 1999; First Amended Complaint filed April 7, 1999; Second Amended Complaint filed September 17, 2001.

number of attempts to replicate the success of the Spanish and Argentine investigations. The most important was the complaint made by Rigoberta Menchú, Nobel peace prize winner and indigenous rights activist, involving Guatemala.

The Guatemalan experience

On its merits the Guatemalan case is stronger than those of the Southern Cone. According to the UN-sponsored Historical Clarification Commission (CEH), some 200,000 people have died in Guatemala since 1960, the vast majority of them killed or disappeared by the military as part of systematic anti-subversive campaigns.[50] As importantly, the commission found that the military had committed genocidal acts against the country's Mayan indigenous population in four areas of the country. The report, along with abundant other documentation, made the characterisation of the crimes as genocide within the meaning of Spain's jurisdictional statute a relatively simple matter. In addition, with respect to the non-Mayan victims (about half the cases presented in Spain involved non-Mayans) the plaintiffs relied on a theory similar to that used successfully in the Argentine cases – the perversion of national security doctrine to leave outside the military concept of 'nation' anyone who posed a challenge to military rule.[51] Evidence of torture, disappearances, summary execution and the like had also long been documented by domestic and international human rights groups and by international observers.

Rigoberta Menchú's complaint in December 1999 to the Audiencia Nacional alleged crimes of genocide, torture and state terrorism.[52] It sought an overall condemnation of Guatemala's recent history, in essence asking the court to give judicial weight to the complete findings of the CEH Report. The complaint named 8 defendants who exercised state functions between 1978 and 1986, including three successive heads of state: retired Generals Romero Lucas García, Efraín Ríos Montt and Oscar Humberto Mejía Victores. Also named were the Lucas-era Ministers of Defence and Army Chief of Staff and three high-ranking police officials. Ríos Montt is head of the Guatemalan Congress.

The complaint referred specifically to crimes connected to Spain, including the storming of the Spanish Embassy in January 1980 in which 36 persons died, including Rigoberta Menchú's father and three Spaniards, the murder of three Spanish priests in Quiche in 1980 and 1981, and the abduction and disappearance of another in the capital, also in 1981. The complaint also recounted the

50 Commission for Historical Clarification, *Guatemala: Memory of Silence* (New York, 1999), available at http://hrdata.aaas.org/ceh/report/english/concl.html.
51 Auto de la Sala de lo Penal de la Audiencia Nacional, 6 Nov. 1998.
52 Available at http://www.frmt.org.mx

torture and death of Menchú's mother and two brothers. Over the next few months, a broad array of Guatemalan and Spanish organisations and individuals presented other cases to the judge for investigation, including massacres of peasant villages, killings of well-known political opponents and disappearances, all characterised as part of the overall genocidal and terrorist scheme.

On 27 March 2000, Judge Ruiz Polanco, despite the objections of the Spanish Public Prosecutor's office, accepted jurisdiction over the case. The Prosecutor's office, as it had in the Chilean and Argentine cases, appealed. Many of the arguments about Spanish jurisdiction over extra-territorial genocide were a repeat of those used in earlier cases. However, the Public Prosecutor's office added a new emphasis to the contention that the Guatemalan courts were perfectly capable of judging these crimes, and that therefore Spain should avoid potentially relitigating the same crimes or producing inconsistent outcomes. The Prosecutor pointed to Guatemala's 1996 Law of National Reconciliation, which provides amnesty but exempts the crimes of genocide, torture and forced disappearance, and to two cases where courts had recently convicted low-ranking military officers in human rights-related crimes.

The twelve judges of the Audiencia Nacional's Penal Chamber decided on December 13 2000 to deny Spanish jurisdiction over the case 'at this moment'.[53] The panel, the same that decided the earlier Southern Cone cases, reaffirmed that Spain has jurisdiction over cases of genocide, terrorism and torture committed abroad. However, the court said, that jurisdiction is necessarily subsidiary to national jurisdictions. Otherwise, the Genocide Convention provision (art. 6) that establishes the courts of the place where genocide occurred or an international criminal court as the proper forums for trial would be meaningless. The court also pointed to the structure of the then pending International Criminal Court as evidence that the subsidiarity principle was well-established in international criminal law.[54] That principle could only be overcome if it were shown that the domestic courts were unable to exercise their jurisdiction, either because a law (like the amnesty laws in Argentina and Chile) impeded it, or because the judicial authorities 'are subject to pressure by governmental or de facto powers, such that it can rationally be concluded that in this climate of official persecution or fear the judicial function cannot feasibly be carried out with the serenity and impartiality necessary to judge.'[55] In the Guatemalan case

53 Auto de la Sala de lo Penal de la Audiencia Nacional, 13 Dec. 2000.
54 Under the ICC's 'complementarity' regime, the Court can only act when national courts are unable or unwilling to do so. See Rome Statute of the International Criminal Court, Art. 17 (1998).
55 Audiencia Nacional, Sala de lo Penal, Pleno, Rollo Apelación No.115/2000-12-13, Causa D. Previas 331/99, Jdo. Central Numero Uno.

there was no legal impediment to prosecution, and unlike in the Southern Cone cases not enough time had gone by since the 1999 Clarification Commission's report (which the judges seemed to use as the demarcation of the post-conflict era) to show conclusively that the judiciary was unable to act. Therefore, jurisdiction was denied and the case was to be shelved, although the decision did leave open the possibility of reopening it at some point in the future.

Given the compelling facts of genocide in Guatemala, as well as the existence of a fair amount of evidence to suggest that the Guatemalan courts *have* actually been subjected to a climate of fear and persecution,[56] why did the court decide to shut down the investigation? The most obvious explanation has to do with the concern, increasingly voiced in Spanish legal and political circles, that the Spanish courts are becoming a kind of 'mini-ICC' that will be overwhelmed by cases asking Spain to right injustices around the world. The court needed to send a signal limiting future cases without undermining its prior jurisprudence. Another line of explanation focuses on the weaknesses of the Guatemalan case: in trying to encompass potentially tens of thousands of acts to be investigated, over a long period of time, and including cases (like the Dos Erres massacre) that *are* now under investigation in Guatemala, the case may have seemed too unwieldy to the judges. The Guatemalans, moreover, are in a much weaker position than the Argentines or Chileans in Spain: there are few Guatemalan exiles in Spain, most survivors are Mayan peasants rather than well-placed middle-class urbanites, and few Spaniards know or care much about the country's recent history. There is no core group of lawyers both steeped in Spanish law and with personal and intimate knowledge of Guatemala's recent history and 'who's-who'.

The Guatemalan decision raises more questions than it answers for recent cases. How much time needs to go by before a court can legitimately conclude that the domestic courts are deliberately avoiding investigations? How much intimidation need be shown? The danger is that by using written amnesties as a bright line, the court has merely set up a situation where governments seeking impunity will avoid formal amnesties, and rely on informal, unwritten means such as intimidation or corruption to keep cases from coming before independent judges. The resulting impunity will be harder to challenge outside the country. This is a particular concern as the scope of the Argentine and Chilean amnesty laws are challenged, more and more successfully, in the domestic courts of those countries. At some point soon, national courts will have to grapple with the same issues raised by the International Criminal Court Statute's

56 Nathanael Heasley et al., 'Impunity in Guatemala: The State's Failure to Provide Justice in the Massacre Cases,' *American University International Law Review*, vol. 16, 2001, pp. 1115-1194.

rules on complementarity: when is the territorial state 'unable or unwilling' to prosecute? The legitimacy and ability of national courts, even more than an international court, adequately to do so, is highly uncertain.

The private plaintiffs in the Guatemalan case then appealed to the Spanish Supreme Court, arguing there is no basis in either Spanish or international law for the court's findings on the subsidiarity of jurisdiction, and that in any case the court erred in finding that not enough time had gone by, or that it was possible to freely bring prosecutions, within Guatemala. On 25 February 2002, more than two years later, the Supreme Court decided by an 8:7 vote to partially overturn the lower court decision. The majority held, in short, that only cases with a clear tie to Spain, through the nationality of either complainant or defendant, could proceed. It therefore threw out all the genocide and terrorism charges, leaving only the charges of torture of Spanish victims, including the staff of the Spanish embassy and four priests. The dissent argued that the majority's jurisdictional requirement of a tie to Spain contradicted both the language and the spirit of Spanish law, and that instead the court should engage in a case by case, prudential, practical inquiry into whether the case was closely tied enough to Spanish interests. Thus the fears of advocates that the court would backtrack on earlier endorsements of universal jurisdiction were realised.

Conclusion

The Spanish judicial investigations into the crimes of the Argentine and Chilean military, and especially the detention of Pinochet in London, revitalised the idea of universal jurisdiction and touched off both related and unrelated cases in many parts of the world. I have not discussed the attempted prosecution of Hissène Habré in Senegal, nor the series of cases before the Belgian courts.

Most importantly, the Pinochet case has played a catalytic role in stimulating and accelerating judicial investigations in the 'target' countries. There have been some places where the jurisprudence of the Spanish courts has been taken up by other magistrates, but the effects of the case are less a question of advances in legal theory than in the realm of the imagination. It is true that the Spanish court's finding that the amnesty laws of Chile and Argentina were inapplicable because they violated international law has helped domestic trial judges in those countries bolster the legal argumentation to invalidate those laws. Judge Cavallo's decision in Argentina invalidating the laws on *punto final* and due obedience cites extensively from Judge Garzón's *autos*. However, Argentina had its own jurisprudence on the importance of international law, on the need to comply with the resolutions of the Inter-American Commission and Court on Human Rights, and on the imprescriptability of crimes against humanity. Similarly, Judge Guzmán could rely on existing Chilean penal law in finding that disappearances are continuing crimes, and therefore not subject to either amnesty laws or statutes of limitation so long as the body does not appear.

Rather, the effects were political and moral. The Spanish cases reduced the governments' ability to overtly oppose domestic prosecutions, they legitimised human rights cases in the eyes of judges and made those cases seem worthwhile (or even 'sexy'), they gave new vigour to local human rights movements and victims' associations. In short, they changed the perception of the possible. That is their greatest merit.

CHAPTER II

The Pinochet case and the changing boundaries of democracy

Alexandra Barahona de Brito

This chapter explores the impact of the Pinochet case, and more widely, of the transnational pursuit of justice for past human rights violations, on democratic governance. It is argued that the case and others like it present two main challenges. First, they challenge 'pacted' transitions, or more generally, national elite pacts which violate international human rights or general civil and political rights standards. This means that an initially 'restricted' democracy is not challenged by an increased 'power of the people' *nationally*, but by the force of an emerging *international* quasi-citizenship, based on the equal or even superior legitimacy of a new human rights creed.

Second, the case and others like it promote or are characterised by a 'judicialisation' of politics, whereby national courts, when in concurrence with international norms, are able to gain a force beyond frontiers never witnessed before. This challenges the central role of the executive in domestic and international policy where human rights are concerned, signalling a shift from the very executive focused approach of the transitional period, and posing questions regarding the nature of the role of democratic states in international life.

It is further argued that these trends are a product of various factors that are changing sovereign boundaries. This, in turn, alters the nature of the relationship between democratic governance and international politics, raising the question of the long-term legitimacy and efficacy of national democratic governance and the related problem of global governance. For, if the authority of democratic national executives is challenged by global or regional norms, it is also the case that there are as yet no comparable accountable, global or regional democratic or representative institutions that can take the role of representation of a new 'global citizenry'.

Transnationalising the search for justice: four cases

A brief overview of four cases in the Southern Cone: Argentina; Brazil; Uruguay and Chile shows that before the arrest of General Pinochet in London there was already a well-established trend to seek out justice in extra-national arenas. The constraints imposed by negotiated transitions had limited progress toward justice for past human rights violations. As the relatives of the victims of repression continued to seek avenues to vindicate their claims they found foreign allies and began to take legal action beyond national boundaries. The strength of their claims has been based on the international and regional human rights commitments adopted by each country since transition to democracy.

The search for truth and justice can be summarised schematically into four dynamics that in some cases correspond to phases. Although these phases are not chronologically similar in each case, and there is considerable overlap between one phase and another (which is why dynamics may be a more appropriate term), it is nonetheless useful to present the dynamics of the search for truth and justice in this way in order to convey the tension and complementarity between official policies (or lack thereof) and civil society responses.

The first phase occurs when national official initiatives are undertaken during the immediate post-transitional period. These initiatives establish the 'parameters' for action and counter-action, which civil society and other non-executive actors contest, react to or collaborate with. This is generally the period when a 'peace vs. stability' debate dominates, and it becomes apparent that the search for justice will be limited by political considerations. The second phase, also during the early transitional period, is characterised by the emergence of civil society actions pursuing justice and truth. Arguments of duty to punish are counterposed to 'stability' arguments. The groups favouring truth and justice often make use of various legal or political 'loopholes' in the wall of impunity. Governments respond by making some concessions but also by closing other avenues to justice, either in order to avoid de-stabilisation, or out of lack of interest or sympathy with the cause of the victims and their relatives.

The third phase is characterised by the search for extra-national avenues for the pursuit of truth and justice. NGOs, courts and other allies 'go transnational' in the absence of satisfactory national responses. This occurs in the post-transitional period, with arguments shifting to the legitimacy of the sources of justice/law. The final phase is still underway and will continue for a long time to come if the continued search for and trials of Nazi war criminals are indicators to go by. All instruments, avenues and actors are combined (national official, national and transnational civil society and regional or international official instruments) in variable ways and with varying intensity in each setting. This is the period of democratic 'consolidation', during which the recognition predominates that there is possible compatibility between retroactive justice and democracy, but also a realisation of the inevitably selective and limited nature of justice, even when political will is available.

Argentina

In Argentina, after the establishment of a truth commission and trials under the Alfonsín transitional presidency, President Menem issued pardons by decree law in October 1989 and January 1991, freeing all military officers jailed for human rights violations. In response, the human rights movement worked with sectors within the national legislature, the judiciary, local and state authorities, journalists, academics and other professional associations, to seek compensation, find the dead, and bring violators to court. More importantly for the argument presented here, these actors and organisations also appealed to international sources of authority to contest impunity.

Following decisions by the Inter-American Human Rights Court (IAHRC), a 1991 presidential decree and three subsequent laws of 1991, 1994 and 1995 were passed to provide financial assistance to all former political detainees, and to the parents and children of the disappeared. The Secretaría de Derechos Humanos (SDH) was established to continue with investigations for purposes of compensation. By September 1998, it had received over 13,000 applications for compensation from former political prisoners and processed 7,000 when the right to apply expired. It also received thousands of requests from the relatives of the disappeared. As of February 1998, US$ 655,574,539 had been paid out and it was estimated that total reparations would amount to US$ 750 million by 2000. In 1992, the IAHRC also ruled against the presidential pardons. It stated that the relatives had a 'right to know' the whereabouts of the disappeared. In 1996 it called on Argentina to investigate their fate and establish a truth commission to that end. Under pressure from the Inter-American system, as well as relatives' organisations such as the Grandmothers of the Disappeared, in 1992 the government created the National Commission for the Right to Identity. It works with the National Genetic Databank, and has played a crucial role in investigations into the location of children of disappeared people illegally adopted by military families. Thus, international and regional obligations, as well as international diplomatic and regional legal pressures, and transnational prosecution efforts have given impetus to the work of domestic human rights organisations (HROs) and gradually weakened the initially adversarial position of the government. The ratification of regional and international human rights instruments did not allow the executive to simply dismiss challenges to the legitimacy of political decisions favouring impunity.[1]

Alongside official pressure from the Inter-American human rights system, Argentine repressors have come under attack from transnational *ad hoc* coalitions of victims and relatives. These groups have made use of the national adoption of human rights instruments that counter decisions favouring impunity. One such group, the European Coalition against Impunity in Argentina, created in 1998, brings together NGOs from Belgium, France, Germany, Italy and Sweden, among other countries, and has sought justice for the more than 500 European citizens murdered by the military regime. European courts have initiated proceedings against or investigations about Argentine repressors in France,[2] Italy,[3] Germany,[4] Honduras, Spain, Sweden and the USA.[5] Some former military officers have been tried and sentenced *in absentia*, while others have international arrest warrants pending against them. Argentine courts have also requested the extradition of former Chilean repressors in cases of human rights violations that took place on Argentine soil, including the assassination of General Carlos Prats in Buenos Aires.

Spanish judge Baltazar Garzón initiated the best-known transnational proceeding in 1997, in connection with which by 1999 there were 98 arrest warrants for military officers and civilians outstanding.[6] The support of international

---

1 Douglass Cassell, 'Lessons from the Americas: Guidelines for International Response to Amnesties for Atrocities,' *Law and Contemporary Problems*, vol. 59, issue 4, 1996, pp. 197–230.

2 Retired Captain Alfredo Astíz was tried in absentia on 16 March 1990 and condemned to lifelong imprisonment for participation in the torture and disappearance of two French nuns. Astíz is also wanted in Sweden for the abduction a 17-year old student. Other French suits were filed in 1999 against Eduardo Massera, Antonio Bussi, Carlos Suárez Masón.

3 More than 200 people of Italian descent were disappeared in Argentina. In 1997 (over twenty years after the pro-justice campaign began) the first preliminary hearings were held on the homicide of six Italian citizens involving seven military officers. Since then, suits have been filed against forty officers, but only fifteen cases are still underway. The others were closed. See: www.derechos.org/nizkor/italia/acusados/imputados.html

4 Prosecution efforts were initiated in 1998, headed by the Coalition Against Impunity formed in March of that year and made up of over fifteen lawyers, human rights and church related organisations. 75 Germans or individuals of German descent were disappeared during the Dirty War.

5 There have been no criminal prosecutions in the USA, but individuals have made use of the Alien Tort Claims Act to prove civil liability and gain compensation for violations. In a landmark suit of 1994, a US court tried the Argentine government for abuses committed against one of its citizens forcing it to pay a settlement, and admit to torture as well as abuse and fraud.

6 In 1998, the Spanish Audiencia Nacional (AN) issued an international arrest warrant for former junta member general Leopoldo Galtieri (who has since died) and nine other Argentine officers for crimes committed against Spanish nationals. By December 1998, Judge Baltazar Garzón was investigating 152 officers.

actors and institutions has been crucial in giving continued hope to domestic HROs. It has helped to persuade them to continue to dedicate important political and institutional resources to the issue. It has also given supporters of the cause new instruments to pressure the government. In 1999, for example, two congressional deputies presented a judicial complaint against Menem and two of his ministers for violating the treaty for judicial co-operation with Spain in the case.[7]

Brazil

Brazilian repressors have not been the objects of transnational prosecution efforts as yet. Learning from its neighbours, Brazil has been careful to ratify regional human rights instruments with reservations, precisely to exclude the possibility of a retroactive application. This was the case when it accepted IACHR jurisdiction in 1998. At the same time, the military amnesty law of 1979, which was negotiated between the outgoing regime and opposition forces to ensure that all politicians formerly barred from political activity would regain full civil and political rights, has never been seriously contested. The struggle of the relatives has centred on a search for the truth rather than punishment and on achieving state recognition of responsibility and compensation for the deaths of the detained and disappeared. This may change.

The first signs of a new pursuit of domestic justice emerged in 1999. Following a 13-year campaign by Torture Never Again groups and various medical associations, disciplinary proceedings were initiated against 26 physicians who had worked in military prisons and were involved in torture.[8] The Rio Centro case of April 1981, when two bombs exploded in a shopping centre full of left-wing concertgoers, also killing one law enforcement officer and wounding another has been reopened. In addition, it looks increasingly possible that the hitherto unassailable amnesty of 1979 will be challenged as a result of external events. As in the case of Argentina and indeed all the countries of the Southern Cone involved in the network, the discovery in 1992 in Paraguay of documents relating to Operation Condor has produced new transnational investigations, both in Latin America and Europe.[9] Operation Condor refers to an operation whereby the Chilean DINA (Directorate of National Intelligence) co-ordinated international repressive campaign across borders, not only in the Southern Cone but also as far afield as Embassy Row in Washington and Rome. In May 2000 the Federal Chamber of Deputies established an eleven member Special

7 See:www.derechos.org/nizkor/arg/espana/menem.html

8 Larry Rohter, *New York Times*, 11 March 1999.

9 On the request for Operation Condor documents in the Spanish-Argentine case see: www.derechos.org/nizkor/arg/espana/condor.html

Commission to investigate the 1976 death of former president João Goulart in 1976 and the fate of other political leaders who died around the same time in suspicious circumstances, in the light of facts that have emerged about Operation Condor.[10] Although suits have yet to be filed at home or abroad, new information continues to emerge and may yet lead to pressures to reopen old cases.

Uruguay

Successive Uruguayan governments since 1989 successfully resisted the search for truth and justice led by human rights NGOs and some left wing personalities from the Blanco and left parties, aided by a 1989 amnesty law which was ratified by a closely fought plebiscite. (It is important to note that the fact that the decision to give up the search for justice was accepted through a democratic vote means that its legitimacy cannot be questioned in the same way that a presidential pardon might be). Despite this impediment to justice and truth, the relatives of the dead and tortured continued to pressure the government. They were aided by diplomatic pressure from various European countries and international organisations. National HROs appealed also to the IAHRC against the amnesty law and both the IAHRC (1992 and 1993) and the UN Commission for Human Rights ruled that the government should derogate the amnesty law and carry out investigations.

However, unlike the situation in Argentina, state authorities ignored both rulings, while repressors have escaped transnational prosecution efforts. Nonetheless, relatives have continued with their attempts to locate the bodies of the disappeared. Their demands have centred on a 'loophole' in the amnesty law that, while precluding trials, states that the government is obliged to promote the investigation of the whereabouts of the disappeared. Popular support for truth is high. In 1997, a reported 54% of people polled were in favour of locating the bodies and investigating how they died, while 8% wanted at least the former. Only 14% felt that the amnesty had closed the matter and 10% that further investigations would be dangerous.[11] The election as president of Colorado Party leader Jorge Batlle brought about a surprising shift in the position of the state with regard to truth seeking. A Comisión por La Paz was established in August 2000, presided over by the Archbishop of Montevideo, to investigate the whereabouts of Uruguayans who disappeared in Uruguay and Argentina between 1973 and 1985. The Commission report was handed in to then president Batlle in October 2002. The Commission received more than 200 *denúncias* of disappearances (39 in Uruguay and 170 in Argentina). In April 2003, the government accepted the conclusions of the report, thus officially recognising

10 See: www.pdt.org.br/jgmort.htm
11 Poll carried out by *Factum* in urban and rural areas, published in *Brecha* 596, 2 May 1997.

for the first time that the disappeared died following kidnapping and torture in clandestine detention centres by the military. The report confirmed that 81 Uruguayans (26 in Uruguay and 55 in Argentina) had disappeared under these conditions. The bodies were exhumed in 1984, incinerated and their ashes thrown in the Plate River. The government said it would take responsibility for the deaths in Uruguay and may follow the report recommendation for compensation for the relatives of the disappeared. At the same time, in an important break with impunity, that same month, the courts sentenced the former Minister of Foreign Relations (1972-1976), Juan Carlos Blanco, for ordering the detention of Elena Quinteros, who disappeared during the dictatorship after being kidnapped from the Uruguayan Embassy in Venezuela in June 1976. The Uruguayan courts also asked the US and Argentine governments for information in connection with the assassination of former legislators, Zelmar Michelini and Héctor Gutiérrez Ruiz who were kidnapped in Buenos Aires in 1976.

Chile

In Chile, the inability or unwillingness of successive governments since 1990 to abolish the 1978 Amnesty Law, which covers all human rights violations committed between 1 September 1973 and 10 March 1978, meant that justice was generally not accessible to victims and their relatives. Although the state set up a Corporation to investigate cases additional to those verified by the Truth Commission, and established a programme of monetary and social compensation, actual trials have been difficult to pursue successfully. Despite this limitation, Chile now has the highest number of officers and violators in general in jail for human rights crimes (crimes committed after the amnesty were not covered). Indeed, that the first such case was a success was largely due to transnational pressure – the US insistence on the trial and punishment of those responsible for the Letelier-Moffit assassination in Washington DC in 1976. This was the first case of international terrorism on US soil, only a few miles from the White House, a fact that has taken on added meaning following the terrorist attacks in the US on 11 September 2001.

On 30 May 1995, the Supreme Court confirmed the sentences against former DINA head Manuel Contreras and Colonel Pedro Espinoza for that crime. The major case, however, of which the Pinochet case is a product, is the Spanish suit, filed in May 1998, accusing the general and others of the deaths of 200 people during Operation Condor. Subsequently, various proceedings and extradition requests have been initiated against human rights violators by countries including Austria, Belgium, Canada, Denmark, France, Germany, Italy, Norway, Switzerland, Sweden and the United Kingdom, as well as the US. Some prosecution efforts had already been undertaken in the USA following the

Letelier-Moffit assassination, leading to the imprisonment of individuals who carried out the bomb attack. As a result of Spanish prosecution efforts and of renewed pressure from the relatives of US victims, the investigation was reopened, under the aegis of the Federal Prosecutor of the District of Colombia, Roscoe Howard, with the US Department of Justice. In February 2002, a group of 25 congressmen called for the speedy conclusion of that investigation by bringing to trial all those involved, invoking the new anti-terrorist language of the post 11-September world. As of June 2003, no indictments had been made, although, ironically, in July 2001, the US Immigration and Naturalisation Service (INS) released Virgilio Paz Romero, one of the material authors of the assassination. After confessing to participation in the crime in 1991, he completed six years of a twelve year sentence and was then put under INS guard. He was released after the US Supreme Court ruled unconstitutional the INS detention of an immigrant for more than six months. The following month José Dionisio Suárez Esquivel was also released following (he had been detained in 1990 and served time until 1997) for the same reason.

US victims of the Chilean repression also included Charles Horman, about whom the Costa Gavras film *Missing* was made, and Frank Teruggi, who were both executed at the National Stadium in Santiago in 1973, as well as Ronnie Moffit who was killed with Letelier in the 1976 car-bombing. In Italy, former DINA agent Michael Townley was sentenced to 18 years on 11 March 1993 for the attempted assassination in Rome of Chile's former vice-president, Bernardo Leighton, and his wife, Ana Fresno, in 1975. On 24 June 1995 General Manuel Contreras was sentenced to 20 years *in absentia* for the same crime. The Pinochet arrest served to revitalise the search for justice within Chile. Despite the anti-climactic resolution by the British government, the courts began to show much greater willingness to try cases. Although the Amnesty Law led to the closure of court cases investigating 170 disappearances, one sixth of the total number of cases under investigation (HRW, 1999), in 1998–1999, five generals, including a former member of the military junta, approximately 30 active duty and retired officers were arrested and jailed for human rights crimes. Further, as of June 2003 an estimated 299 cases had been presented against Pinochet and others.[12] This was not only the result of the Pinochet arrest. It was essentially the product of a longer-term trend within the Supreme Court. As pro-regime judges retired, a new Court composition meant that a more favourable (to victims) interpretation of the Amnesty Law began to emerge.

What may be observed, then, through an examination of the cases of Argentina, Brazil, Chile and Uruguay, is a tendency for human rights activists to seek

12 See http://www.fasic.org

extra-national arenas for justice and truth when national avenues are unavail-able or deemed unsatisfactory. At the same time, the force of transnational prosecution efforts serves to revive the search for justice domestically, gener-ating a two way dynamic towards justice. This effect is clearly greater in Argentina and Chile. In large part, this can be attributed to the lesser number of foreign victims in Brazil and Uruguay, the fact that these dictatorships were not as well known or internationally scrutinised, and because neither developed human rights movements as strong and with such international name recogni-tion as those of Chile and Argentina. Even so, even in Brazil and Uruguay, this two way dynamic tells us a lot about the shifting locus of sovereignty and demo-cratic authority. The following two sections of this chapter explore these issues.

Elite pacts and popular sovereignty: who are 'the people'?

Conflict over the Pinochet case was not between states violating the sover-eignty of another state, as the Chilean government often claimed. Nor was it a manifestation of 'imperialism'. Some Spaniards wanted the general to return home as much as some Chileans did. Other Chileans, however, allied them-selves with other Spaniards and Europeans because they wanted the General to be tried in the name of a principle that they felt 'trumped' that of national sovereignty: universal jurisdiction for crimes against humanity.

Latin American governments submitted to such pressures have tended to resist the logic of universal jurisdiction because it is perceived to impinge on national sovereignty and pose a threat to political decisions and national 'elite pacts' based on an at least partial closure of the past. The ethical-juridical logic of transnational prosecution efforts challenges the logic of political accommo-dation and compromise behind transitional pacts and consensus-building mechanisms in circumstances where outgoing authoritarian actors still retain a measure of power. Such prosecution efforts also take beyond sovereign boundaries what were once national struggles between executives, on the one hand, and judiciaries and human rights organisations on the other. In sum, the authority, legitimacy and stability of national executives and of transitional 'foundational' political pacts is challenged as national and international actors work in alliance to contest the terms according to which transitions to demo-cracy in the region were carried out.

This raises a key question: which is more legitimate, a sovereign popular decision or international human rights law? How do we reconcile the two? Does a majority democratic decision taken in a conditioned national context rule supreme, or should it be 'trumped' by a minority will to pursue justice in an open international context? At the time of Pinochet's arrest, Chile was a democracy. According to classic democratic theory, sovereignty was held by the people within a bounded territorial unit. Chile's people implicitly opted for near impunity by accepting a transition, framed by various transitional provisions of the Constitution of 1980, which ensured a step-by-step passage to a 'protected democracy'. They accepted a constitution that ensured the continued power of the military and the right in the political system, and which protected the great majority of human rights violators from justice. They accepted a threshold for constitutional reform that did not allow reform without right-wing support. They accepted a voting system that ensured the over-representation of the right in the legislature and the existence of nine appointed senatorial positions, four of which are nominated by the Armed Forces and the Supreme Court. This sovereign choice meant that it was impossible to derogate the Amnesty Law, or to reform the military justice system to ensure that human rights cases would be heard in the civilian courts. Thus, the Supreme Court, which co-operated with the regime and helped to legitimise it, initially sent the great majority of cases to the military courts where they were closed with a 'preventive' application of the amnesty law.

If most Chileans accepted all this as part of a 'transitional deal', what right do other Chileans have to contest that decision outside Chilean borders? There are legitimate grounds for their action. First, the Chilean dictatorship produced an estimated 200,000 exiles, almost two per cent of the population.[13] These individuals settled in up to 140 countries, the majority in Europe. Exiles, as well as individuals with dual nationality, have a right of recourse to national courts for redress, even if their rights have been violated elsewhere. For these individuals and those supporting them, popular sovereignty would seem to be conceived of as lying less in their right to vote, and more in their right to justice, a good which they must gain by resorting to international institutions and norms.

Second, foreign institutions can pronounce on the legitimacy of democratic decisions adopted within the national sphere, because national governments have given them the right to do so. Although there was no exact precedent for trying a Head of State in the particular circumstances surrounding the Pinochet case, prosecution of crimes against humanity is based on well-established principles to which all the state parties involved in this particular case are subject.[14] The ratification of human rights treaties is one form of concession of sovereignty (of the right to treat ones citizens as one pleases), as is the emergence and

13 Thomas Wright and Rody Oñate, *Flight from Chile: Voices of Exile* (Albuquerque, 1998), p. 91.
14 For details see: AI 'United Kingdom Universal Jurisdiction and Absence of Immunity for Crimes Against Humanity,' January 1999 at http://www.amnesty.org.uk/news/pinochet/report.html.

reinforcement of regimes of conditionality. These constitute an admission by states that sovereignty cannot be absolute, particularly where human well-being and core values are concerned. The democracy protecting regimes within the EU, the Council of Europe, the Organisation for Security and Co-operation in Europe (OSCE), as well as the Organization of American States (OAS) and the Rio Group among others, for example, indicate that democratic nations accept that non-intervention cannot be an argument when human well being is at stake.

Thus, the sovereign right of the people has a dual residence. It resides in the national government house, but also in a nebulous house of international citizenship built out of an evolving international human rights law.

Shifting sovereign boundaries and the impact on democratic governance

The phenomenon outlined above is the product of wider changes, both domestic and international. I will outline four factors, which I will call 'revolutions' because of the depth of their present, and above all potential, impact.

First, there is the 'human rights revolution' which, from the early 1970s onwards introduced the discourse and practice of human rights firmly into the international arena. The discourse of human rights 'has narrowed the gaps between state and society, and between state and world, by providing a common normative currency that is exchanged by government, international institutions, and civil society.'[15] The human rights revolution is not just discursive, but also legal, normative and institutional. Court jurisprudence around the world is questioning the principles of 'immunity from jurisdiction' and 'immunity of state agencies' from prosecution for wrongdoing. Normatively, the revolution consists of conventions and instruments for the promotion and protection of human rights within the United Nations and regional organisations in Latin America, Europe and even Africa. Since 1993, the UN Vienna Human Rights Conference Declaration and Programme of Action states that the universality of human rights is 'beyond question', and further places States under the obligation to promote 'universal respect for, and observance and protection of, all human rights and fundamental freedoms for all.'

Institutionally, the first attempts since 1945 to bring grave human rights crimes to justice, the International Criminal Tribunals for the Former Yugoslavia (ICTFY) and Rwanda (ICTR), make modestly credible for the first time the claim that such egregious human rights crimes will be taken seriously internationally. These courts demonstrate the existence of a post-Cold War linkage between security and justice and the importance attached to the rights of

15 Richard Falk, *Human Rights Horizons: The Pursuit of Justice in a Globalising World*. (London, 2000), p. 54.

individuals above and beyond their membership of a sovereign community. Further, the establishment of the ICC is perhaps the clearest indicator that the concern of the international community with gross violations is not *ad hoc* but permanent.

Second, there is the 'democratic revolution'. Processes of democratisation or re-democratisation in various parts of the world from the 1980s onwards have consolidated and given renewed force both to the notion of human rights and to civil society networks defending human rights. Democracy is the form of government that most bases itself on the notion of individual rights and as such, is most likely to offer (although it does not guarantee) the conditions for the realisation of basic rights (including the right to justice). By promoting the core value of the rule of law, of the presumption of innocence, of fair trial and adequate legal defence, it is the system most sympathetic to the search for justice at the national and international levels. At the same time, democracy 'frees' civil society from the constraints that it suffers under totalitarian or authoritarian political conditions, and allows it to participate more freely and effectively at all levels of the decision-making process.

Further, democracy perhaps more than any other regime type tends to force governments to widen the circle of participation in decision-making to other actors, allowing civil society actors in the form of non-governmental organisations to participate in the formulation of policy. As democracies and their relations with the outside world have become more permeable and complex, authority and legitimacy are spread and shared unevenly among various actors, ranging from individuals mobilised around universal ethical issues, to partially autonomous sub-regions within nations, to professional associations with strong international links. Human rights organisations have thus gained increased recognition by governmental actors in the elaboration of national, regional and international human rights platforms.

This shift in the nature of international decision-making by democratic states means that national executives now have to achieve legitimacy in new ways. They can no longer appeal to a nebulous but unitary notion of 'the national interest' because they are no longer its sole owners. They must struggle with and co-opt other actors, both national and international, with a recognised 'right' to defining what has now become a shifting and comprehensive entity, partly defined by groups whose legitimacy is sometimes inferior, sometimes equal to, or that even sometimes 'trumps' that of national executive authority. In this context, myriad actors can set in motion events that have a significant impact on inter-state relations.

This brings us to the third 'revolution', the emergence of transnational activist networks.[16] The challenges posed by transnational prosecution efforts have emerged not only because there are democracies and independent judiciaries on a world-wide scale never witnessed before or a set of international human rights laws and norms which now has unprecedented force. They emerge because these norms, democracies and judiciaries now exist in conjunction with another key phenomenon. This is the appearance of groups or individuals linked to *ad hoc* but powerful transnational coalitions that actively pursue normative goals such as human rights causes, which have the legal expertise, know-how and financial capacity to take such cases to court.

Prosecution efforts against human rights violators have been advanced by mixed transnational coalitions, which include exiles, judges, Church and human rights related non-governmental organisations, consuls and ambassadors, forensic scientists, psychologists specialising in the trauma of torture and disappearance, and left-wing political parties linked to the victims of repression. NGOs and their allies are playing a growing role in international litigation, participating in the proceedings of permanent international courts, as *amicus curiae*, contributing to the solidity of the jurisprudence of court decisions. Litigation has increased in all international courts, particularly human rights cases. Since the 1980s NGO pressure has been crucial in pushing US federal courts to pursue civil suits against human rights violators in accordance with the provisions of the 1793 Alien Tort Claims Act and the 1992 Torture Victims Protection Act. Individuals accused of grave human rights violations from various Latin American and other countries have been tried and millions of dollars awarded in damages. In Europe, since the early 1990s, courts have criminally pursued Rwandans, Bosnian Serbs and former Latin American military officers and government officials for human rights crimes.[17]

The Pinochet case is only the most famous of these cases. It boosted the notion that, in the absence of a working ICC, the courts of any country could legitimately try the subject of any other country for crimes against humanity and other gross human rights violations. Although Pinochet was returned to Chile and will not be judged there, the affirmation of extra-territorial jurisdiction against arguments of sovereignty, the denial of immunity to a former head of state, and the acceptance of broad definitions of genocide and terrorism by the Spanish courts were of crucial importance.[18]

Such networks are supported by, and their legitimacy to intervene has also

---

16 See Margaret E. Keck and Kathryn Sikkink, *Activists Beyond Borders: Advocacy Networks in International Politics*. (Ithaca, NY, 1998).

17 See Naomi Roht-Arriaza, 'The Role of International Actors in National Accountability Processes,' in Alexandra Barahona de Brito et al. (eds.), *The Politics of Memory: Transitional Justice in Democratising Societies* (Oxford, 2001), pp. 40–64

18 *Ibid.*

been fortified by, the existence of a global public that is quickly mobilised on human rights issues, and by new communications technologies, allowing an abuse in any country to be rapidly known throughout the globe. The 'snowball' effect set in motion by this precedent is notable. Examples include the Senegalese arrest in 2000 of the former leader of Chad, Hissène Habré for torture, the Mexican arrest in 2000 of Miguel Angel Cavallo, an Argentine military officer accused by a Spanish court of genocide, terrorism and torture, and the accusations levelled against Israeli premier, Ariel Sharon, in Belgium in 2001.[19]

National courts, international jurisdiction

One manifestation of the problems introduced by this new context may be seen in the role of the judiciary. In today's world of plastic sovereignty, where 'the rights of human rights' transcend national boundaries, the authority of the judiciary has spilled out beyond national frontiers and is challenging that of national executives in the international arena. The growing scope and power of national courts is the second area in which one can see challenges to traditional conceptions of democratic authority and to the executive branch as the unchallenged institutional state actor in international affairs. Here, one must look at two issues: one is the relationship between national executives and judiciaries and their respective roles in the foreign arena, and the second is the legitimacy of national judiciaries as administrators of international law.

As far as the first is concerned, the Pinochet case illustrates how difficult it has become for governments to restrict decision-making to executive arenas. The days are gone when governments monopolised the world stage. Like all institutions, national executives struggle to maintain their prerogatives. One of these prerogatives, already partly contested in this age of public opinion politics, powerful non-governmental organisations and interest groups, is control over foreign policy. In a world of strictly delineated sovereignty, judicial independence is not a factor in inter-state relations. Judges can and do enter into conflict with executives, but those conflicts are restricted to the national sphere. They are about defining the nature of democratic politics within states. The principle and practice of universal jurisdiction, however, is allowing national judiciaries to take a front seat in international relations with unpredictable consequences.

The fact that judiciaries may affect foreign policy decisions is a cause of concern for executives governing democratic polities. One of the fundamental characteristics of democracies is the separation of powers. As the executors of policy in democratic nations, national executives cannot but accept judicial

19 Human Rights Watch, *Human Rights Watch Annual Report, 2001* (New York, 2001).

independence. Yet their authority as the classic representatives of 'the national interest' in a world where inter-state relations unfold between sovereign states is weakened. Hence the dilemma and loss of authority suffered by Prime Minister Aznar during the Pinochet case, and his call to the judiciary to respect the jurisdiction of the executive in foreign policy-making. In August 1999, he appealed indirectly to Judge Garzón, stating that 'Spain's foreign relations, including relations with Chile, are the responsibility of the government of the nation and not of some court.' However, the slightest hint of a negotiated solution to the Pinochet case, in the form of the announcement of possible 'friendly arbitration' between Spain and Chile, met with immediate opposition from both progressive and conservative sectors of the Spanish judiciary, and had to be dropped.

One must ask, however, how legitimate the new role being played by national courts is. How much power should be granted to courts and individuals pursuing transnational justice for human rights violations? Should countries become subject to the jurisprudence and rules of procedure of the courts of other countries? Spanish prosecution efforts were possible because of the *acción popular* provision, which permits the filing of suits by third parties when the crime in question is deemed to be in the public interest. This provision allowed an association of magistrates, the Union of Progressive Spanish Magistrates (UPFE) to file suits in April 1996 against Chilean military officers in Chile, and made way for other organisations to pursue the cases also. Thus, on 5 July 1996 the Spanish United Left (IU), the Chilean association of the families of the detained-disappeared and the Salvador Allende Foundation for the Defence of Human Rights filed a suit against Pinochet. Thus ended the first part of a 25-year search for legal recourse by Juan Garcés, former advisor to Allende and president of the Foundation, to make Pinochet accountable.

Should not national prosecution efforts in such cases be centralised in the hands of Supreme Courts to ensure consistency? In the view of the Chief Prosecutor of the Spanish Audiencia Nacional (AN) only the Supreme Court should have undertaken the Pinochet investigation. The Spanish President of the General Council of the Judiciary and the AN, on the other hand, opined that judges are free to act and that the AN could legitimately act in the case.[20] Which argument is valid?

More fundamentally, how legitimate or credible are judicial decisions on human rights cases by courts with different views and in countries where jurisprudence is made on a case-by-case basis? While the AN was busy doing its best to prosecute human rights crimes in Chile, another lower court in Spain

20 For the jurisdictional dispute between Judge Baltazar Garzón and the Fiscalía, see: Margarita Lacabe, 'The Criminal Procedures against Chilean and Argentinean Repressors in Spain' at http://www.derechos.net/marga/papers/spain.html

refused to respond positively to a Portuguese extradition request for a former agent of the Portuguese political police, Rosa Casaco. He stood accused of torturing and assassinating Humberto Delgado, an opposition presidential candidate in 1958. Regardless of the respective merits of each decision, there is clearly a problem in terms of consistency of rulings. Perhaps even more contradictory was the decision of the same AN to dismiss the suit for human rights crimes filed against Fidel Castro and other members of his government, on the grounds that he was not prosecutable as a head of state. In sum, high levels of judicial power in conflict with the interests of the executive raises the problem of dual legitimacy. Who, after all, governs at home and abroad, in whose name and with what aims?

Obstacles in the way of universal justice

Despite these promising, albeit complex, developments, there are a number of obstacles to establishing consistent and effective avenues for the pursuit of justice. First, there is the fact that access to international justice or compensatory action to victims of violations is deeply unequal, to the extent that it may be largely unavailable, to individuals around the globe. This is the result of a cumbersome, politicised and inadequate international institutional framework, of a lack of financial clout on the part of the UN and regional human rights bodies pursuing justice, and of the inability of transnational networks to address all past crimes against humanity. The Garzón process, for example, has been largely symbolic in its effects. Garzón requested the extradition of an Argentine officer, Miguel Angel Cavallo, residing in Mexico, a request interpreted favourably by a Mexican judge in January 2001, and upheld by the Mexican Supreme Court in June 2003. He has also gained custody of former navy captain Adolfo Scilingo, but this is only because Scilingo confessed to his acts in Argentina in 1998 and voluntarily presented himself in Spain for questioning. Garzón has gained custody over none of the other 98 Argentine *extraditables* who refuse to leave their country to avoid arrest. Limiting the freedom of movement of former torturers does constitute some sort of victory, but the perception of ineffectiveness and selectivity is essentially true, and detracts from the credibility of claims to 'universal justice.'

Transnational prosecutions in national courts are also open to the charge of hypocritical selectivity and instrumentalisation of law by the 'powerful'. The Spanish never tried to come to terms with a repressive past. Should their amnesty law be overturned by a Chilean court engaged in the trying of a Nationalist or Communist partisan crime against humanity? Indeed, why Pinochet and not others? The French parliament applauded the decision of the House of Lords, but it has allowed 'Baby Doc' Duvalier to continue to live in France in impunity.

Second, there is the still central role of the state in international relations, and the continued attachment to notions of national sovereignty and the pursuit of 'the national interest' above and beyond the limits imposed by human rights law. As Falk notes 'sovereignty has been legally interpreted in a manner that accommodates claims of responsibility and accountability.' Yet legal accommodation 'needs to be distinguished from political accommodation, and it is here that the apparent tension between geopolitical realities and wider patterns of responsibility and accountability exposes the fearful inadequacy of international society.[21] The key problem is that power in the international system is not distributed equally.

There are two manifestations of what I call 'old territorialities' relevant for this discussion. The first is 'traditional "South" anti-interventionist nationalism' (in which sovereignty is defended against the perceived onslaught of 'conditionality' in the name of freedom from various forms of intervention). The second, from the 'North', is encapsulated in the phrase: 'I make the rules but they do not apply to me.' Superior economic, political and international power is taken advantage of to exempt oneself from rules one claims to be universal. It confirms that some countries are more sovereign than others. The best example of this is the United States, which is simultaneously the prime world rule-maker historically and also the country that most resists allowing those rules to apply to itself.[22] Resistance to a new universal jurisdiction is not only the reaction of non-democratic actors and guilty parties. It is also 'a product of the perception that the discourse of universal jurisdiction is ill prepared to deal with the realities of a world governed by uneven power relations and weak instruments for the effective pursuit of universality.'[23]

In sum, there is a highly problematic relationship between a more interventionist ethos to fulfil a wider conception of justice and the way that the international system is structured today. There is the fact of inequality among states in the international system, the potential instability caused by the weakening of the principles of sovereignty and non-intervention in such a context, and the tension between self-interest and equanimity or consistency when determining the grounds for interventionism. These competing claims reveal that we live in a world of a nascent individual-oriented 'universal jurisdiction', but also of a state-oriented ethos that denies fledgling instruments for the enforcement of

21 Richard Falk, *Human Rights Horizons*, p. 71.

22 Alexandra Barahona de Brito, 'A integração regional e a expansão da jurisdição universal: a União Europeia e o Mercosul,' in IEEI (ed.), *O novo multilateralismo: perspectiva da União Europeia e do Mercosul*. (Lisbon, 2001), pp. 133–74.

23 *Ibid.*

that jurisdiction full accountability and enforcement capabilities.

Conclusion

The Pinochet case will be remembered as one of the most important case histories in the prosecution of human rights. Unprecedented, it provoked myriad and protracted legal and political conflicts among the parties involved. Legal opinion was and continues to be divided between those who favour the primacy of international human rights law and those who view as unacceptable the action of national courts or who argue that under current conditions international law is not sufficiently clear to permit extradition and prosecution.

The Pinochet case raises questions about the locus of sovereignty and the competing rights of different actors to define where sovereignty resides and where its limits lie. More specifically, it portrays a world of inter-state relations between democratic nations with their sovereign power self-restricted by universal ethical values and international legal commitments. They are right, those who claim that the actions of the Spanish judiciary constituted a violation of sovereignty; but so were those who supported its efforts. The leopard is changing its spots, but it is far from losing them. The case and the conflicts surrounding it reveal a world poised between the logic of state sovereignty and universal jurisdiction, and demonstrate the changing nature of foreign policy-making and international law-making, particularly where human rights are concerned. An international society is emerging where the logic of national sovereignty no longer rules supreme but in which the instruments to pursue universality are still weak and often contradictory. It is a world in which such a situation such as the Pinochet case could conceivably happen, but not as yet one in which it could take place without causing deep controversy.

The creation of the ICC is a major step forward for the human rights and international humanitarian law, and required a long hard struggle between 'universalists' and those jealously guarding sovereign prerogatives. But the ICC is not useful in dealing with suits presented against former human rights violators, as it does not have retroactive jurisdiction. However, individuals cannot be stopped from taking their cases to court. This means that the pursuit of justice will continue to be messy and complicated, testing the ability of executives, judiciaries and informal transnational coalitions to negotiate the complex path between two kinds of sovereignty claims.

Traditionally, the key actors involved in any process of democratisation have been national civil and political societies and states. Today, such processes are being de-territorialised to some extent, as a growing number of transnational or international actors gain increasing influence over domestic political outcomes. Democratic deepening has become linked with exogenous events and forces that operate outside the boundaries of the state. To cite Richard Falk, 'as the clarity of statism recedes in an era of globalisation, the essential character of sovereignty becomes more and more elusive and subject to re-negotiation by the play of political forces, moral attitudes and prevailing perceptions.' While sovereignty is still paramount, it 'can no longer be reduced to territoriality; it now includes elements of normativity (human rights, humane governance, human dignity) and functionality (non-territorial centres of authority and control).'[24]

To quote Held from his study of the links between democratic and global governance, 'What is the contemporary meaning of citizenship and citizenship rights? Is the principle of territorial representation the single most appropriate principle for the determination of the basis of political representation? Are there duties beyond borders? If so, what are the political and legal implications of these duties?'[25] Indeed, 'The very idea of consent through elections, and the particular notion that the relevant constituencies of voluntary agreement are the communities of a bounded territory or a state, become problematic as soon as the issue of national, regional and global interconnectedness is considered and the nature of a so-called relevant community is contested.'[26] As the Pinochet case demonstrates, 'the meaning and place of democratic politics ... have to be rethought in relation to overlapping local, national, regional and global structures and processes.'[27]

In short, the practice and theory of citizenship and rights is shifting as a result of changes in the political, juridical and economic boundaries of the nation-state. Ensuring rights and access to justice challenges traditional conceptions of political sovereignty; it makes the business of nations the business of the international community. While the nation state is still the prime location of allegiance, a new form of transnational 'popular sovereignty' or citizenship can be seen in the making. However, this transition is far from complete, and leaves open, for the time being at least, questions of democratic authority and governance.

---

24 Richard Falk, *Human Rights Horizons*, p. 70.
25 David Held, *Democracy and the Global Order: From the Modern State to Cosmopolitan Govern-*
    ance. (London, 1995), p. x.
26 *Ibid.*, p. 18.
27 *Ibid.*, p. 21.

CHAPTER 12

International law after the Pinochet case

Antonio Remiro Brotóns

A hundred years ago international law treated people in a cavalier fashion unless they happened to be foreigners with a passport from what was then a boss country. Then the mere *interest* of lesser countries in these exalted foreigners could be considered unfriendly, if not outright interference. On the other hand, respect for fundamental human rights has today become an obligation *erga omnes* of the state, and in situations where large-scale systematic violation of such rights has occurred – when an international crime has been committed – international law endeavours to pursue the responsibility of both the state and state officials to its ultimate conclusion by propitiating the practice of an international criminal jurisdiction that is not conditioned by where the crime was committed nor by the nationality or domicile of the accused, and that is free of the immunities that have traditionally ensured the impunity of states and their representatives. The Pinochet case, a wind reaping a whirlwind, undoubtedly tested the authenticity and extent of this process.[1]

This chapter will address three issues: how far can individuals responsible for international crimes be criminally investigated on the basis of the principle of universality; how far does the immunity of agents of other states extend; and what relationship needs to be established between state judges and international tribunals in the suppression of this criminality? It will be argued that recent events in judicial practice have been bittersweet in that discriminatory attitudes may be observed in the investigation of crimes and criminals; international criminal jurisdiction and international tribunals have been undermined, and are not immune to influence from agents of Empire; and there has been partial use of these tribunals as a political tool, to the detriment of the impartial and universal administration of justice.

---

1 See Antonio Remiro Brotóns, *El caso Pinochet. Los límites de la impunidad* (Madrid, 1999).

The principle of universal criminal jurisdiction

The initial debate underpinning the Pinochet case concerned the degree to which the exercise of criminal jurisdiction founded on the principle of universality conforms to international norms. The position of the Spanish judges, although uncommon, is not unique. For example, the French *Cour de Cassation*, in a judgement of 6 January 1998 (the case of *Dupaquier, Kalinda and others v. Wenceslas Munyeshyaka*), acknowledged the competence of the French courts to try crimes committed in Rwanda in 1994 by Rwandans against Rwandans.[2] On 11 April 2000, an examining magistrate of the court of first instance in Brussels issued an international arrest warrant against the Foreign Minister of the Democratic Republic of Congo, Yerodia Abdoulaye Ndombasi, with a view to requesting his extradition for crimes against humanity and war crimes allegedly committed prior to his coming into office. The Belgian Law of 16 June 1993, which was modified by that of 10 February 1999 regarding the suppression of serious violations of international humanitarian law, established its jurisdiction in accordance with the principle of universal jurisdiction without making the exercise of this jurisdiction conditional on the alleged criminal's presence in Belgium (article 7).

Regarding Pinochet the Chilean government insisted on the practically exclusive jurisdiction of the Chilean courts by invoking a principle of territoriality stemming directly from sovereignty. The International Court of Justice could have made a pronouncement concerning this if Chile had eventually brought an action against Spain. However, once Pinochet was back in Chile, the Chilean government did not persevere with the *principlist* attitude that it had been preaching, and practical considerations concerning the defence of his congressional privilege prevailed. The international arrest warrant subsequently issued by a Belgian judge against the minister Ndombasi did give cause for pronouncement by the court when the Democratic Republic of the Congo, on 27 October 2000, brought an action against Belgium. The Congo argued that, *inter alia*, article 7 of the relevant Belgian law, together with the arrest warrant that applied this, were a violation of: (1) the principle according to which a state cannot execute its power over the territory of another; and (2) the principle of sovereign equality of states (article 2.1 of the Charter of the United Nations). However, the Congo then abandoned this rationale and requested that the order be annulled merely on the basis of the personal inviolability and immunity from

---

2 *See* Brigitte Stern, 'La compétence universelle en France: le cas des crimes commis en ex-Yugoslavie et au Rwanda,' *German Yearbook of International Law*, vol. 40, 1997, pp. 280–99; Denis Alland and Frédérique Ferrand, 'Jurisprudence Française en matière de Droit International Public,' *Revue Générale de Droit International*, vol. 102, no. 3, 1998, pp. 828 ff.;.

criminal jurisdiction of the minister, who by then had changed ministerial post from foreign affairs to education.[3] Thus the court's final judgement was based only upon the second line of argument.

Nevertheless, even though the court made no pronouncement on the issue of entitlement to exercise universal jurisdiction, certain judges have done so in declarations, separate or dissenting opinions, revealing a disparity in their points of view. Some of these opinions, for example, those made by President Guillaume and Rezek, have been negative. Judge Ranjeva came to the same, almost regretful, conclusion given that substantive international law is as it is and not otherwise. However, the majority of those who have expressed their view agree with the idea of universal jurisdiction over international crimes in international law. These include judges Higgins, Kooijmans and Buergenthal in a joint opinion, judge Koroma in a separate opinion, judge Al-Khasawneh, at least implicitly, in his dissenting opinion, and the ad hoc judge Van den Wyngaert, who also dissented. This does not mean, however, that, if the court had been obliged to make a pronouncement, the affirmative position would have prevailed. Seven of the judges who participated in the deliberation and decision-making process remained silent.

In order to elucidate this issue it is first necessary to determine whether states are *obliged* to include a jurisdictional precedent based on the principle of universality in their legal system. The answer is that at present this obligation only derives from the provisions of the international treaties to which a state adheres.

In this respect, in relation to *war crimes*, the Geneva Convention of 12 August 1949 and the additional Protocol I of 8 June 1977 oblige the parties to the convention to pursue serious infringements of their regulations applicable in international armed conflicts on the basis of the principle of universal jurisdiction.[4] Given the very high level of participation in these instruments,[5] it can be said that state judges virtually all over the world have the jurisdiction to

3 *Arrest Warrant of 11 April 2000* (Democratic Republic of the Congo v. Belgium), Judgement of 14 February 2002, available at http://www.icj-cij.org/icjwww/idocket/iCOBE/iCOBEframe.htm

4 Convention (I) for the Amelioration of the Condition of the Wounded and Sick in Armed Forces in the Field (II) or the Amelioration of the Condition of Wounded, Sick and Shipwrecked Members of Armed Forces at Sea articles 50 and 51; Convention (III) relative to the treatment of prisioners of war, articles 129 and 130; Convention (IV) relative to the protection of civilian persons in time of war, articles 146 and 147; Protocol additional to the Geneva Conventions of 12 August 1949, and relating to the Protection of Victims of International Armed Conflicts (Protocol I), of 8 June 1977; article 85.

5 On 8 March 2002, there were 189 States parties to the Geneva Conventions, the same number of members in the UNO; the number of States party to Protocol I was 159.

investigate these crimes wherever they are committed and whatever the nationality and domicile of the subjects.[6]

Nevertheless, the great majority of treaties concerned with the criminal investigation of international crimes or crimes against the fundamental interests of the international community do not go so far. Their *modus operandi* generally boils down to: (1) the obligatory setting up of state jurisdiction over the crimes or infringements, taking into account where these were committed and, according to circumstance, the nationality and/or residence of their active and/or passive subjects; (2) the obligation of the authorities of the place where the accused have been arrested either to facilitate any extradition requested by the authorities of the state (or states) under the obligation of criminal investigation, or to carry out this investigation themselves (*aut dedere aut iudicare*); and (3) the acceptance of any other basis for jurisdiction decided by the States parties to the treaties.[7]

Does this last point mean that states have *carte blanche* to include a principle of universal jurisdiction in their system of criminal suppression? Is state jurisdiction in accordance with general international law in allowing for the criminal investigation of those responsible for international crimes carried out by foreigners abroad?

6 In less demanding terms, the Convention on the elimination and suppression of the crime of apartheid of 30 November 1973 also imposes on parties to the Convention the adoption of measures to investigate this crime on the basis of the principle of universality. *See* article IV*b* of the Convention, which over one hundred States are party to, although excluding the United States, Canada and members of the European Union.

7 *See* for example, the New York Convention for the Prevention and Punishment of Crimes against Internationally Protected People, including Diplomatic Agents of 14 December 1973, article 3.3; the New York Convention against the Holding of Hostages of 17 December 1979, article 5.2; the United Nations Convention against Torture and Other Cruel, Inhuman or Degrading Treatment or Punishment of 10 December 1984, article 5; the United Nations Convention for the Security of United Nations Personnel and Associated Personnel of 9 December 1994, article 10.4. Also, the Montreal Convention on the Suppression of Unlawful Acts against the Security of Civil Aviation of 23 September 1971, article 5.3; the Vienna Convention for the Physical Protection of Nuclear Materials of 26 October 1979, article 8.3; the Montreal Protocol for the Suppression of Acts of Unlawful Violence committed in Airports serving Civil Aviation of 24 February 1988, article III; the Rome Convention for the Suppression of Unlawful Acts against the Security of Maritime Navigation of 10 March 1988, article 6.5; the Rome Protocol for the Suppression of Unlawful Acts against the Security of Fixed Platforms located on the Continental Shelf, of the same date, article 6.5; the United Nations Convention against Unlawful Traffic in Narcotic Drugs and Psychotropic Substances of 20 December 1988, article 4.2.b; Convention against the Recruitment, Use, Financing and Training of Mercenariesof 4 December 1989, article 9.3; the United Nations Convention for the Suppression of Terrorist Acts with Bombs of 12 January 1998, article 6.5; the New York Convention for the Suppression of the Financing of Terrorism of 10 January 2000, article 7.6; the Convention against Transnational Organised Crime of 15 November 2000, article 15.6.

The answer is no in relation to the crime of aggression. The international crime codification project of the International Law Commission (1996) only acknowledges the competence of state judges to try their national citizens as an alternative to international tribunals (article 8). As the commission pointed out, the rule is justified because the question of individual responsibility for this crime cannot be resolved without preliminary consideration being given to the question of aggression having been committed by a state, which, left in the hands of state tribunals, would be contrary to the fundamental principle of international law *par in parem imperium non habet* (an equal has no dominion over an equal) and, moreover, would have serious consequences for international relations and international peace and security. The recognised faculty of a state's courts to try its own national citizens on the highly improbable hypothesis of their being considered guilty of aggression is justified on the basis that there is no obligation to determine beforehand any aggression committed by another state and this should not affect relations with third-party countries.

In relation to genocide, the most characteristic and serious of the crimes attributed to General Pinochet by the Spanish judges and ruled out right from the beginning by the British authorities (as far as the extradition that was being requested was concerned), spokespersons for the Chilean government – on the basis of article 6 of the 1948 Convention[8] – pointed to the exclusive competence of the Chilean courts given the failure over the intervening fifty years to set up an international court. This interpretation received the not inconsiderable backing of the International Law Commission itself, which in the commentary to article 8 of the 1996 codification project appears to take for granted the restrictive effect *inter partes* of article 6 of the 1948 Convention in relation to universal jurisdiction provided for by customary international law. This view won over the Ministerio Fiscal (Office of the Prosecutor) in Spain, Lord Slynn of Hadley in the UK, (the president of the first House of Lords panel to deal with the case) and, for reasons that were more explicable, the *ad hoc* judge Professor Kreça in The Hague, appointed by the International Court of Justice at the instigation of Yugoslavia, who were being taken to court by Bosnia-Herzegovina in relation to application of the Convention.

However, this interpretation is unacceptable because, if admitted, not even the state of the person who commits genocide in foreign territory could exercise jurisdiction in conformity with the *active personality* principle. What is clearly not acceptable is a grammatical and logical interpretation leading to manifestly

---

8 According to which, 'Persons charged with genocide or any of the other acts enumerated in article III shall be tried by a competent tribunal of the State in the territory of which the act was committed, or by such international penal tribunal as may have jurisdiction with respect to those Contracting Parties which shall have accepted its jurisdiction'.

absurd results that contradict the objectives being pursued, as the International Court of Justice itself has stressed on occasions when the 1948 Convention has come up for judgement or a decision.[9] It is clearly absurd for parties to a convention for the investigation of a particularly serious international crime to renounce a faculty that provides for such an investigation; it is absurd for states that are not parties to a mechanism of multilateral co-operation to have juris-dictional means that parties to that mechanism renounce; it is absurd for universal jurisdiction to be denied to parties to the 1948 Convention on genocide while at the same time it is declared in relation to any other crime, crimes against humanity or war crimes, with which it is also frequently connected. At all events, it would be disheartening if the *obligation* to accept its jurisdiction that is imposed on the country in which the genocide is committed were to be converted into the *privilege* of monopolising it.

In the process of consolidation of universal jurisdiction over international crimes, the transcendent decision of the Supreme Court of Israel in *Attorney General of Israel v. Eichmann* (1962) is considered to be of particular import-ance.[10] Lord Millett emphasised this on submitting his vote in the House of Lords Judicial Committee in the Pinochet case (decision of 24 March 1999). Whilst the means used to transfer the former head of department IV D-4, who was in charge of implementing the Final Solution, to Israel have been doctrin-ally criticised, as Millett pointed out, Israel's right to affirm its jurisdiction (even though it did not exist as a State when Eichmann committed his misdeeds) has never been questioned, not on account of the historic link between this State and the Jewish people as the district court considered, but rather due to the nature of Eichmann's crimes, the victims of which had also included non-Jewish groups.[11]

9 In the consultative opinion of 28 May 1951 on the *Reservations to the Convention against Genocide*, the Court emphasised the importance of the obligatory character of the principles on which the Convention is based, the universal condemnation of genocide and the co-operation required to free mankind from such a scourge (*Reports ICJ*, 1951, p. 23); in the sentence of 11 July 1996 in the matter of *the application of the Convention for the prevention and suppression of the crime of genocide* (Bosnia-Herzegovina v. Yugoslavia) the Court affirmed the *erga omnes* character of the rights and obligations laid down in the Convention and verified that the obligation of preventing and penalising the crime of genocide is not territorially limited (*Reports ICJ*, 1996, p. 616, par. 31).

10 Eichmann was kidnapped in the Republic of Argentina and transferred to Israel where he was judged, condemned and finally executed. *See Attorney General v. Eichmann*, Jerusalem District Court (1961) 36 ILR 18, 39, and Supreme Court of Israel (1962) 36 ILR 277, 304. The relations between the Republic of Argentina of Israel, which were damaged by this unlawful coercive act, improved when Israel apologised to the Republic of Argentina, and so went some way to providing satisfaction (*see* resolution 138-1960 of the Security Council).

11 The Eichmann case was corroborated in United States by *Demjanjuk v. Petrovsky* – (1985) 603F. Supp.1468 aff d. 776 F. 2d. 571- a case in which proceedings were under way con-

In the opinion of Lord Millett, crimes prohibited by international law are covered by universal jurisdiction in conformity with customary international law when two conditions are complied with: (1) the crimes must be contrary to a peremptory norm of international law (*ius cogens*);[12] and (2) the crimes must be sufficiently serious and have been carried out on such a scale that they can be justly perceived to be an attack on the international judicial order; isolated criminal acts, even those committed by state officials, are insufficient.[13]

From here on, whether or not the courts of a State will have extraterritorial jurisdiction over international crimes will depend on its internal law and on the constitutional handling of the relations between customary international law and the criminal jurisdiction of the courts.[14]

In Spain the judges of the Audiencia Nacional convincingly endorsed the operative consequences of the principle of universality in the proceedings against the Chilean and Argentine military juntas, although the fear of its becoming the planetary refuge for lost causes of all types (at least in Latin America) prompted the *Sala de lo Penal* (Criminal Chamber of the Spanish National Court) to hold back when attempts were made to proceed against crimes of the Guatemalan military. This retreat did not signal a rejection of the principle of universality, but resulted from an assessment of the criterion of subsidiarity, which had always underpinned the pursuit of specific cases.[15] When the judiciary of the

---

cerning a petition for extradition from Israel where the court considered the principle of universal punishment to be applicable, with the observation that: 'International law provides that certain offences may be punished by any state because the offenders are enemies of all mankind and all nations have an equal interest in their apprehension and punishment'.

12   This condition is well supported by precedents and doctrine. In *Prosecutor v. Anto Furundžija* (10 December 1998), to quote a recent example, it says, 'At the individual level, that is, of criminal liability, it would seem that one of the consequences of the jus cogens character bestowed by the international community upon the prohibition of torture is that every state is entitled to investigate, prosecute, and punish or extradite individuals accused of torture who are in a territory under its jurisdiction'. See International Court for the former Yugoslavia, matter IT-95-17/1-T, *Prosecutor v. Anto Furundžija*, 10 December 1998.

13   This condition is implicit in the original restriction of universal jurisdiction to war crimes and crimes against the peace, in the court's reasoning in the Eichmann case and in the definitions adopted in the more recent statutes of the international tribunals for the former Yugoslavia and Rwanda.

14   In the case of Great Britain, Lord Millett specified that the statutory legal grounds for criminal jurisdiction are complemented by common law, of which customary international law forms part, from which, in the judge's opinion, the English courts have, and have always had, extraterritorial criminal jurisdiction with regard to crimes where universal jurisdiction applies in conformity with customary international law.

15   *See* legal grounds ten of the ruling of 27 March 2000, Juzgado Central de Instrucción no. 1 of the Audiencia National, and two and three of the ruling of 13 December 2000 of the Criminal Chamber Sala de lo Penal, Audiencia National.

country where the crime took place is dealing with a case, there is enforced abstention of any other; in this respect, in practice there is preferential exercising of jurisdiction in Spain and the Sala de lo Penal (Criminal Chamber) of the Audiencia Nacional admits that article 6 of the 1948 Convention 'imposes the subsidiarity of action of jurisdictions that are different to those laid down by the provision so that the jurisdiction of a State must abstain from exercising said jurisdiction over events that constitute genocide that is being tried by courts in the country where they occurred or by an International Criminal Court'.[16]

In the Pinochet case the Chamber did not consider that this situation applied. In the Guatemalan case, it reiterated that the inactivity of the judicial organs in the country where the crimes were perpetrated is a necessary condition for the exercising of universal jurisdiction; inactivity understood as being when these organs are subjected to pressure by governmental powers, or the powers that be, and there is an atmosphere of relentless harassment or fear such as to prevent the proper performance of judicial functions, or when legislation is enacted that provides protection for those in the dock. In the Guatemalan case, however, unlike the Pinochet case and that of the Argentine military juntas, the Chamber (ruling of 13 December 2000) did not believe this condition to be fulfilled. Although the Chamber's assessment of the circumstances in which justice is administered in Guatemala is highly debatable, and was possibly determined with the intention of preventing the organs of the Spanish judiciary from becoming a court on call for all international crimes that have taken place in Latin America, the soundness of the argument is, nevertheless, unquestionable.

Victims of crimes against the peace and security of mankind, and their legal representatives, in principle base their choice of court on practical grounds. Lawsuits are not conducted abroad when there are credible and functioning courts in the country in which the events occurred, and where those who are allegedly responsible are physically present. In the same way, a judge who is approached merely on grounds of universal jurisdiction will not spend his/her time taking difficult legal proceedings when a juez natural (a competent, independent and impartial judge or court) is available where the acts were committed, and even less so when the accused are not in the judge's country. A judge lawfully entitled to act on the basis of the principle of universal investigation will evaluate the appropriateness of exercising his/her jurisdiction if the presence of the accused is deemed to be highly improbable and consequently there is an equally high probability of the injunctions being shelved.

The connection often proposed between the principle of universal jurisdiction and the presence of the person allegedly responsible for the crime in the

16 See legal grounds two of the ruling of 5 November 1998.

territory of a State (iudex aprehensionis) is not correct if the aim is to claim that the person's presence is, according to international law, a necessary prerequisite on which to base jurisdiction.[17] As was demonstrated in the Pinochet case, the movements of alleged criminals beyond safe places of refuge, and police and judicial co-operation in extradition proceedings, diminish the importance of their presence in the committal proceedings, and, of course, show the inconsistency of this circumstance as an essential element of jurisdiction, although they do reinforce the role of extradition as determinant in the course and efficient administering of justice. As the Pinochet case has demonstrated, this poses numerous problems (double jeopardy, the prescription of criminal responsibility, government involvement in the final decision, etc) which cannot be addressed here.

A series of immunities

One controversial issue has been the series of immunities of foreign state agents facing actions for international crimes before judges considered in principle to have the relevant competence. A key issue is whether and how far forms of immunity that are customarily and conventionally recognised in the central organs of state entrusted with international relations (Head of State, Head of Government, Foreign Minister), diplomatic and consular organs and agents and components of special missions, operate when their beneficiaries are accused of these crimes.

---

17 In support of the thesis that extends the principle of universality to jurisdiction over the place of apprehension, mention is usually made of the projected convention on criminal jurisdiction, developed in 1935 by the *Harvard Research in International Law* ('Draft Convention on Jurisdiction with respect to Crime,' *AJIL* (1935), suppl., pp. 437–635), where article 10 affirms that the principle of universality can only be invoked if the foreign national is present in a place subject to the authority of the State that assumes jurisdiction, with the presence of the accused being the grounds provided. However, irrespective of the date of this private project, which is prior to regulatory developments concerning crimes against the peace and security of mankind, and its consideration of a circumstance – the presence of the accused in the court – which in the United States judicial system transcends such international criminality in such a way that on occasions bounty hunters, police and even members of the armed forces have not hesitated in forcibly transferring foreign citizens to the territory of the United States to bring them before judges. These have then proceeded according to the doctrine *male captus, bene detentus* ('badly captured, well detained' – the principle that permits the trial of an improperly arrested person) to justify the exercising of jurisdiction. The requirement that the accused be present has nothing to do with jurisdictional grounds but with the legal proceedings and pronouncement of sentence in default, which many legislative bodies, including the Spanish (article 841 of the *Ley de Enjuiciamiento Criminal* – Law of Criminal Prosecution), do not in principle allow.

One result of the Pinochet case has been that this matter has been exhaustively debated in recent years at the highest formal level, i.e. that of Head of State.[18] Claims that criminal responsibility does not apply on the basis that the acts concerned corresponded to the exercising of an agent's functions must be ruled out. The recognition of immunity is incompatible with the very idea of the crimes investigated and the characteristic functions of an agent of the state in conformity with international law. Moreover, once the accused resigns (or is removed from office), investigations are no longer affected by the principle of sovereign equality as the alleged criminal loses all representational status, no matter how formal this was.

What is the situation, however, whilst the agent is still in office? If the criminal investigation falls to an international tribunal, then immunity is not operative. This was already stated in the Statutes of the Nuremberg Tribunals (London Agreement of 8 August 1945) and Tokyo (agreement of 19 January 1946) and more recently in the Statutes of the International Tribunals for the former Yugoslavia (article 7.2) and Rwanda (article 6.2) and the Statute of the International Criminal Court itself (article 27). Slobodan Milosevic, as President of the FRY, was put on trial in May 1999 by the International Tribunal for the former Yugoslavia and he has been imprisoned in Scheveningen (Netherlands) for some time, in custody of the court.

Nevertheless, there continues to be noteworthy resistance at state level to put a stop to the series of immunities enjoyed by officially admitted and accredited foreign agents accused of international crimes, even where that jurisdiction is accepted. Not even the International Criminal Court has received reassurances that states parties to the Court will hand over those appearing in lists of accused if they have internationally recognised immunity.[19] In the Pinochet case, the law lords, who were divided on many points, did agree on the immunity of Heads of State in office. In Spain, the Plenary Session of the Criminal Chamber

---

18 See Andrea Bianchi, 'Immunity versus Human Rights: The Pinochet Case,' European Journal of International Law, vol. 10, no. 2 (1999), pp. 237–78; Christian Dominicé, 'Quelques observations sur l'immunité de juridiction pénale de l'ancien chef d'Etat,' Revue Générale de Droit International Public, vol. 103, no. 2, 1999, pp. 297–308; Pierre-Marie Dupuy, 'Crimes et immunités, ou dans quelle mesure la nature des premiers empêche l'exercise des secondes,' Revue Générale de Droit International Public, vol. 103, no. 2, 1999, pp. 289–96; John R.W.D. Jones, 'Immunity and "Double Criminality": General Augusto Pinochet before the House of Lords,' in S. Yee and W. Tieya (eds.), International Law in the Post-Cold War Worlds: Essays in Memory of Li Haopei (London and New York, 2001); Jan Klabbers, 'The General, the Lords and the Possible End of State Immunity,' Nordic Journal of International Law, vol. 68, no. 1, 1999, pp. 85–95; Ana Gemma López Martín, 'Las inmunidades del Derecho internacional: su aplicación en España,' Cuadernos de Derecho Público, vol. 6 (1999), pp. 139–57.

19 See article 98 of the Statute of the International Criminal Court.

of the Audiencia National, in a decision (*auto*) of 4 March 1999, affirmed this same immunity in an absolute way as a result of the recognition of the foreign state and its corollaries with respect to the principle of sovereignty and sovereign equality.[20]

More recently, the sentence of the French *Cour de Cassation* of 13 March 2001 has been seen as the first crack in this wall of criminal immunity. Although the *Cour de Cassation*, on the basis of the immunity of Heads of State, accepted the appeal against the sentence of the *Chambre d'Accusation* of the *Cour d'Appel* of 20 October 2000 (which related to the criminal responsibility of Libyan Muamar El Gaddafi in the terrorist attack on a UTA plane which exploded over the Tenere desert (Niger) on 19 September 1989 with one hundred and seventy dead), the *Cour* made note of contingent limits to such immunity on the basis of the general principles of international law (which the crime that the Libyan leader was accused of did not exceed).[21]

This interpretation of the sentence by the *Cour de Cassation* is, however, more arbitrary than anything else. Both the examining magistrate and the judge of second instance had rejected the immunity of a foreign Head of State suspected of involvement with the destruction of property caused by an explosive substance in a terrorist action that resulted in death. The *Cour de Cassation* corrected the lower organs: 'en l'état du droit international, le crime denoncé, quelle qu'en soit la gravité, ne relève pas des exceptions au principe de l'immunité de juridiction des chefs d'Etat étrangers en exercise'. ('In the state of international law, the crime reported, whatever its seriousness, does not admit exceptions to the principle of immunity of jurisdiction of existing foreign heads of state.')

Furthermore, the International Court of Justice made an authoritative pronouncement on the matter in its decision over the suit that the Democratic Republic of the Congo had filed against Belgium, mentioned above. Belgian law expressly excludes the immunity of state officials accused of international crimes,[22] and, on this basis, the then Congolese Foreign Minister was made subject to an international arrest warrant.[23] According to the Congo, 'by issuing and internationally circulating the arrest warrant of 11 April 2000 ... Belgium committed a violation ... of the rule of customary international law concerning the absolute inviolability and immunity from criminal process of incumbent

---

20 See *Fundamentos de derecho* (precedents) four and five of the *auto* of 4 March 1999.
21 See Salvatore Zappalà, 'Do Heads of State in Office Enjoy Immunity from Jurisdiction for International Crimes? The Ghadaffi Case before the French Cour de Cassation,' *European Journal of International Law*, vol. 12, no. 3 (2001), pp. 595–612...
22 Law of 16 June 1993, modified by that of 10 February 1999, article 5.
23 See above.

foreign ministers'. The Court upheld this view with thirteen votes for and three against. There is no exception to this as long as the accused person holds a position which carries immunity from criminal jurisdiction, such as that of Foreign Minister, not even in the case of alleged implication in international crimes. Either stepping down or being removed from office, the renunciation of immunity by the State being represented or judicial investigation by the State or some form of universal jurisdiction, if there is one, is necessary in order to get around impunity.

The brilliant formulation of the judges in minority who were against the claim[24] or the reservations of certain judges in the majority[25] concerning the excessive scope of immunity according to the Court can certainly be remarked on. Nevertheless, the emphatic nature of the decision and the size of the majority endorsing it send a clear signal that the main judicial organ of the United Nations does not wish to subject the stability of international relations to disturbances originating from the decentralised judicial investigation of crimes, no matter how abject they be.

Universal jurisdiction: an international criminal court

From a comparative point of view, legislative differences and the different judicial traditions of states leads to discrimination in the treatment of those accused. Examples can relate to issues including: differences in the way that crimes are classified; the termination of criminal responsibility; exemptions and extenuating circumstances; the catalogue of applicable penalties that may or may not include the death penalty and the possibility of benefiting from significant reductions in sentences through the acceptance of guilt or by collaborating with the prosecution. All this must lead to very different sentences and, with them, unequal treatment amongst those accused in different countries, even without entering into the matter of the examining capabilities and the impartiality and independence of the judges. Hence, the principle of universal jurisdiction has been criticised because it may allow alleged criminals to find the most appropriate forum in order to obtain acquittals, light punishment or the benefits of being pardoned by allied or friendly governments and/or judicial powers that lack any real independence. This kind of *forum shopping* must be opposed with measures that revise *non bis in idem*, (the principle that no-one can be tried a second time on the same charge) together with the extraterritorial effectiveness of reprieves and the postponement of sentences that would appear, in any case, to be more appropriate to an international tribunal.

24 Judges Oda, Al-Khasawneh; *ad hoc* judge Van den Wyngaert.
25 Judges Higgins, Kooijmans and Buergenthal.

Apart from these problems, when judges and courts in third party countries decide to make up for the deficiencies of the more natural forums of jurisdiction, conflict in interstate relations is inevitable if, and when, the authorities of the country in which the crime is committed (and/or of the nationality of the perpetrators) look unfavourably on the prosecution of its (former) rulers in other states, especially if this means by-passing measures that are regarded as being a direct expression of its sovereignty.[26] Such conflict becomes more profound if circumstances make enforcement feasible over and above the trial and sentencing.

International tribunals would enable these obstacles to be overcome or at least mitigated. Anticipated by the Allies during the Second World War, such tribunals were set up at the end of the war in Nuremberg and Tokyo to judge important criminals of war from the defeated Axis powers. Unfortunately, advances in the codification of types of criminal act have not been followed in the same way by establishment at the international level of suppressive mechanisms endowed with sufficient guarantees. The establishment of an international tribunal stagnated for almost fifty years until tribunals were created for the former Yugoslavia (res. 827 of 25 May 1993) and Rwanda (res. 955 of 8 November 1994) following a decision by the Security Council, within the context of the competencies attributed to it in chapter VII of the Charter to stand up to and defy threats and violations of peace and acts of aggression. It was mainly the Western countries, led by the United States, who obstructed the more advanced projects, the same countries that later on would be hastily looking for ways to put Saddam Hussein on trial (*in absentia?*) or to pursue the warlord Aidid in the streets of Mogadishu, looking to arrest him in the hope that he would be charged, tried and punished, by who nobody exactly knew, for his alleged responsibility for the armed attacks on UN Blue Helmets from 3 July to 5 July 1993 (resolution 837, of 6, of the Security Council).

26 The point is illustrated by the letter sent by the Chilean Foreign Minister, Insulza, to the Secretary General of the UNO, Kofi Annan, on 22 December 1998, where he pointed out that: 'In societies that are pacifically passing from an authoritarian regime to a democratic one, tension is inevitably produced between the need for justice to be dealt with regarding all of the human rights violations and the exigency of attaining national reconciliation. Surmounting this tension' in the opinion of the Foreign Minister, 'is a very delicate task that can only be undertaken by the people in the country in question' and, in the specific case of Pinochet, the attempts to try him outside of Chile 'produce serious disturbances to the process of democratic transition and national reconciliation'. Of course, admitted the Foreign Minister, 'it is essential for unresolved matters to be investigated, especially the cases of people who disappeared during the 1970s, with justice being carried out within the framework of Chilean legislation,' but 'external intervention in this matter, for whatever intention by those who have instigated this, does not help any of these objectives and, on the contrary, contributes to the polarisation of society and will aggravate the differences that still exist amongst the Chilean people for many years to come'.

It appears that there is now also a desire to assuage the feelings of guilt that remained after the genocide in Cambodia, which was officially condemned by the General Assembly in 1974,[27] by organising a mixed jurisdiction (Cambodian-International) or to apply the *ad hoc* model tried in Yugoslavia and Rwanda in other countries, such as Sierra Leone, although in these cases such measures would be undertaken at the request or through negotiation with the local governments.[28] Still, the wish to prevent improvisation, together with the convenience of setting up a permanent, comprehensive and international judicial institution to avoid accusations of political manipulation, revived and gave urgency to the dormant project of the International Law Commission. The project, after being accepted by a committee of governmental representatives, enabled the diplomatic conference in Rome to adopt, on 17 July 1998, the Statute of the International Criminal Court, which came into existence on 11 April 2002, with over sixty states subscribing to it.

The judging of these criminals does not necessarily require the setting up of these costly mechanisms. However, the punishment of criminals responsible for the most serious crimes *en masse* needs to be exemplary, objective and transparent, and subject to the jurisdiction of international institutions. In this respect, the setting up of tribunals for the former Yugoslavia and Rwanda has been positive, although it has seemed on occasion that, over questions of agenda and timetable, political considerations have sometimes prevailed over those of the administration of justice,[29] and the concern remains that the setting up of *ad hoc* tribunals is seen by some as a means of preventing their wider use.

It is not a question now, however, of evaluating the pros and cons of the new Court in assisting states in the investigation and punishment of serious offenders. Nor is it a matter of noting that, apart from the crimes originating from the armed conflicts in the former Yugoslavia and those that occurred in Rwanda in 1994, there is no international tribunal today to which crimes committed prior to the coming into force of the Statute of Rome, with all its limitations, may be

---

27 Resolution 3238 (XXIX). Then, resolution 44/22.

28 At the request of the Security Council (resolution 1315 of 14 August 2000), the Secretary General of the United Nations negotiated an agreement with the government of Sierra Leone to set up a tribunal to try those responsible for international crimes that occurred in the civil conflict in the country from 30 November 1996 onwards. When definite voluntary contributions were pledged and became available to set it up and for financing over the first few years, the Secretary General authorised it to begin its activities in 2002.

29 Particular criticisms were aimed at the fact that the Office of the Prosecutor did not want to open an investigation on the alleged war crimes committed by NATO and some of its member States with the bombing of Yugoslavia in the spring of 1999 (which could be called the *crimes of the benefactor*) nor the crimes committed in Kosovo following the retreat of the Yugoslav armed force (*crimes of the victims*).

submitted. The Court will be able to try, amongst other things, genocide and crimes against humanity committed after this date[30] on condition – in the case of crimes against humanity – that the state where they were committed, or the state of which the accused is a national, is party to the Statute.[31] This is in addition to the political preconditions and conditions accepted by the Statute that limit the actual possibilities of the International Criminal Court jurisdiction.[32]

What needs to be established now is that the ongoing development and consolidation of the punishment norms for crimes against the peace and security of mankind must in no way be tied to progress along the path to universal jurisdiction. This process, which is highly positive but limited and incomplete, has not prevented states from endowing their own judges with the competence to investigate these crimes irrespective of where they occurred. It is also important that the denial of criminal immunity to the representatives and officials of foreign states accused of crimes against the peace and security of mankind should not be strictly tied to the jurisdiction of international criminal tribunals, even where the accused no longer occupy the positions that led to the concession of such immunity.

The creation and operation of international tribunals for the former Yugoslavia and Rwanda has not prevented the sentencing of convicted perpetrators of crimes committed in these countries by judges in other countries. Belgium provides an example. While the International Tribunal for Rwanda – whose mandate was limited to the crimes committed during 1994 – clearly moves sluggishly, on 8 June 2001 a Brussels court declared four Rwandans, including one former minister and two Benedictine nuns, guilty of genocide on the basis of the verdict of a citizens' jury.

It is worth drawing attention to this since the Chilean government, motivated by the Pinochet case, felt compelled to set up a broad political front against the principle of universal jurisdiction. The offensive became particularly apparent in a letter sent by Chilean Foreign Minister Insulza to the Secretary General of the UN on 22 December 1998. Here it was argued that universality of criminal jurisdiction would lead to international anarchy and would violate the sovereignty and legal equality of States if applied unilaterally, that is, by state judges. According to the Foreign Minister's letter, one of the challenges facing the UN in the new millennium is 'how to ensure full respect for human rights and prevent the impunity of those who transgress them without sacrificing the governing principles of international relations that, like veritable norms of *jus cogens*, have been incorporated into article 2 of the Charter of the

---

30   *See* articles 11, 22.1 and 24.1 of the Statute of the Court.
31   *See* article 12.2 of the Statute of the Court.
32   *See* articles 12–16 of the Statute of the Court.

United Nations'; Chile, the charter states, has an interest in the setting up of the International Criminal Court and that it exercise its functions as soon as possible, and 'it is concerned at how States acting individually try to usurp its powers'.

In his letter the Chilean Foreign Minister tries to overcome the negative image of a government which protects an alleged criminal like General Pinochet, by invoking the exemplary judicial performance of Chile in subsequent years. He refers in this context to its dealings with the civil responsibilities deriving from the human rights violations perpetrated under the Pinochet regime, to its search for truth and reconciliation through a national commission of legal entities (the Rettig Commission) that pioneered the handling of this kind of problem (and produced a report on 9 February 1991) and to its ratification of numerous treaties on human rights, including its signing of the Statute of the International Criminal Court. The letter insists on the Chilean government's *principlist* attitude and also projects a certain sense of victimisation in its idea of the powerful, cloaked in the flag of universality, as selective bringers to account of the weak.

Along the same line of argument, there are those, such as Lord Slynn of Hadley, who propose that the denial of criminal immunity to the representatives and officials of foreign States accused of crimes against the peace and security of mankind be firmly linked with the jurisdiction of international tribunals. They maintain that this should be the case even where the positions that justified the concession of such immunity are no longer held, and interpret the precautionary measure according to which the governmental status of somebody who is allegedly guilty does not prevent proceedings being taken against him, as the exception to an unshakeable rule, and not the proof that the rule has changed in accordance with the spirit and objectives now being pursued.

These tenets are arbitrary. In truth, when the preparation of some conventions is examined and it is decreed that whoever has committed the crimes will be punished, whether they are rulers, state officials or private individuals, it can be seen what was really meant was not the pursuit and punishment of rulers and state officials (the essence of the crime) but that of private individuals. In this same respect, the International Law Commission agreed in 1985 that the codification project of crimes against the peace and security of mankind had to consider the responsibility not just of the authorities but also of any individual involved in them.

A continuous succession of international and regional multilateral treaties has been laid down over a long period. These treaties have made proposals and committed States to combating the different typical forms of crime against the peace and security of mankind by developing their laws and judges, by declaring the most serious crimes to be imprescribable, their prosecution to be universal, their sentences harsh, the official or public nature of guilty individuals to be immaterial and merely to add to the seriousness of their crimes, etc.

It is reiterated in the introductory considerations of the latest important instrument, the Statute of the International Criminal Court, that the most serious crimes that distress the international community cannot remain unpunished; that effective jurisdiction requires national measures and the reinforcement of international co-operation; that the parties are determined to put an end to impunity; and that the *duty* of each State is to *exercise its criminal jurisdiction* over those who perpetrate these crimes,[33] with an insistence that the role of the Court be clearly expressed in article 1 of the Statute.[34]

It would be cynical to think that all this effort was merely rhetoric conditional upon the non-application of the laws by judges preferring to attend to matters of more immediate and local interest, or that these laws would be applied only with the consent of the authorities of the country in which the crimes were committed, by those who committed them or by those who succeeded those who committed them, that is to say, by those who drew the short straw.

In political terms, it is understandable that the Belgian Foreign Minister advised against what he called 'the perverse effects of (Belgian) law' when an official visit by the head of the Israeli government, Ariel Sharon, was cancelled since a statute did not provide him with immunity from a charge against him presented before the Belgian courts concerning his alleged responsibility in the crimes that occurred in the Palestinian refugee camps of Sabra and Chatila in 1982.[35] Since then, the filing of a number of cases in the Belgian courts naming high-profile individuals including President George Bush and US General Tommy Franks (commander of US forces in the recent Iraq war) has increased both the Belgian government's embarrassment and pressure from the United States, which froze funding for a new NATO headquarters in Brussels and threatened to boycott NATO meetings at the existing HQ. In June 2003 the Belgian government announced its decision to amend the 1993 law that allows universal jurisdiction, limiting its application to cases involving Belgian citizens.

If a state has incorporated the principle of universal criminal jurisdiction, it obviously cannot suggest, should a judge decide to apply these laws, that they merely exist to satisfy a certain moral aesthetic or that those most responsible for criminal acts – all the more serious when committed from within and with the might of the State – continue to be protected from prosecution on the basis

---

33 *See* paragraphs four, five and six of the introduction to the Court Statute.

34 The complementary character of the International Criminal Court regarding national criminal jurisdiction, stated in article 1, is expressly underlined in paragraph ten of the introduction to the Court Statute. *See* also articles 17–19.

35 *See El País*, 9 June 2001, p. 8.

of outmoded regulations that see human rights as the *domaine reservé* of each sovereign.

The establishment of a permanent International Criminal Court cannot be used to bring up short the processes by which social movements, NGOs and the media have pushed judges and courts in individual states to assume and exercise the principle of universal jurisdiction, especially when the Statute of the ICC is by no means exhaustive, and has put limitations on the crimes it can deal with subject to jurisdiction.

In fact, in order to attract the Clinton Administration, which was under pressure from the Pentagon and the Republican majority in Congress who demanded guarantees that *not one US citizen* could be put on trial without the authorisation of the United States, the project of the Statute of the International Criminal Court was weakened. Finally, certain subtypes of the crimes concerned were presented in more restrictive terms than those permitted by other international Conventions already in force, with the crime of aggression being put to one side for at least seven years,[36] while contracting States were also allowed to *opt out* for a period of seven years in relation to war crimes that had occurred on their territory or that were attributed to their national citizens.[37] In any case, the competency of the Court was limited to crimes committed subsequent to the Statute coming into force.[38]

Nor is this all. Unless it is the Security Council, acting within the context of chapter VII of the Charter, that makes the accusation and orders an investigation by the Office of the Prosecutor, the exercising of the competency of the Court is subject to a prior double condition, namely, that the State in which the crime has been committed or, alternatively, the State of the nationality of the accused, is party to the Statute (or accepts the jurisdiction of the Court),[39] and that the Security Council does not exercise its recognised faculty whereby it can request the suspension of an investigation or of a trial for renewable periods of twelve months.[40] Moreover, the Prosecutor cannot officially start an investigation without the authorisation of the Pre-Trial Chamber.[41]

---

36 *See* articles 5.2, 121 and 123 of the Statute of the Court.

37 *See* article 124 of the Statute of the Court. The United States government wanted more, i.e. a renewable decennial moratorium for all crimes apart from genocide.

38 *See* articles 11, 22.1 and 24.1 of the Statute of the Court.

39 The United States government tried to make the consent of the State of the accused's nationality essential in any case to exercise jurisdiction.

40 The United States government tried to make authorisation from the Security Council a *conditio sine qua non* for starting an investigation, which would have enabled it to have recourse to the privilege of veto as a permanent member of the Council, to short-circuit cases that affected its interests or those of its preferential allies, particularly Israel.

41 *See* articles 12–16 of the Statute of the Court.

When the period in which the Statute was open for signing came to an end on 31 December 2000 the number of signatories stood at one hundred and thirty-nine. The United States, Israel and the Islamic Republic of Iran were *last day signatories*. The signing of the Statute does not of course guarantee that a country becomes a contracting State and party to the Statute. It can in fact be considered to be good public relations for a country and, above all, help to keep that country involved in the development and enforcement of statutory measures which it might subsequently be able to twist to its own ends. This is what has been termed 'one foot in, one foot out' or *ambivalent multilateralism*. Nevertheless, a signatory has both rights and duties, including that of abstaining from acts that frustrate the object and purpose of the signed treaty as long as it does not make clear its intention to not be party to it.[42] The Bush administration has since made very clear its belligerence toward the statute, mounting an increasingly aggressive campaign to undermine it and to secure bilateral deals ensuring the exemption of US citizens from its jurisdiction.[43]

Conclusion

Reference is frequently made to the double and apparently contradictory accusation of the 'judicialisation of politics' and the 'politicisation of justice' (a 'dictatorship of the judges') in order to disguise inconvenience or displeasure at the independent action of the judiciary while paying scrupulous respect to the principle of legality (but not perhaps that of opportunity). Henry Kissinger – in an article published in *Foreign Affairs* entitled 'The Pitfalls of Universal Jurisdiction' – warns against 'the tyranny of judges' and 'the dictatorship of the virtuous' as having often led to 'inquisitions and even witch-hunts', in which light he criticises the judicial actions of Spain and England in the Pinochet case. The former Secretary of State under President Nixon, who has been accused of behind the scenes involvement in the fall of President Allende and the repression carried out by the Chilean military junta, must perforce be an interested party. Along the same line of argument, there are those who have maintained that the

---

42 *See* article 18.a of the Vienna Convention on the Law of Treaties of 23 May 1969. Although the United States is not party to this Convention, as is the case with many other treaties, there is general opinion that the aforementioned rule is declarative of a general norm of international law.

43 For a discussion of US hostility to the court see Marc Weller, 'Undoing the global constitution: UN Security Council action on the International Criminal Court,' *International Affairs*, vol. 78, No. 4 (2002), pp. 693-712; Jamie Mayerfeld, 'Who Shall be Judge: The United States, the International Criminal Court and the Global Enforcement of Human Rights,' *Human Rights Quarterly*, vol. 25, 2003, pp. 93-129.

price of the process of democratisation is the impunity of tyrants – an impunity that commissions of historical truth subsequently endeavour to compensate for – and they accuse those who refuse to pay this price of political prejudice and grandstanding. In this respect, it is worth following the financing and news coverage of events like the Congress of Democracy (Warsaw, June 2000) where self-proclaimed representatives of 'civil society' turned on experienced politicians and influential speakers with the message *¡viva la transición democrática, abajo la justicia universal!* (Long live the democratic transition, down with universal justice!)

Certainly, judicial activism in defence of human rights and the discovery of international law by state judges willing to increase their independence from political circles *tout court* does imply a shift in power that at times has put politicians in a tight spot. Stimulated by social and non-governmental organisations and progressive news media, these judges have taken international norms and dragged them out of the splendid isolation in which they were languishing as a result of the lack of awareness and of conviction that existed in the privileged world of the law. However, one should not get carried away, applauding the transnational judges in their tense struggle with the rules of judicial aid and the co-operation of other judicial and non-judicial authorities. Drawing attention to the scalps taken may distract attention from areas of greater interest and seriousness, and also displaces responsibility away from developed countries (who judge) to developing countries (who are judged).

Many people who accuse state justice applied to international crimes, under the protection of the principle of universal jurisdiction, of politicisation and who try to obstruct its development also invoke the setting up of an international criminal jurisdiction on condition that its actions are under the control of political organs. The position of the spokespersons of the Clinton Administration in the process of preparing the Statute of the International Criminal Court was very revealing in that it upheld a judicial model that is dependent on the Security Council (that is, on its permanent members) for all its initiatives and that is only applicable *to others*. The Bush administration has gone further, manifesting outright hostility toward the Court. With two hundred thousand armed units in other parts of the world, there is no good international or foreign court to judge US soldiers for the crimes they may commit in the missions they are entrusted with. It has even been claimed that humanitarian interventions may be at risk because the more respectable states will not want to commit their units to operations that end up being jeopardised by zealous prosecution. In the face of the hostility of the United States, the members of the European Union adopted a 'common position' in support of the prompt implementation of the statute and the Court.[44] More recently, however, under renewed pressure from the Bush administration supported by the UK government, the EU has agreed to allow its members to sign individual immunity agreements with the US to protect US personnel from prosecution by the ICC, despite the fact that the judicial services of the Commission, even the European Parliament, considered such agreements to be incompatible with the ICC Statute and, it should be added, with the leading role of the European Union in the setting up of the Court. Not only that. The European members of the UN Security Council voted for resolution 1422 (2002) of 12 July, by which the Council requests 'that the ICC, if a case arises involving current or former officials or personnel from a contributing State not a Party to the Rome Statute over acts or omissions relating to a UN established or authorised operation, shall for a twelve-month period starting 1 July 2002 not commence or proceed with investigation or prosecution of any such case, unless the Security Council decides otherwise'. The Council expressed the intention to renew this request each 1 July for further 12-month periods 'for as long as may be necessary'. In June 2003 the UN Security Council duly renewed the resolution, despite the misgivings expressed by Kofi Annan.[45] Resolution 1422 represents a clear move away from the authority given to the Security Council by article 16 of the Rome Statute. This bodes ill for the credibility of the Court and of the European Union and its member states.

---

44 Common position on 11 June 2001. Circulated as a document of the General Assembly of the United Nations in relation to the matter 162 of the programme ('Setting up of the International Criminal Court') at the request of the Permanent Representative from Belgium exercising the half-yearly Presidency of the European Union (A/55/1020, 26 July 2001). This common position was confirmed and reinforced to 20 June 2002.

45 Kofi Annan, statement to the Security Council, 12 June 2003, available at http://www.un.org/apps/sg/sgstats.asp?nid=389

Select bibliography

Alba, Víctor, *El militarismo* (México: UNAM, 1960)

Albi, Julio, *La defensa de las Indias (1764–1799)* (Madrid: ICI, Ediciones Cultura Hispánica, 1987)

Allamand, Andrés, *La travesía del desierto* (Santiago: Editorial Aguilar, 1999)

Alland, Denis and Frédérique Ferrand, 'Jurisprudence Française en matière de Droit International Public', *Revue Générale de Droit International*, vol. 102, no. 3, 1998, pp. 825–32

Alonso, José Ramón, *Historia política del ejército español* (Madrid: Editora Nacional, 1974)

Americas Watch Report, *Human Rights since the Plebiscite 1988/1989* (New York: Americas Watch, 1989)

Americas Watch Report, *Chile in Transition* (New York: Americas Watch, 1989)

Angell, Alan, 'What Remains of Pinochet's Chile?', Occasional Paper No. 3, Institute of Latin American Studies, University of London, 1993

Angell, Alan and Benny Pollack, 'The Chilean Presidential Elections of 1999–2000 and Democratic Consolidation', *Bulletin of Latin American Research*, vol. 19, no. 2, 2000, pp. 357–78

Archer, Christon I., *The Army in Bourbon Mexico, 1760–1810* (Albuquerque: University of New Mexico Press, 1977)

Astrosa Herrera, Renato, *Código de Justicia Militar Comentados*, 3a edición (Santiago, Editorial Jurídica, 1985)

Astrosa Herrera, Renato, *Jurisdicción Penal Militar* (Santiago: Editorial Jurídica, 1973), included in *Código de Justicia Militar Comentados*

Barahona de Brito, Alexandra, 'The Southern Cone', in Barahona de Brito *et al.*, *The Politics of Memory* (New York: Oxford University Press, 2001).

Barahona de Brito, Alexandra, 'A integração regional e a expansão da jurisdição universal: a União Europeia e o Mercosul', in IEEI (ed.), *O novo multilateralismo: perspectiva da União Europeia e do Mercosul* (Lisbon: Principia, 2001)

Barahona de Brito, Alexandra *et al.* (eds), *The Politics of Memory: Transitional Justice in Democratising Societies* (Oxford: OUP, 2001)

Barrio Reyna, Alvaro del and José Julio León Reyes, *Terrorismo, ley, antiterrorista y derechos humanos* (Santiago: Universidad Academia de Humanismo Cristiano, 1991)

Beckett, Andy, *Pinochet in Piccadilly* (London: Faber and Faber, 2002)

Bell, John, *Policy Arguments in Judicial Decisions* (Oxford: Clarendon, 1993)

Bianchi, Andrea, 'Immunity versus Human Rights: The Pinochet Case', *European Journal of International Law*, vol. 10, no. 2 (1999), pp. 237–78

Birnbaum, Michael, 'Pinochet and Double Criminality', *Criminal Law Review*, March, 2000, pp. 127–39

Branch, Taylor and Eugene M. Propper, *Labyrinth* (New York: Penguin Books, 1983)

Brazier, Rodney, *Constitutional Reform* (2nd edn, Oxford: OUP, 1998)

Brisard, Jean-Charles and Guillaume Dasquié, *Ben Laden. La verité interdite* (Paris, 2001)

Brody, Reed and Michael Ratner (eds), *The Pinochet Papers: The Case of Augusto Pinochet in Spain and Britain* (The Hague/London/Boston: Kluwer, 2000)

Brown, Cynthia, *Human Rights and the 'Politics of Agreements'. Chile During President Aylwin's First Year* (Washington, DC: Americas Watch, July 1991)

Bulnes Aldunate, Luz, *Constitución Política de la República de Chile* (Santiago: Editorial Jurídica, 1981)

Byers, Michael, 'The Law and Politics of the Pinochet Case', *Duke Journal of Comparative and International Law*, Spring/Summer, 2000

Caffarena de Jiles, Elena, *El recurso de amparo frente a los regímenes de emergencia* (Santiago: Editorial Jurídica, 1957)

Campbell, Leon, *The Military and Society in Colonial Peru, 1750–1810* (Philadelphia: American Philosophical Society, 1978)

Cassell, Douglass, 'Lessons from the Americas: Guidelines for International Response to Amnesties for Atrocities', *Law and Contemporary Problems*, vol. 59, issue 4, 1996, pp. 197–230

Cavallo, Ascanio, Manuel Salazar and Oscar Sepúlveda, *La historia oculta del régimen militar* (Santiago, Chile: Editorial Grijalbo, 1989)

Chile, *Ordenanza Jeneral del Ejército* (Santiago: Imprenta de la Opinión, 1940)

Chile, *Código Procesal Penal* (Santiago: Ediciones Publiley, 2000)

Christiansen, E., *The Origins of Military Power in Spain, 1800–1854 9* (London: Oxford University Press, 1967)

Commission for Historical Clarification, *Guatemala: Memory of Silence* (New York: United Nations, 1999)

Contreras, Héctor and Mónica González, *Los secretos del comando conjunto* (Santiago: Las Ediciones del Ornitorrinco, 1991)

Correa, Jorge, 'Cinderella stays at the party. Judicial power in Chile in the nineties', in Paul Drake and Iván Jaksić (eds), *El modelo chileno. Democracia y desarrollo en los noventa* (Santiago: LOM Ediciones, 1999)

Covarrubias y Leyva, Diego de, *Practicarum quaestionum* (Salamanca: Andreas de Portonariis, 1560)

Colegio de Abogados, *Justicia militar en Chile* (1990) (Santiago: Imprenta Montegrande SA).

Corporación Nacional de Reparación y Reconciliación, *Los estados de excepción en Chile* (Santiago, 1996)

Davis, Madeleine, *The Pinochet Case* (London: Institute of Latin American Studies, Research Paper no 53, 2000)

Davis, Nathaniel, *The Last Two Years of Salvador Allende* (Ithaca, NY: Cornell UP, 1985)

Detzner, John A., *Tribunales chilenos y derecho internacional de derechos humanos* (Santiago: Comisión Chilena de Derechos Humanos, 1988)

Dinges, John and Landau, Saul, *Assassination on Embassy Row* (New York: Pantheon Books, 1981)

Dominicé, Christian, 'Quelques observations sur l'immunité de juridiction pénale de l'ancien chef d'Etat', *Revue Générale de Droit International Public*, vol. 103, no. 2, 1999, pp. 297–308

Drake, Paul and Iván Jaksić (eds), *El modelo chileno. Democracia y desarrollo en los noventa* (Santiago: LOM Ediciones, 1999)

Dupuy, Pierre-Marie, 'Crimes et immunités, ou dans quelle mesure la nature des premiers empêche l'exercise des secondes', *Revue Générale de Droit International Public*, vol. 103, no. 2, 1999, pp. 289–96

Ensalaco, Mark, *Chile Under Pinochet: Recovering the Truth* (Philadelphia: University of Pennsylvania Press, 2000)

Escalona, Camilo, *Una transición de dos caras* (Santiago: LOM Ediciones, 1999)

Falk, Richard, *Human Rights Horizons: The Pursuit of Justice in a Globalising World.* (London: Routledge, 2000)

Feitlowitz, Marguerite, *A Lexicon of Terror: Argentina and the Legacies of Torture* (New York: OUP, 1998)

Fisher, John R., Allan J. Kuethe, and Anthony McFarlane (eds), *Reform and Insurrection in Bourbon New Granada and Peru* (Baton Rouge: Louisiana State University Press, 1990)

Fox, Hazel, 'The First Pinochet Case: Immunity of a former Head of State', *International and Comparative Law Quarterly*, vol. 48, Part 1, Jan. 1999

Frühling, Hugo, Carlos Portales and Augusto Varas, *Estado y fuerzas armadas* (Santiago: Editorial Sudamericana, 1982)

Funke, Manfred, *Starker oder schwacher Diktator? Hitlers Herrschaft und die Deutschen,* (Düsseldorf, 1989)

García-Gallo, Alfonso, *Los orígenes de la administración territorial de las Indias* (Madrid: Rivadeneyra, S.A, 1944)

García-Gallo, Alfonso (1966), *Los orígenes españoles de las instituciones americanas, estudio de derecho indiano* (Madrid: Rivadeneyra, S.A, 1966)

Garretón, Manuel Antonio, Roberto Garretón and Carmen Garretón, *Por la fuerza sin razón. Análisis y textos de los bandos de la dictadura militar* (Santiago: LOM Ediciones, 1998)

Garcés, Juan, *Allende et l'expérience chilienne* (Paris: Presses de Sciences Po, 1976)

Gazmuri, Cristián, Patricia Arancibia and Alvaro Góngora, *Eduardo Frei Montalva y su época* (Santiago: Aguilar, 1996)

González Morales, Felipe, Jorge Mera Figueroa and Juan Enrique Vargas Viancos,

Protección democrática de la Seguridad del Estado. Estados de excepción y derecho penal político (Santiago, Universidad Academia de Humanismo Cristiano, 1991)

Grant, E., 'The Questions of Jurisdiction and Bias', in D. Woodhouse, *The Pinochet case: a Legal and Constitutional Analysis* (Oxford: Hart Publishing, 2000)

Grotius, Hugo, *De Iure Belli ac Paci* (Paris, 1625). Trans. Francis W. Kelsey, *The Law of War and Peace* (New York: Bobbs-Merrill, 1925)

Harrington, Edwin and Mónica González, *Bomba en una calle de Palermo* (Santiago: Editorial Emision, 1987)

Harris, Robin, *A Tale of Two Chileans: Pinochet and Allende* (London: Chilean Supporters Abroad, 1999)

Haushofer, Karl, *Der Kontinentalblock: Mitteleuropa–Eurasien–Japan* (Munich: Zentral-verlag der NSDAP, 1941). French edition, Haushofer, Karl, *De la géopolitique* (Paris: Fayard, 1986)

Hazell, Robert (ed.), *Constitutional Futures: A History of the Next Ten Years* (Oxford: OUP, 1999)

Heasley, Nathanael *et al.*, 'Impunity in Guatemala: The State's Failure to Provide Justice in the Massacre Cases', *American University International Law Review*, vol. 16, 2001, pp. 1115-1194

Held, David, *Democracy and the Global Order: From the Modern State to Cosmopolitan Governance* (London: Polity Press, 1995)

Hilbink, Lisa, 'Un Estado de Derecho no liberal', in Paul Drake and Iván Jaksic (eds), *El modelo chileno. Democracia y desarrollo en los noventa* (Santiago: LOM Ediciones, 1999)

Hilbink, Lisa, 'An Exception to Chilean Exceptionalism? The Historical Role of Chile's Judiciary', in Susan Eva Eckstein and Timothy P. Wickham-Crowley (eds), *What Justice? Whose Justice? Fighting for Fairness in Latin America* (Berkeley: University of California Press, 2003)

Hodges, Donald, *Argentina's 'Dirty War': An Intellectual Biography* (Austin: University of Texas Press, 1991)

Honduran National Commissioner for the Protection of Human Rights, *The Facts Speak for Themselves* (New York: CEJIL/Human Rights Watch, 1994)

House of Representatives, *The Hinchey Report on CIA Activities in Chile* (Washington, DC: the House of Representatives 2000)

Human Rights Watch, 'The Pinochet Case – A Wake-up Call to Tyrants and Victims Alike', http://www.hrw.org/campaigns/chile98/precedent.htm

Human Rights Watch, *Human Rights Watch Annual Report, 2001* (New York: Human Rights Watch, 2001)

Huneeus, Carlos, *La Unión de Centro Democrático y la transición a la democracia en España* (Madrid: Centro de Investigaciones Sociológicas-Siglo XXI Editores, 1985)

Huneeus, Carlos, 'Las elecciones en Chile después del Autoritarismo', in Silvia Dutrenit, *Huellas de las transiciones políticas* (Mexico: Instituto Mora, 1998)

Huneeus, Carlos, 'Technocrats and Politicians in an Authoritarian Regime; The "ODEPLAN Boys" and the "Gremialists" in Pinochet's Chile', *Journal of Latin American Studies*, vol. 32, issue 2, May 2000, pp. 461–501

Huneeus, Carlos, *El régimen de Pinochet* (Santiago: Editorial Sudamerica, 2001)

Huneeus, Carlos, 'La derecha en el Chile después de Pinochet: el caso de la Unión Demócrata Independiente', *Working Paper*, No. 285, July 2001, Helen Kellogg Institute for International Studies, University of Notre Dame

International Commission of the Latin American Studies Association, *The Chilean Plebiscite: a first Step towards Democratisation* (Pittsburgh: LASA, 1989)

Jones, John R. W. D., 'Immunity and "Double Criminality": General Augusto Pinochet before the House of Lords', in S. Yee and W. Tieya (eds), *International Law in the Post-Cold War World: Essays in Memory of Li Haopei* (London and New York: Routledge, 2001)

Kant, Immanuel, *Perpetual Peace: A Philosophical Sketch* (Könisberg: Friedrich Nicolovius, 1795 and 1796)

Keck, Margaret E. and Kathryn Sikkink, *Activists Beyond Borders: Advocacy Networks in International Politics* (Ithaca, NY: Cornell UP, 1998)

Kissinger, Henry, *Does America Need a Foreign Policy? Toward a Diplomacy for the 21st Century* (New York: Simon and Schuster, 2001)

Kissinger, Henry, 'The Pitfalls of Universal Jurisdiction', *Foreign Affairs*, vol. 80, no. 4 (2001), pp. 86ff

Klabbers, Jan, 'The General, the Lords and the Possible End of State Immunity', *Nordic Journal of International Law*, vol. 68, no. 1, 1999, pp. 85–95

Kuethe, Allan J., *Military Reform and Society in New Granada, 1773–1808* (Gainesville: University Presses of Florida, 1978)

Kuethe, Allan J., *Cuba, 1753–1815, Crown, Military and Society* (Knoxville: University of Tennessee Press, 1986)

Lacabe, Margarita, 'The Criminal Procedures against Chilean and Argentinean Repressors in Spain', at www.derechos.net/marga/papers/spain.html

Lahera, Eugenio, and Ortúzar, Marcelo. 'Military Expenditures and Development in Latin America', *CEPAL Review*, no. 65, Aug. 1998, pp. 15–30

Landau, Saul, *Orlando Letelier, testimonio y vindicación* (Madrid: Siglo XXI, 1996)

Larraín, Felipe and Rodrigo Vergara, *La transformación ecónomica de Chile* (Santiago, CEP, 2000)

Lechner, Norbert and Pedro Guell, 'Construcción social de las memorias de la transición chilena', in Amparo Menéndez and Alfredo Joignant (eds), *La caja de Pandora* (Santiago: Editorial Planeta, 2000)

Linz, Juan J. and Alfred Stepan, *Problems of Democratic Transition and Consolidation* (Baltimore: The Johns Hopkins University Press, 1996)

Lira, Elizabeth and Brian Loveman, 'Derechos humanos en la "transición" modelo; Chile 1988–1999', in Paul Drake and Iván Jaksić (eds), *El Modelo Chileno: Democracia y Desarrollo en los Noventa*, (Santiago: Ediciones LOM, 1999)

Lira, Elizabeth and Brian Loveman, *Las ardientes cenizas del olvido: Vía chilena de Reconciliación Política 1932–1994* (Santiago: LOM Ediciones, 2000)

López Dawson, Carlos, *Justicia y derechos humanos*, 2nd edn (Santiago: Instituto para el Nuevo Chile, 1986)

López Dawson, Carlos, *Instrumentos internacionales de derechos humanos vigentes en Chile* (Santiago: Comisión Chiena de Derechos Humanos, 1994)

López Dawson, Carlos, *Justicia militar. Una nueva mirada* (Santiago: Comisión Chilena de Derechos Humanos, 1995)

López Martín, Ana Gemma, 'Las inmunidades del Derecho internacional: su aplicación en España', *Cuadernos de Derecho Público*, vol. 6 (1999), pp. 139–57

Loveman, Brian, *The Constitution of Tyranny. Regimes of Exception in Spanish America* (Pittsburgh, PA, University of Pittsburgh Press, 1993)

Loveman, Brian, '"Protected Democracies" and Military Guardianship: Political Transitions in Latin America, 1978–1993', *Journal of InterAmerican Studies and World Affairs*, vol. 36, issue 2, 1994, pp. 105–89.

Loveman, Brian, *For la Patria: Politics and Armed Forces in Latin America* (Wilmington, DE: Scholarly Resources, 1999)

Loveman, Brian and Elizabeth Lira, *Las ardientes cenizas del olvido: Vía chilena de reconciliación política 1932–1994* (Santiago: LOM Ediciones, 2000)

Loveman, Brian, *Chile. The Legacy of Hispanic Capitalism*, 3rd edn (New York: Oxford University Press, 2001)

Loveman, Brian, 'Historical Foundations of Civil–Military Relations in Spanish America', in David Pion-Berlin (ed.), *Civil–Military Relations in Latin America: New Analytical Perspectives* (Chapel Hill: University of North Carolina Press, 2001), pp. 246–74

Loveman, Brian and Elizabeth Lira, *Arquitectura política y seguridad interior del Estado 1811–1990* (Santiago: Dirección de Bibliotecas, Archivos y Museos (DIBAM), Centro de Investigaciones Diego Barros Arana, 2002)

Lynch, John, *Bourbon Spain 1700–1808* (London: Basil Blackwell, 1989)

Lynch, John, *Caudillos en Spanish America 1800–1850* (New York: Oxford University Press, 1992)

McAlister, Lyle, *The 'Fuero Militar' in New Spain, 1764–1800* (Gainesville: University of Florida Press, 1957).

McSherry, J. Patrice, *Incomplete Transition. Military Power and Democracy in Argentina.* (New York: St Martin's Press, 1997)

Malamud, Carlos (ed.), *El caso Pinochet. Un debate sobre los límites de la impunidad*, Papeles de Trabajo, Instituto Universitario Ortega y Gasset, Madrid, 2000.

Martínez Bañón, Rafael and Thomas M. Barker (eds), *Armed Forces and Society in Spain, Past and Present* (New York: Columbia University Press, 1988)

Mera Figueroa, Jorge, *La justicia militar en Chile* (Santiago, FLACSO, 2000)

Mayerfeld, Jamie. 'Who Shall be Judge?: The United States, the International Criminal Court and the Global Enforcement of Human Rights', *Human Rights Quarterly* vol. 25, (2003), pp. 93–129

Ministerio de Defensa Nacional, El Salvador, *Doctrina militar y relaciones ejército/socieded* (El Salvador, 1994)

Molina Jonson, Carlos. (Lt. Col.), *1973: Algunas de las razones del quiebre de la institucionalidad política* (Santiago: Estado Mayor General del Ejército de Chile, 1987)

Moulián, Tomás, *Chile actual. Anatomía de un mito* (Santiago: LOM Ediciones, 1997)

Norden, Deborah, *Military Rebellion in Argentina. Between Coups and Consolidation* (Lincoln, NE: University of Nebraska Press, 1996)

Nunn, Frederick M., *Yesterday's Soldiers, European Military Professionalism in South America, 1890–1940* (Lincoln, NE: University of Nebraska Press, 1983)

Paley, Julia, *Marketing Democracy: Power and Social Movements in Post-Dictatorship Chile*, (California: University of California Press, 2001)

Pereira, Anthony and Jorge Zaerucha, *The Protected Step-Child: Military Justice in Chile* (Unpublished paper, LASA Conference, Washington DC, 2001)

Pérez, Mónica and Felipe Gerdtzen, *Augusto Pinochet: 503 días atrapado en Londres* (Santiago: Editorial Los Andes, 2000)

Pion-Berlin, David (ed.), *Civil–Military Relations in Latin America. New Analytical Perspectives* (Chapel Hill: University of North Carolina Press, 2001)

Portales, Felipe, *Chile: una democracia tutelada* (Santiago: Editorial Sudamericana, 2000)

Putnam, Robert D., *Bowling Alone: The Collapse and Revival of American Community* (New York: Simon & Schuster, 2000)

Quinn, Robert J., 'Will the Rule of Law End? Challenging Grants of Amnesty for the Human Rights Violations of a Prior Regime: Chile's New Model', *Fordham Law Review*, vo. 62 (1994), p. 905

Rawnsley, Andrew, *Servants of the People: The Inside Story of New Labour* (London: Penguin Books, 2000)

Remiro Brotóns, Antonio, *El caso Pinochet. Los límites de la impunidad* (Madrid: Biblioteca Nueva, 1999)

Report by the National Commission for Truth and Reconciliation (*Comisión Nacional de Verdad y Reconciliación*) (Place: Publisher, Date)

Report by the Vicariate of Solidarity of the Archbishop of Santiago (*Vicaría de la Solidaridad del Arzobispado de Santiago*) (Place: Publisher, Date)

Reydams, Luc, 'Universal Criminal Jurisdiction: The Belgian State of Affairs', *Criminal Law Forum*, vol. 11, no. 2 (2000).

Robertson David, *Judicial Discretion in the House of Lords* (Oxford: Clarendon, 1998)

Robertson, David, 'The House of Lords as a Political and Constitutional Court: Lessons from the Pinochet Case', in Diana Woodhouse (ed.), *The Pinochet Case: A Legal and Constitutional Analysis* (Oxford: Hart Publishing, 2000)

Rodríguez, Laura, 'The Spanish Riots of 1766', *Past and Present*, vol. 59, May 1973, pp. 117–46

Roht-Arriaza, Naomi and Lauren Gibson, 'The Developing Jurisprudence on Amnesty', *Human Rights Quarterly*, vol. 20 (1998), p. 843

Roht-Arriaza, Naomi, 'The Role of International Actors in National Accountability Processes', in Alexandra Barahona de Brito et al. (eds), *The Politics of Memory: Transitional Justice in Democratising Societies* (Oxford: OUP, 2001), pp. 40–64

Rojas B., Paz *et al.*, *Tarda pero llega. Pinochet ante la justicia española* (Santiago: LOM Ediciones, 1998)

Rojas, Francisco and Carolina Stefoni (eds), *El 'caso Pinochet'. Visiones hemisféricas de su dentención en Londres* (Santiago, FLACSO, 2001)

Scelle, Georges, *Manuel de Droit International Public* (Paris: Domat-Montchrestien, 1948)

Senate Select Committee on Government Operations with Respect to Intelligence Activities, *Alleged Assassination Plots Involving Foreign Leaders* (Washington, DC: US Printing Office, 1975)

Stepan, Alfred, *Rethinking Military Politics, Brazil and the Southern Cone* (Princeton: Princeton University Press, 1988)

Stern, Brigitte, 'La compétence universelle en France: le cas des crimes commis en ex-Yugoslavie et au Rwanda', *German Yearbook of International Law*, vol. 40, 1997, pp. 280–99

The Lifting of Senator Augusto Pinochet's parliamentary immunity. Supreme Court of Justice (Place: Publisher, Date).

Thompson, I. A. A., *War and Government in Habsburgh Spain, 1560–1620* (London: Athlone Press, 1976)

Turns, David. 'Pinochet's Fallout: Jurisdiction and Immunity for Criminal Violations of International Law', vol. 20, *Legal Studies*, vol. 4, Nov. 2000, p. 579.

Valenzuela, J. Samuel, 'La Constitución de 1980 y el inicio de la redemocratización en Chile', in Torcuato Di Tella (ed.), *Crisis de representatividad y sistemas de partidos políticos* (Buenos Aires: Grupo Editor Latinoamericano, 1998), pp. 149–95

Valenzuela, J. Samuel, 'Los escollos de la redemocratización chilena', *Boletín SAAP*, vol. 5, no. 9, Spring 1999, pp. 111–25

Verbitsky, Horacio, *The Flight: Confessions of an Argentine Dirty Warrior* (New York: New Press, 1996)

Verdugo, Patricia, *Los zarpazos del Puma* (Santiago, Chile: CESOC, 1989)

Vergara, Carlos, 'Reacciones del gobierno chileno durante el caso Pinochet', in FLACSO Chile (ed.), *Chile 1999–2000: Nuevo Gobierno: desafíos de la reconciliación* (Santiago: FLACSO, 2000)

von Beyme, Klaus, *Vom Faschismus zur Entwicklungsdiktatur – Machtelite und Opposition in Spanien* (Munich: Piper, 1971)

Warbrick, Colin, 'Extradition Law Aspects of Pinochet 3', *International and Comparative Law Quarterly*, Oct. 1999

Weeks, G., *The Military and Chilean Democracy*. Unpublished paper: Latin American Studies Association Conference, Chicago, 1998

Weller, Marc, 'Undoing the global constitution: UN Security Council action on the International Criminal Court', *International Affairs*, vol. 78, no. 4, 2002, pp. 693–712

Weller, Marc, 'On the Hazards of Foreign Travel for Dictators and Other International Criminals', *International Affairs*, vol. 75, no. 3, 1999

Wilde, Alex, 'Irruptions of Memory: Expressive Politics in Chile's Transition to Democracy', *Journal of Latin American Studies*, vol. 31, no. 2 1999, pp. 473–500

Wilson, Richard, 'Prosecuting Pinochet: International Crimes in Spanish Domestic Law', *Human Rights Quarterly* 21 (1999)

Woodhouse, Diana (ed.), *The Pinochet Case: A Legal and Constitutional Analysis* (Oxford: Hart Publishing, 2000)

Wright, Thomas and Rody Oñate, *Flight from Chile: Voices of Exile* (Albuquerque, 1998)

Zappalà, Salvatore, 'Do Heads of State in Office Enjoy Immunity from Jurisdiction for International Crimes? The Ghadaffi Case before the French Cour de Cassation', *European Journal of International Law*, vol. 12, no. 3, 2001, pp. 595–612

Zoglin, Kate, 'Paraguay's Archive of Terror: International Cooperation and Operation Condor', *University of Miami Inter-American Law Review*, vol. 32 (2001), p. 57

Zuñiga San Martín, Ana María, *Legislación sobre seguridad del estado, control de armas y terrorismo* (Santiago, Editorial Jurídica de Chile, 1985)

RELEVANT WEB SITES

www.derechos.org/nizkor/arg/espana/menem.html
www.derechos.org/nizkor/arg/espana/condor.html
www.pdt.org.br/jgmort.htm
www.amnesty.org.uk/pinochet/report.html

Index

Note: an entry in *italic* indicates reference to a footnote on that page